D1600540

MAKING OFFICERS OUT
OF GENTLEMEN

MAKING OFFICERS OUT OF GENTLEMEN

Military Institution-Building in India, c. 1900–1960

VIPUL DUTTA

OXFORD
UNIVERSITY PRESS

OXFORD
UNIVERSITY PRESS

Oxford University Press is a department of the University of Oxford.
It furthers the University's objective of excellence in research, scholarship,
and education by publishing worldwide. Oxford is a registered trademark of
Oxford University Press in the UK and in certain other countries.

Published in India by
Oxford University Press
22 Workspace, 2nd Floor, 1/22 Asaf Ali Road, New Delhi 110 002, India

First Edition published in 2021

ISBN-13 (print edition): 978-0-19-013022-0
ISBN-10 (print edition): 0-19-013022-9

ISBN-13 (eBook): 978-0-19-099395-5
ISBN-10 (eBook): 0-19-099395-2

Typeset in Bembo Std 10.5/13
by The Graphics Solution, New Delhi 110 092
Printed in India by Rakmo Press, New Delhi 110 020

Contents

Acknowledgements

I consider myself fortunate to have received an incredible amount of inspiration from so many people. First, I want to thank Professor Sunil Khilnani and Professor Srinath Raghavan for their academic support during my doctoral years at King's College London, UK, where I studied aspects of military educational and institutional reform as part of my thesis that later provided the inspiration for this book. I also want to express deep gratitude to Dr Rudra Chaudhuri, without whom I could not have developed my research ideas to their fullest extent.

Dr Nilanjan Sarkar in London helped me navigate my early years in the UK. His advice on the course of my academic journey has been invaluable and I am indebted to his unfailing kindness. This work has also refined, immeasurably, its scope in shaping current debates on institutional and educational reforms because of insights received from Professor Joya Chatterji at the University of Cambridge, UK, Dr Yasmin Khan at the University of Oxford, UK, and Professor Ashley Jackson at King's College London, UK. I have also benefitted immensely from the discussions I have had with Dr Jahnavi Phalkey on the nature of institutional growth in Indian history, and I am thankful for her encouragement and advice.

I was taught by an exceptional set of teachers at the University of Delhi and Jawaharlal Nehru University (JNU), New Delhi, India, prior to joining King's. Professor Mahesh Rangarajan has had an extraordinary impact on my growth as a scholar. His commitment to encourage others in walking the extra mile to achieve excellence in research, institution building, and public engagement has been a ceaseless source of inspiration and mentorship for me. Professor Amar Farooqui at the

University of Delhi first spotted my interest in military history and encouraged me to read further on the subject. I am indebted to the support that he extended to me years ago.

I am deeply thankful to Dr Anirudh Deshpande, one of a handful of military historians in India, who has been so generous in sharing his knowledge and experience of rigorous engagement with questions of Indian military policy. His generosity, kindness of spirit, and the support he has extended to students and early career researchers like me is invaluable. Professor Sucheta Mahajan at JNU remains a steadfast supporter of all her students and I am lucky to have received her guidance while being at the Centre for Historical Studies. I am also grateful for the support received from scholars and experts at the Institute for Defence Studies and Analysis, New Delhi, India (now Manohar Parrikar Institute for Defence Studies and Analysis), where I was briefly stationed as a visiting fellow in early 2014.

Over the course of a few years, many people and institutions have shared their time and resources with me including Sqn Ldr Rana Chhina at the United Service Institution of India, Delhi, Professor Kaushik Roy, Professor Peter Stanley, Professor Brian Holden-Reid, Professor Tarak Barkawi, Dr Chandar Sundaram, Professor Harsh Pant, Dr Anit Mukherjee, Dr Walter Ladwig III, Dr Gavin Rand, the Alkazi Foundation for the Arts, New Delhi, and Kamaldeep Sandhu. I apologize for not being able to name everyone here and I humbly acknowledge my debt to all of them. In particular, the archivists, librarians, and subject-matter experts at the British Library, London; the National Archives, Kew; the Liddell Hart Centre for Military Archives, London; the National Army Museum, London; and archival repositories at the University of Cambridge, University of Manchester, and the London School of Economics and Political Science played a big role in helping me navigate their extensive collections. Dr Alan Jeffreys at the Imperial War Museum, London, helped me understand the intricacies of the Indo-UK defence relationship in the early twentieth century. I am also deeply grateful to the staff at the National Archives of India, the Nehru Memorial Museum and Library, and the Historical Section of the Ministry of Defence in Delhi, especially Dr Narendra Yadav.

This book could not have been conceived and written without the company of close friends in Delhi and London. My home in London for over 3 years—Goodenough College, complete with its fellow residents and friends, support staff, and former director Maj. Gen. Andrew Ritchie (retd) offered a safe and warm environment for research.

Teaching, working, and undertaking research at the Indian Institute of Technology Guwahati, India, has been a privilege. I thank the director, deans, head of the department, staff, students, and colleagues, especially Professor Arupjyoti Saikia and Dr John Thomas, for their warm support. Nandini Ganguly at Oxford University Press has been extremely helpful and I am grateful for her patience and sustained interest in this work. I am also thankful to the editorial support lent by Smita Mathur and the team at OUP.

I am lucky to have the support of a loving family including my parents Brig. Vinod Dutta (retd) and Vidhu Dutta, and Varun, my brother. Three generations within my family have served with the Indian Armed Forces, including the decades-long service of my grandfather Maj. Gen. Purushottam Dutta (retd). As a historian, it is both a source of immense pride and responsibility.

This book is dedicated to my mother.

Abbreviations

ABCA	Army Bureau of Current Affairs
AFRC	Armed Forces Reconstitution Committee
AHQ	Army headquarters
BL	British Library
BSc	bachelor of science
CENTO	Central Asia Treaty Organization
CFI	Custodian Force India
CLA	Central Legislative Assembly
CO	commanding officer
COS	chief of staff
DSSC	Defence Services Staff College
ECO	emergency commissioned officer
FM	field marshal
GHQ	General headquarters
GoI	Government of India
GS	General Staff
HMSO	Her Majesty's Stationery Office
ICC	Imperial Cadet Corps
ICO	Indian Commissioned Officer
IMA	Indian Military Academy
INA	Indian National Army
IOR	India Office Records
ISF	Indian States Forces
ISPCC	Inter-Service Pre-Cadet College
JDC	Joint Defence Council
JUSII	*Journal of the United Services Institute of India*

KCIO	King's Commissioned Indian Officer
KCO	King's Commissioned Officer
MBE	Member of the British Empire
MEO	Military Evacuation Organisation
MLA	Member of Legislative Assembly
MPhil	master of philosophy
MS	military secretary
NAI	National Archives of India
NAM	National Army Museum (London)
NATO	North Atlantic Treaty Organization
NCO	non-commissioned officer
NDA	National Defence Academy
NDC	National Defence College
NMML	Nehru Memorial Museum and Library
NNRC	Neutral Nations Repatriation Commission
NWA	National War Academy
OBE	Order of the British Empire
OTC	Officers' Training Corps
PoW	prisoner of war
RAF	Royal Air Force
RIAF	Royal Indian Air Force
RIN	Royal Indian Navy
RTC	Round Table Conference
SEATO	South East Asia Treaty Organization
SWJN	*Selected Works of Jawaharlal Nehru*
TNA	The National Archives (Kew, UK)
TOP	*Constitutional Relations between Britain and India: The Transfer of Power 1942–7*
VCO	Viceroy's Commissioned Officer
WO	warrant officer

Introduction

This book focusses on the emergence of a series of key officer-training and 'feeder'[1] establishments from the early to mid-twentieth century in India.[2] In doing so, it aims to highlight the military policies that were pursued in the subcontinent at this time, with special regard to the administration of these military institutions,[3] most of which were built or reorganized in response to official and political demands for greater

---

[1] The term 'feeder' networks or 'feeder training colleges/institutions/academies' will be used in this volume to refer to the military schools and colleges that emerged between the late nineteenth and early twentieth centuries in the subcontinent to train and educate sons of aristocrats, and later sons of commissioned and non-commissioned Indian Army personnel in order to prepare them for a career in the Indian Army.

[2] A part of this book focusses on the early twentieth-century history of those territories and regions in South Asia that, after 1947, became grouped into two new nation-states—India and Pakistan. Therefore, terms such as 'India', 'Indian', or even the 'Indian Army' will apply—in accordance with the historical sources referred to in this work—to the subcontinent. Except in those instances where it will be specified as referring to India and/or Pakistan, the institutions discussed after 1947 are those that belong to the post-Independence Indian State's armed forces.

[3] I will use the term 'military institution(s)' throughout this volume in the context of 'embedded' institutions within the Indian military, that is, the inter-service training, feeder, and instructional academies, with or without the powers of awarding commissions to potential officers. While several historians have written at length on the 'institution' of the Indian military and its associated aspects 'as a whole', there is little by way of explaining the emergence of these 'embedded' institutions within the Indian military.

and rapid 'Indianization' of the military. It argues that twentieth-century officer Indianization, that is, the gradual replacement of British officers with Indian men having equivalent powers of command,[4] has to be studied and examined in the context of the larger military institution-building processes in the subcontinent in order to comprehensively understand the nature, pace, and character of Indianization policies. This is because an unrelenting focus on the politically driven demands to rapidly Indianize the officer cadre of the military in the existing historiography has ignored the wider significance of the critical administrative and institutional challenges that were encountered in meeting the demands for more Indian officers. In the wake of addressing those institutional challenges, Indianization policies were transformed and considerably broadened in scope to include key aspects and practices relating to officer training and education.

This volume will highlight that beneath the political rhetoric and the 'narrow preoccupation'[5] with demanding greater Indian representation in the Indian military lay a wide network of military schools, colleges, and commissioning academies, which were the primary sites engaged in herculean efforts to churn out trained Indian men. It, therefore, will reveal the twin overlooked aspects related to military Indianization. First, it will illuminate the missing 'institutional' element in military Indianization discussions, and second, it will argue how each successive wave of military institution-building in the subcontinent laid the basis for the next round of institutional reform and

---

[4] A King's/Queen's commissioned officer could essentially exercise command over both junior Indian and British officers and subalterns. This was in contrast to several other and controversial commissions such as the Viceroy's Commission, which only allowed its holder to exercise authority over Indians and exempted British officers and other variously commissioned or non-commissioned British recruits from their powers of command.

[5] Apurba Kundu, *Militarism in India: The Army and Civil Society in Consensus* (London and New York: Tauris Academic Studies, 1998), p. 39. Kundu has remarked that even though some nationalist leaders grouped as the 'instrumental gradualists'—that is, members who were most interested in military affairs—did achieve important gains in 'expanding Indian participation in the armed forces', their 'narrow preoccupation' with opening up particular positions to Indians eventually came to be seen as a 'drag' on the goal of independence.

innovation to take place, thereby, pointing at certain regional, 'Princely', and state-centred contexts in which military Indianization and military institution-building came to be discussed. In elaborating my argument, I offer a detailed analysis of the early evolution and development of India's military institutional network by means of a series of case studies. These case studies will demonstrate the transformative impact that military training institutions and the Indianization policies had on each other as more Indian officers were being inducted.

A brief overview[6] of the basic chronology of the emergence of the military academies this book examines helps to reveal their centrality in the history of the Indian military and the subcontinent more broadly. This volume will study the Indian Military Academy (IMA, established in 1932 in Dehradun), the National Defence Academy (NDA; inaugurated in 1949, later relocated to Khadakvasla, near Pune [previously Poona]), and the National Defence College (NDC; established in 1960 in New Delhi). These are the flagship inter-service training and instructional spaces of the officers belonging to the Indian military, which were set up in the twentieth century.

The book, however, will commence with a brief overview of the earliest institutional appearances in the subcontinent in the late nineteenth century that coincided with the initial expressions of governmental interest in Indianization (theme of Chapter 1). Beneath the twentieth-century network of military academies lay an intricate web of military feeder and preparatory schools and colleges, which began to appear in the subcontinent from the latter part of the nineteenth century. A significant number of these feeder institutions were established to cater to the princely states. However, by 1925, a renewed phase of expansion of these institutions, coupled with the formation of newer military colleges, took place. This new phase of military institution-building in the subcontinent raised multiple issues of official concern. The challenges of providing a suitable education relevant both for military and non-military workplaces; the question of 'ethnicity' and 'martial suitability' of candidates; as well as the institutional identity of these colleges and schools with respect to the larger military academies and civilian institutional educational network transformed and complicated the discourse on military Indianization, which is often

---

[6] Please also see Appendix at the end.

characterized only as part of 'some reward'[7] due to India after the First World War.

The management of this feeder college network of the late nineteenth century set the context for the discussions on the formation and expansion of the higher military officers' academies that began to appear after 1932. The connection between the feeder and higher institutions was evident in the ways in which the administrative and functional challenges of the latter were addressed by an institutional overhaul in the workings of the former. In 1925, for instance, when a committee was appointed by the government to study both the existing recruitment practices and the feasibility for an Indian officers' academy like Sandhurst in the UK, the report recommended an educational reorganization of the feeder network to augment its capacity in graduating more rigorously trained candidates for military service. Likewise, the struggles of the NDA, the Indian Staff College, and the NDC after Independence to align and enhance their military educational programmes by seeking affiliation with civilian universities spoke to the concerns of the earliest military institutional network set up in the subcontinent that dealt with similar questions in significant detail. Thus, military Indianization held within itself a wide range of complex institutional issues that have not been adequately studied before.

Studying the Indian military principally through its training and feeder institutions is important in order to analyse the 'responses' that these institutions evoked from the government and the military authorities to address the institutional challenges associated with the task of training more Indians. These 'responses' were a crucial factor in engineering, what Linda Colley has termed as the 'volte face', wherein the Indian Army turned from being an 'imperial lackey' to a 'focus of national pride'.[8] Studying the responses to institutional problems complicates the transition of the Indian military by moving

---

[7] John Gaylor, *Sons of John Company: The Indian and Pakistan Armies, 1903–91* (Tunbridge Wells: Spellmount Ltd., 1992), p. 2.

[8] Linda Colley, 'The Indian Armed Forces and Politics since 1947: Putting Difference in Context', Jawaharlal Nehru Memorial Lecture, 24 April 2003. Available at https://www.cambridgetrust.org/assets/documents/Lecture_25.pdf https://www.cambridgetrust.org/partners/jawaharlal-nehru-memorial-lectures; accessed on 20 August 2020.

away from the neat periodization of 'colonial' and 'post-Independence' phases of military administration, and highlights the process of military Indianization as a continuous process through the decades of colonial and post-Independence rule.

Indianization, I will also argue, demanded discussions on generating 'structures' and plans to situate the emerging cadre of Indian officers in the larger educational, inter-service context of military services so as to augment and enhance their military training. This was felt necessary to bolster the pace of the replacement of British officers as well as impart a distinct but globally aligned set of skills to the Indian officers who could hold their own in a future military force, irrespective of the polity within which the military would function—whether colonial, dominion, or a future national 'Indian' armed force. This global connection in imparting a professionalized system of military education also led to similar reforms in other parts of the Empire, chiefly in West Africa, whose own demands for expanding the officer corps in the 1940s compelled the Colonial Office in London to seek the assistance of the Indian government to manage 'Africanization'.

Indianization, therefore, is a vital indicator of the ways and means through which the State (whether colonial or the post-1947 Government of India [GoI]) managed a developing cadre of Indian military officers, which had started to replace their British counterparts in the early twentieth century. This 'replacement' necessitated the adoption of policies and measures to sustain the rate at which this process was to proceed: revealing the 'insights' into not just 'colonial rule', as Sumit Sarkar had perceptively noted on the nature of military policy, but also the workings of the post-Independence Indian State.[9]

The steady increase in the number of Indian candidates desirous of becoming officers gave rise to a host of new issues relating to what it really meant to be a part of an 'Indian', and later 'national' military force.[10] These new ties of belonging necessitated, after 1947, the

---

[9] Sumit Sarkar, *Modern India: 1885–1947* (New Delhi: Macmillan, 1983), p. 16.

[10] See, for instance, GB 133 AUC/1193, Letter from Jawaharlal Nehru, Member for External Affairs and Commonwealth Relations in the Interim Government of India (GoI), to Auchinleck, 12 September 1946, Field Marshal (FM) Auchinleck Papers, The John Rylands Library (Special Collections),

formation and expansion of newer military institutions of training for senior military officers that could bring together members and knowledge regimes from a wide range of inter-governmental departments to focus on aspects of national security and defence. Additionally, it also meant retrieving the military from a purely 'militaristic' occupational role-profile and locating it in a context in which it could develop and function alongside civilian structures of governance.[11]

A combination of issues arising out of the chaotic and contradictory processes of replacement of British officers necessitated frequent rounds of administrative overhauling of military institutions. This was done so as to link the changing occupational and operational expectations of an 'Indianized' officer corps with the constantly evolving academic and institutional space that military academies inhabited. This book will therefore highlight the 'officer–institution' interface from early to mid-twentieth century, where the two seemingly parallel but reformatory streams of officer Indianization and institutional reform converged to offer a new understanding of the wider implications of the military Indianization. Therefore, studying the institutional history of the Indian military is essentially a study of the transformational interactions that took place between the 'officer' and the 'academy' when both categories were undergoing critical shifts in their meaning and scope.

The theme of an 'Indianized force' occurs across a wide range of memoirs of former Indian officers, but they do not adequately refer to the enormous challenges that were associated with these institutions. Indianization, if ever analysed, is discussed mainly in terms of a 'tardy' progress in 'introducing Indian King's Commissioned Officers into the

---

University of Manchester Library, UK. In order to 'infuse a new nationalist spirit in the ranks of the Indian Army', Nehru remarked in this letter, it was essential to remove it from communal associations and racist interests and resist its employment in policing foreign territories. Nehru also suggested that it was necessary to 'man the Indian Army with Indian nationals from top to bottom' with the British element staying only in an advisory capacity.

[11] Report in *The Hindustan Times*, 7 October 1949. Nehru remarked that the role of defence services had changed under the present circumstances and they were required to think it a part of their duty to do 'social service' to the nation and extend a helping hand towards the process of 'nation-building'.

positions of British officers'.[12] The reasons for this 'tardy' progress do not go beyond the familiar British 'uneasiness' about 'giving officer training to Indians'—a reason that gets replicated in the historiography on Indian military Indianization because of its reliance on these sources to a considerable extent. Early institutional sites, mainly the feeder schools and colleges, go largely unreported in the memoirs. The reasons for these gaps are significant.

Many of the earliest King's Commissioned Indian Officers (KCIOs) liked to start their account with their experiences of Sandhurst, perhaps signalling a distinct, personal break in their lives while moving away from India. The memoirs deal with the various aspects of their lives in England. For instance, Gen. Thimayya, a senior ranking Indian officer, trained at Sandhurst, 'began to understand the nature of British prejudice against Indians at Sandhurst'.[13] Other senior commanders like Harbakhsh Singh, who did not attend Sandhurst, chose to remember the differential terms of service with which they were saddled with in the post-1947 scenario, when their Sandhurst-trained counterparts seemed to have had a tight grip on appointments and promotions.[14] Differences in statuses and appointments of the KCIOs versus Indian Commissioned Officers (ICOs) were a source of much friction in the generation of officers immediately after Independence. The narratives are therefore dotted with personal accounts, which are punctuated by career-related milestones before moving on towards offering battle-centric analyses of post-1947 Indian military campaigns in which most of these officers took part.

More importantly, the reason as to why military training feeder institutions are neglected in personal memoirs is because many of the earliest King's Commissioned Officers (KCOs) hailed from privileged families with considerable land and commercial interests, and thus, would not have had to attend the military-feeder institutions that emerged in northwestern India in the early twentieth century, often

[12] Lt Gen. S.L. Menezes, *Fidelity and Honour: The Indian Army from the Seventeenth to the Twenty-First Century* (Delhi: Oxford University Press, 1999), p. 307.

[13] Humphrey Evans, *Thimayya of India: A Soldier's Life*, (Dehradun: Natraj Publishers, 1988), p. 65.

[14] Lt Gen. Harbakhsh Singh, *In the Line of Duty: A Soldier Remembers*, (New Delhi: Lancer Publishers, 2000), p. 385.

moving directly onto regular officers' academies.[15] Indeed, records of these feeder institutions (as I discuss in Chapter 1) attest to a growing 'non-commissioned officer' (NCO) provenance of the cadets, while the princes and children of aristocrats increasingly withdrew from these sites to join other institutions, thereby signalling the slow decline of these feeder institutions—a process that was exacerbated after the First World War. Thus, a combination of institutional decline aided by elitist educational preferences has caused the feeder institutions to be overlooked in the historical analyses.

The little research that does exist on Indian military institutions has been largely produced by the Indian military itself, generally authored by retired functionaries. Unsurprisingly, these works reveal clear biases. The institutional accounts authored by Lal[16] and Raina,[17] for instance, can be loosely regarded as official biographies, and have advanced largely Statist and isolated accounts of institutions such as the NDA, unconnected from the historical waves of transformations that have swept across the Indian military architecture since the late nineteenth century. The sources used for writing these accounts are often not clearly stated and present the history of military institutions

---

[15] The trend may not be uniform, but the profiles of several early ICOs generally reflected a graduate, or at least undergraduate educational qualification. Gen. Thimayya, who went on to become the army chief, came from a prosperous family of coffee planters from southern India (Evans, *Thimayya of India*). Gen. (later FM) K.M. Cariappa, who was the first Indian commander-in-chief of the Indian Army, also hailed from a prosperous Coorgi family of the south, with roots in the provincial state services of the princely state of Mysore (I.M. Muthanna, *General Cariappa: The First Indian Commander-in-Chief* [Mysore: Usha Press, 1964]). Gen. J.N. Chaudhuri, also army chief (B.K. Narayan, *General J.N. Chaudhuri: An Autobiography* [Delhi: Vikas, 1978]), was schooled in England, while Gen. Harbakhsh Singh, senior army commander, studied at Government College, Lahore, before joining the IMA. For a detailed review of the earliest batches of KCOs, their political leanings and motivations behind joining the military, see Kundu, *Militarism in India*, pp. 33–8.

[16] Kishori Lal, *The National Defence Academy* (Pune: Parashuram Process Publishers, 1999).

[17] T. Raina, *Cradle for Leadership: The National Defence Academy—A History, 1949–1996* (New Delhi: Oxford University Press, 1997).

interspersed with chronological milestones like Independence or the post-1947 military campaigns.

Joanna Bourke[18] has criticized the persistence of these 'institutional bonds' between historians and the military establishment. Bourke is one of the leading voices of the school of new military historians that breaks with the 'drum and trumpet' school of military history in favour of important though neglected research agendas such as gender relations during wartime. Peter Karsten, writing in 1984, also defined the academic concerns of the emerging crop of 'new historians' relating to the relationship between military systems and the 'greater society'.[19] Karsten's succinct definition was symptomatic of the major trends in historical writings of the period, when fascinating studies of the military started to emerge from outside the discipline of history.

However, Jeremy Black's critique of the 'new military history' (also known as the 'war and society' approach), being inconsistently involved in the analyses of the elements of 'culture' in relation to the military, puts this historiographical tradition in a critical perspective.[20] Black also contends that the approach betrays a western bias, and argues that the methodologies typified by this school pose a 'risk' towards 'demilitarizing the subject'.[21] The claim of Eurocentrism is evident in much of the early historiography on military practices and warfare, but the claims of 'demilitarization' seem far-fetched. This is because 'wartime activities', as the historian Yasmin Khan notes, do not easily fit into dominant national or global narratives but straddle different historiographical 'impulses'.[22] Newer histories of the ways in which

---

[18] Joanna Bourke, 'New Military History', in *Palgrave Advances in Modern Military History*, ed. Matthew Hughes and William J. Philpott, pp. 258–80 (Basingstoke and New York: Palgrave Macmillan, 2006).

[19] Peter Karsten, 'The "New" American Military History: A Map of the Territory, Explored and Unexplored', *American Quarterly* vol. 36, no. 3 (1984): 389–418.

[20] Jeremy Black, *Rethinking Military History* (London and New York: Routledge, 2004), p. 54.

[21] Black, *Rethinking Military History*, p. 54.

[22] Yasmin Khan, 'Remembering and Forgetting: South Asia and the Second World War', in *The Heritage of War*, Key Issues in Cultural Heritage Series, ed. Martin Gegner and Bart Ziino, pp. 177–93 (Abingdon and New York: Routledge, 2012), p. 183.

militaries function should be welcomed as an opportunity to widen the horizons of understanding how armed forces locate themselves in non-military contexts.

Much of the scholarly literature on the Indian military has revolved around studying the impact of major political events on the organization, ever since it came under the East India Company's administration in the early seventeenth century.[23] However, the institutions which make up the armed forces have not been critically analysed. The reasons for this neglect are revealing. One of the recurring leitmotifs in the analyses was the 'nationalist historiography', which portrayed the struggles for an Indian Army staffed with 'Indian' officers as one of the key demands of the larger pan-India movement, aimed at securing independence from Britain. The induction of more Indian officers then became a function of the agitation to secure more representation in bodies that were ostensibly set up to serve India, but, in the absence of a sufficient number of Indians, were made to serve colonial interests. The range of early twentieth-century travails of the Indian military have been too easily assimilated into nationalist terms and reduced simply to serve as evidence of Britain's political subjugation of the subcontinent. Military institutions, therefore, are important sites to probe and unpack the hitherto 'linear' narrative on Indianization, which regards the reason for 'withholding' Indians from all opportunities for military officer training as part of a 'consistent' colonial policy.[24]

In the latter part of the twentieth century, especially during the decades of the 1970s and 1980s, newer methodologies to understand Indian history emerged, which attempted to look at the regional and local interface between politics and its public constituents. These new developments also transformed the study of Indian military. Examples of new work that has emerged from these developments include studies focussed on soldiers (as opposed to officers) and their welfare; migration of soldier-labourers during the Great War;[25] and probing

---

[23] Foremost in this section of the military historiography is Philip Mason, *A Matter of Honour: An Account of the Indian Army, Its Officers and Men* (London: Jonathan Cape, 1974).

[24] Capt. G.V. Modak, *Indian Defence Problem* (Poona: Capt. G.V. Modak, 1933), p. 308.

[25] Radhika Singha, 'The Great War and a "Proper" Passport for the Colony: Border-Crossing in British India, c.1882–1922', *Indian Economic and Social*

instances of military unrest, legal arbitration, and administration in non-urban spheres during and after the World Wars.[26] A critical study of the military's officer-production spaces can provide a fuller explanation for the military's and the Indian polity's transitions in the twentieth century, but such a study has been missing from the Indian military historiography's list of priorities.

FRAMEWORKS OF INDIAN MILITARY HISTORIOGRAPHY

The bulk of scholarship on the Indian military tends to fall into one of three distinct but inter-related frameworks. The first framework deals with aspects of tactical and battle-centric episodes in the life of the Indian military, and the second framework outlines the military's internal administrative challenges. Yet, neither of these two frameworks is able to sufficiently register how both the characteristic identity of the Indian military and the processes of its Indianization were shaped by the academies and feeder institutions. The third framework—though it does not exclusively deal with military institutions discussed in the thesis—brings together certain key elements from the first two frameworks in order to re-evaluate the 'deterministic' contexts surrounding Indian military. The 'third framework', therefore, helps illuminate the military as a stratified institution comprising a diverse set of sub-structures within it.

The First and Second Frameworks: Understanding Institutional Reform through Episodic Warfare

The first frame in the historiography relates to tactics and operations in which the Indian military has taken part over the course of the

---

History Review vol. 50, no. 3 (2013): 289–315. Also see, Radhika Singha, 'The Recruiter's Eye on "The Primitive": To France—and Back—in the Indian Labour Corps, 1917–18', in *Other Combatants, Other Fronts: Competing Histories of the First World War*, ed. J.E. Kitchen, A. Miller and L. Rowe, pp. 199–223 (Newcastle upon Tyne: Cambridge Scholar Series, 2011).

[26] See, for instance, Tan Tai Yong, *The Garrison State: The Military, Government and Society in Colonial Punjab, 1849–1947* (New Delhi: SAGE, 2005)

past centuries: specifically, the two World Wars and other localized campaigns. The role of the Indian Army's Expeditionary Forces in the First World War,[27] the colonial policies of recruitment and bestowing 'rewards',[28] internal policing[29] in the inter-War period, and 'Frontier warfare'[30] serve as important goalposts to highlight the role that tactical and strategic considerations played in the forging of the Anglo-Indian military relationship in the early decades of the twentieth century.[31]

This military and geo-strategic relationship was complicated further with the onset of the Second World War, as shown by Bayly and Harper's work on the collapse of the British front in Southeast Asia in

---

[27] George Morton-Jack, *The Indian Army on the Western Front: India's Expeditionary Force to France and Belgium in the First World War* (Cambridge: Cambridge University Press, 2014). The list of books on the operational experiences of the Indian Army are too numerous to be listed, and such an exercise is beyond the scope of this book. However, a convenient axis along which the historiography could be accessed is a series of warfare themes like frontier operations, 'learning', doctrinal understanding, and so on. These themes have (and continue to) evoked divergent viewpoints from a range of scholars interested in studying the Indian military. Some representative examples include: Gordon Corrigan, *Sepoys in the Trenches: The Indian Corps on the Western Front, 1914–1915*, (Stroud: Spellmount, 2006); Lt Col S.N. Saxena, *Role of Indian Army in the First World War* (Delhi: Bhavna, 1987); Kaushik Roy, 'From Defeat to Victory: Logistics of the Campaign in Mesopotamia, 1914–18', *First World War Studies* vol. 1 (2010): 35–55; and Peter Stanley, *Die in Battle, Do Not Despair: The Indians on Gallipoli, 1915* (Solihull: Helion, 2015). More recent works also include Vedica Kant, *'If I Die Here, Who Will Remember Me?': India and the First World War* (New Delhi: Roli, 2014) and Santanu Das, *1914–1918: Indian Troops in Europe* (Ahmedabad: Mapin, 2015).

[28] Aravind Ganachari, 'First World War: Purchasing Indian Loyalties: Imperial Policy of Recruitment and Rewards', *Economic and Political Weekly* vol. 40, no. 8, (19–25 February 2005): 779–88.

[29] Srinath Raghavan, 'Protecting the Raj: The Army in India and Internal Security, c. 1919–39', *Small Wars & Insurgencies* vol. 16, no. 3 (2005): 253–79.

[30] Timothy Moreman, *The Army in India and the Development of Frontier Warfare: 1849–1947* (London: Macmillan, 1998)

[31] Shrabani Basu, *For King and Another Country: Indian Soldiers on the Western Front, 1914–18* (New Delhi: Bloomsbury India, 2015), pp. 140–55. Basu outlines the sociocultural fault lines in this relationship, specifically during the time the troops were stationed in Britain receiving medical treatment.

1942–3.[32] Karnad—although it is not central to his narrative—offers a glimpse of the early university-administered training spaces for prospective officers, thereby highlighting the overlooked institutional efforts that struggled to keep pace with the wartime demands for more Indians to man the war front.[33]

Kaushik Roy's prolific scholarship on the state of the Indian Army during the two World Wars and later deals with several themes relating to the tactical and operational exercises of the Indian military.[34] For instance, Roy's 'inter-connected history' offers vital comparisons of the battlefield and institutional effectiveness of the Indian Army across two strikingly diverse theatres of the Second World War:[35] the arid northwest frontier and Southeast Asia. Yet, it does not adequately take note of the earliest network of military feeder institutions that emerged and expanded in the northwest, precisely at this time as a result of the renewed official attention on the strategic implications of the northwest frontier in the early twentieth century. Stephen P. Cohen too has written at length on aspects of Indian and Pakistani armies,[36] tracing the changes underlying transition of the colonial army into a modern-day force as it stands today, through a variety of organizational parameters.

The Second World War[37] also forms an important context to study institutional reform. The War carried vital transformational impulses

---

[32] C.A. Bayly and T.N. Harper, *Forgotten Armies: Britain's Asian Empire and the War with Japan* (London: Allen Lane, 2004). Also see C.A. Bayly and T.N. Harper, *Forgotten Wars: The End of Britain's Asian Empire* (London: Allen Lane, 2007).

[33] Raghu Karnad, *Farthest Field: An Indian Story of the Second World War* (Delhi: 4th Estate/Harper Collins, 2015)

[34] See Kaushik Roy, *The Armed Forces of Independent India: 1947–2006* (Delhi: Manohar 2010) for a discussion on the nature of command and control within the Indian Army in the broader context of counter-insurgency operations.

[35] Kaushik Roy, *Sepoys against the Rising Sun: The Indian Army in the Far East and South-East Asia, 1941–45* (Leiden: Brill, 2016).

[36] Stephen P. Cohen, *The Indian Army: Its Contribution to the Development of a Nation* (Berkeley: University of California Press, 1971). Also see Stephen P. Cohen, *The Pakistan Army* (Karachi: Oxford Pakistan Paperbacks, 1998).

[37] Like the First World War, the Second World War, too, has been a subject of much research into the purely military aspects of the conflict with

for the organizational and training protocols of the Indian military. Tarak Barkawi's work, for instance, has been instrumental in teasing out the complex forces at work in seemingly militaristic and technologically deterministic confines of a war zone to underscore the distinctive ways in which colonial armies such as the Indian Army were trained, organized, and administered.[38]

This strand is further developed in an approach, which may be emblematic, though not fully representative, of what Roy has referred to as the 'Modernisation theory'.[39] Approaches adopted by historians like Gajendra Singh[40] as well as Roy, Liebau, and Ahuja[41] in documenting

---

respect to the Indian Army. One of the most interesting works on the subject is Raymond Callahan, *Churchill and His Generals* (Lawrence: University of Kansas Press, 2007), since it offers a compelling account of the workings and the politics of the higher General Staff (GS) both within the Indian and British armies. Other comprehensive histories like Niall Barr, *Pendulum of War: The Three Battles of El Alamein* (London: Jonathan Cape, 2004); Timothy Moreman, *The Jungle, the Japanese and the British Commonwealth Armies at War, 1941–1945: Fighting Methods, Doctrine and Training for Jungle Warfare* (London: Frank Cass, 2005); and Daniel Marston, *Phoenix from the Ashes: The Indian Army in the Burma Campaign* (Westport, CT: Praeger, 2003) offer robust operational accounts of the Indian Army. T.A. Heathcote, *The Military in British India: Development of British Land Forces in South Asia, 1600–1947* (Manchester: Manchester University Press, 1995) offers a broad, pan-regional assessment of the Indian Army's fortunes in the War and afterwards.

[38] Tarak Barkawi, 'Culture and Combat in the Colonies: The Indian Army in the Second World War', *Journal of Contemporary History* vol. 41, no. 2 (2006): 325–55.

[39] Kaushik Roy (ed.), *War and Society in Colonial India* (Delhi: Oxford University Press, 2006), p. 15. Roy identifies and locates the 'Modernization theorists' within the frameworks of war and society. Stephen Peter Rosen has also analysed the inter-relationships that link social structures with military power within this framework. See Stephen P. Rosen, *Societies and Military Power: India and its Armies* (Delhi: Oxford University Press, 1996), pp. 26–32.

[40] Gajendra Singh, *The Testimonies of Indian Soldiers and the Two World Wars: Between Self and Sepoy* (London: Bloomsbury, 2014).

[41] Franziska Roy, Heike Liebau, and Ravi Ahuja (eds), *'When the War Began We Heard of Several Kings': South Asian Prisoners in World War I Germany* (New Delhi: Social Science Press, 2011).

the testimonies of wartime troops serving abroad (while fighting or in conditions of internment) illuminate the regulatory power of juridical discourses in constraining sepoys' voices, along with their modes of expression and conduct across a broad range of combat theatres during the World Wars. Accounts delving into juridical and epistolary sources also reveal the 'multiple sites of textuality'[42] that letters and other oral military sources acquire over time, thereby complicating the study of troops and their experiences across non-Indian combat theatres.[43] Of course, Omissi's earlier work (recently re-published), which is an edited volume comprising letters written by Indian soldiers during the Great War, reflects a growing scholarly engagement with the cultural and ideographic expressions of military personnel during times of conflicts.[44]

A section of the scholarship within this framework also probes the military relationship of the Raj with the provinces. This relationship was a crucial function of the subcontinent's security, and the colonial State strengthened it by forging important fiscal links with the regions through the mechanisms of military pensions, remittances, and welfare channels.[45] These fiscal regulatory mechanisms had a decisive impact on the communities in the rural hinterlands, especially in Punjab and the northwest, thereby bolstering the military infrastructure in the region. However, existing research has not been able to point out that this military infrastructure was also instrumental in the early

---

[42] Santanu Das, 'Indians at Home, Mesopotamia and France, 1914–1918: Towards an Intimate History', in *Race, Empire and First World War Writing*, ed. Santanu Das, pp. 70–89 (New York: Cambridge University Press, 2011), p. 82.

[43] Claude Markovits, 'Indian Soldiers' Experiences in France During World War I: Seeing Europe From the Rear of the Front', in *The World in the World Wars*, ed. H. Liebau, K. Bromber, K. Lange, D. Hamzah, and R. Ahuja, pp. 29–53 (Leiden and Boston: Brill, 2010).

[44] David Omissi (ed.), *Indian Voices of the Great War: Soldiers' Letters, 1914–18* (Basingstoke: Macmillan, 1999). The book was also part of the gifts that were exchanged between the prime ministers of India and the UK on the occasion of the former's visit to London in November 2015, thus affording a degree of legitimacy to India's nascent commemoration efforts in marking the Great War centenary.

[45] Rajit Mazumder, *The Indian Army and the Making of the Punjab* (Ranikhet, Bangalore: Permanent Black, 2003).

development of military feeder networks that were set up through the utilization of these resources, in collaboration with the Raj's landed magnates and the princes.[46]

The second framework in the historiography deals with military's internal administration and issues related to recruitment of personnel. Not surprisingly, the role of the 'martial race theories' is a recurring theme. Its persistence in the military discourse from the eighteenth century, down to the more contemporary discussions of the State's military relationship with the 'untouchable soldier',[47] undergirds the resonance of caste and ethnicity in the discourse on security. The historian Douglas Peers has argued that by the time India's defence architecture was coming to be regularized to meet with the 'Russian threat' to British interests in the subcontinent in the late nineteenth century, the links between the 'martial race theory' and official imperial security policy were becoming more visible.[48]

Racial undertones in military practices and training were not unique to the subcontinent. Military as well as policing doctrines were extensively mixed with a 'racist contempt' for the enemies which 'helped shape the new brutalities' that were displayed by European armies after 1914.[49] But in the case of India, martial identities were themselves fractured along multiple axes of ethnicities, which have given rise to a number of studies charting the differential experiences of specific communities in military service. Martial race conceptions had implications on the development and perceptions surrounding

---

[46] Ian Copland, *The Princes of India in the Endgame of Empire, 1917–1947* (Cambridge: Cambridge University Press, 1997), p. 33. Copland contends that the princes, 'more than any social group', extended the largest measure of financial support during the First World War.

[47] Stephen P. Cohen, 'The Untouchable Soldier: Caste, Politics and the Indian Army', *The Journal of Asian Studies* vol. 28, no. 3 (1969): 453–68.

[48] Douglas Peers, 'The Martial Races and the Indian Army in the Victorian Era', in *A Military History of India and South Asia: From the East India Company to the Nuclear Era*, ed. Daniel Marston and Chandar S. Sundaram, pp. 34–52 (Westport, CA, London: Praeger Security International, 2007). Also see Channa Wickremesekera, *'Best Black Troops in the World': British Perception and the Making of the Sepoy, 1746–1805* (Delhi: Manohar, 2002).

[49] Mark Mazower, 'Violence and the State in the Twentieth Century', *American Historical Review* vol. 107, no. 4 (2002): 1158–78, 1176.

military workplaces across combat environments, and were 'anchored' in what Radhika Singha has termed as the 'institutional distinctions' between sepoy and follower ranks in the Indian Army.[50] Assessments of communities, such as the case of the Gurkhas[51] as well as comparative studies on other groups like Sikh and Muslim personnel[52] and their career trajectories after Independence, have widened the ambit of military sociological studies focussing on the impact of religious and ethnic identities on 'officership'. Yet, this scholarship, despite its interest in the processes of recruitment, is marked by a remarkable absence of any inclusion of military institutions—the veritable 'factories' for officer production, which constantly juggled between the fluctuating priorities of the pseudo-scientific 'martial list'.

Kaushik Roy, while validating the presence of longer, regional, and early colonial ties to the development of the idea of the 'martial races,'[53] makes an important contribution not just to our understanding of the welfare mechanisms of the Indian military as a critical enabler of troop 'loyalty' and the hegemony of the Raj in the latter half of the nineteenth century,[54] but also in shaping discipline and morale later during the Second World War.[55] However, it is important

---

[50] Radhika Singha, 'Front Lines and Status Lines: Sepoy and "Menial" in the Great War 1916–1920', in *The World in the World Wars*, ed. H. Liebau, K. Bromber, K. Lange, D. Hamzah, and R. Ahuja, pp. 55–106 (Leiden and Boston: Brill, 2010).

[51] Lionel Caplan, 'Martial Gurkhas: The Persistence of a British Military Discourse on "Race"', in *The Concept of Race in South Asia*, ed. Peter Robb, pp. 260–81 (New Delhi: Oxford University Press, 1995).

[52] Omar Khalidi, 'Ethnic Group Recruitment in the Indian Army', *Pacific Affairs* vol. 74, no. 4 (Winter 2001–2): 529–52.

[53] Kaushik Roy, 'Race and Recruitment in the Indian Army: 1880–1918', *Modern Asian Studies* vol. 47, no. 4 (2013): 1310–47

[54] Kaushik Roy, *Brown Warriors of the Raj: Recruitment and the Mechanics of Command in the Sepoy Army, 1859–1913* (Delhi: Manohar, 2008); 'Logistics and the Construction of Loyalty: The Welfare mechanism in the Indian Army, 1859–1913', in *The British Raj and Its Indian Armed Forces, 1857–1939*, ed. P.S. Gupta and A. Deshpande, pp. 98–124 (Delhi: Oxford University Press, 2002).

[55] Kaushik Roy, 'Discipline and Morale of the African, British and Indian Army Units in Burma and India During World War II: July 1943 to August 1945', *Modern Asian Studies* vol. 44, no. 6 (2010): 1255–82. Also see Kaushik

to recognize that the expansion and reorganization of military schools like the Lawrence School network[56] and others that emerged in the latter part of the nineteenth century were also institutional manifestations of the welfare mechanisms of the Raj. These institutions were established and reorganized to cater, in large part, to the Raj's growing military constituencies.

The Third Framework: Understanding Military 'Institutional' Reform Thematically

This volume draws significant thematic and methodological insights from the third framework of Indian military historiography. This framework contextualizes developments within the Indian military in not just political history but also the social history of the subcontinent, thereby integrating military issues into a larger continuum of political, economic, and cultural trends across the subcontinent. Even though the scholarship within this framework makes no direct or detailed references to the military institutions that are presented in this book, it throws up an insightful set of ideas that have shaped some of the central research aims of this volume.

Cantonments, officers' clubs, and 'military hospitals'[57] figure as the three prominent sites in the assessment of colonial military policy on the administrative, cultural-scientific, and functional challenges associated with the management of a wide array of military institutions and institutional practices therein.

Colonial military perceptions and practices also often compartmentalized instances of personalized behaviour and even gender relations. Military prostitution, for instance, was significantly impacted and often regulated as a result of 'sustained militarization' brought about by the

---

Roy, 'Military Loyalty in the Colonial Context: A Case Study of the Indian Army during World War II', *Journal of Military History* vol. 73, no. 2 (2009): 497–529.

[56] Discussed in Chapter 1.

[57] Erica Wald, *Vice in the Barracks: Medicine, the Military and the Making of Colonial India, 1780–1868* (London and New York: Palgrave Macmillan: 2014). Also see Seema Alavi, *The Sepoys and the Company: Tradition and Transition in Northern India, 1770–1830* (Delhi: Oxford University Press, 1995).

Second World War.[58] These features of regulating communitarian self-images were also evident in the vacuous attempts by the State in post-marking identities of the Raj's minorities like the Anglo-Indians. Showering fraught identities from 'above' complicated the process of Indianization significantly, especially when Anglo-Indian men started to sit for examinations for inclusion into Indian military academies.[59]

Social relations and conceptions of class were significantly impacted through the ways in which the boundaries of military spaces like cantonments were 'imagined'. Interestingly, much of this spatial regulation also determined patterns of military institution-building like in the case of feeder colleges, many of which came to be located in elevated areas, mirroring Wald's analysis of the moral and medical concerns, which perceived the 'nucleus of the idea behind hill stations and sanatoriums' as sites for acclimatization for troops.[60] 'Clubbability', too, formed distinctive contours on the fabric of military Anglo-Indian society's convivial networks.[61] These very clubs later became integral appendages of mid-twentieth-century military institutions, and the cultural and symbolic iconography of these spaces lent themselves to the context of Indianization and officer socialization in the twentieth century in unique ways, as shall be discussed in subsequent chapters.

Given my specific focus on the early twentieth century, of particular relevance to my work is David Omissi's monumental sociopolitical history of the Indian Army.[62] The pursuit of what Omissi regards as 'applied military violence' and the institutional liaison of the Indian Army with civilian forces in aid of civil power reflected the carefully 'fostered structures of military collaboration on which' colonial power

---

[58] Yasmin Khan, 'Sex in an Imperial War Zone: Transnational Encounters in Second World War India', *History Workshop Journal* vol. 73, no. 1 (2012): 240–58.

[59] This has been discussed in greater detail in Chapter 2.

[60] Erica Wald, 'Health, Discipline and Appropriate Behaviour: The Body of the Soldier and Space of the Cantonment', *Modern Asian Studies* vol. 46, no. 4 (2012): 815–56.

[61] Mrinalini Sinha, 'Britishness, Clubbability, and the Colonial Public Sphere: The Genealogy of an Imperial Institution in Colonial India', *Journal of British Studies* vol. 40, no. 4 (2001): 489–521.

[62] David Omissi, *The Sepoy and the Raj: The Indian Army, 1860–1940* (Basingstoke: Macmillan, 1994).

rested.[63] These structures of military collaboration have important ramifications for the study of post-Independence officers' academies in general, and the NDA in particular, which had to juggle serious issues of land transfer and State control in the wake of their expansion in the mid-1940s, typifying the historical spectacle of collaboration between the state and central governments in military institution-building.[64]

Chandar Sundaram's wide-ranging scholarship has dealt in great detail with the politics of Indianization policies pursued in the subcontinent. Sundaram's work on early organizational features like the Imperial Cadet Corps (ICC), formed in 1901[65] and instituted with a view towards the implementation of Indianization, offers critical insights into the military policies of early twentieth century. However, his accounts of military Indianization end in the early twentieth century, just at the time when a renewed phase of military institution-building was being planned for the subcontinent for the coming decades. This book extends the chronological and thematic boundaries to offer a more institution-focussed twentieth-century history of the Indian military's Indianization and institutional reform policies.

More recently, Yasmin Khan's work on the Second World War unearths the forgotten voices of some of the key constituents of the military institutional network that were pressed into service after 1939.[66] Khan goes beyond the 'home front' of Britain to offer a critical account of the varied sociological landscapes of this conflict across

---

[63] Omissi, *The Sepoy and the Raj*, p. 234. For an assessment of the internal policing duties of the Indian Army in northern India, please see Gyanesh Kudaisya, '"In Aid of Civil Power": The Colonial Army in Northern India, c. 1919–42', *The Journal of Imperial and Commonwealth History* vol. 32, no. 1 (2004): 41–68.

[64] This has been discussed in Chapter 3.

[65] Chandar S. Sundaram, '"Treated with Scant Attention": The Imperial Cadet Corps, Indian Nobles, and Anglo-Indian Policy, 1897–1917', *The Journal of Military History* vol. 77, no. 1 (2013): 41–70. For an assessment of early Indianization, see Chandar S. Sundaram, 'A Grudging Concession: The Origins of the Indianisation of the Indian Army's Officer Corps, 1817–1917', Unpublished PhD thesis (Montreal: McGill University, 1996).

[66] Yasmin Khan, *The Raj at War: A People's History of India's Second World War* (Gurgaon: Random House India, 2015).

South Asia.[67] Her focus on the stresses and strains of the Indian Medical Service,[68] for instance, uncovers the impact of the Second World War on the sub-structures within the military at this time, and provides a useful context to examine the ways in which War reconfigured the institutional map of the officers' academies.

Srinath Raghavan, in his latest work, situates the Second World War in its sociopolitical and economic context. Raghavan explores the institutional manifestations of wartime resource mobilization in commerce and industry in India to underscore the importance of relinking the conflict with the political economy of the subcontinent.[69] Raghavan also outlines the steady erosion of colonial power in India through an analysis of the politics of Indianization of the armed forces and the political ballast it lent to the nationalist movement.

Alongside the international emergence of ideas on 'development' in the context of post-War reconstruction and displacement,[70] Deshpande[71] and Gupta,[72] in their studies of Indianization, have analysed how military fiscal reform and inclusion of Indian officers in the years leading up to the outbreak of War in Europe was part of a fiercely competitive political process that was dictated by high politics in New Delhi and London.

[67] Also see, for instance, Yasmin Khan, 'The Raj at War A People's History of India's Second World War', Talk at the Oxford University Department for Continuing Education. Available at https://www.youtube.com/watch?v=tPyAnqXrTAA; accessed on 20 August 2020.

[68] Khan, *The Raj at War*, p. 235.

[69] Srinath Raghavan, *India's War: The Making of Modern South Asia, 1939–1945* (Delhi: Allen Lane, 2016).

[70] Yasmin Khan, 'Wars of Displacement: Exile and Uprooting in the 1940s', in *The Cambridge History of the Second World War*, Volume 3, ed. Adam Tooze and Michael Geyer, pp. 277–97 (Cambridge: Cambridge University Press, 2015).

[71] Anirudh Deshpande, *British Military Policy in India, 1900–1945: Colonial Constraints and Declining Power* (New Delhi: Manohar, 2005).

[72] P.S. Gupta, 'The Army, Politics and Constitutional Change in India, 1919–39', in *Power, Politics and the People: Studies in British Imperialism and Indian Nationalism*, pp. 219–39 (New Delhi: Permanent Black, 2001). Also see P.S. Gupta, 'The Debate on Indianisation 1918–39', in *The British Raj and Its Indian Armed Forces, 1857–1939*, ed. P.S. Gupta and A. Deshpande, pp. 228–69 (New Delhi: Oxford University Press, 2002).

Aside from the official accounts edited and compiled by Bisheshwar Prasad,[73] a modest number of critical studies have emerged in recent years on the inter-War institutional evolution of the Indian officer corps. Barua's work, for instance, is one of the most relevant studies to have focussed exclusively on the development and professionalization of Indian officers after the Second World War.[74] Yet, Barua's work limits itself to the early to mid-twentieth-century political movement geared towards Indianization, citing the emergence of the IMA as the denouement of a long struggle to acquire an Indianized force.

Much of the scholarship on Indian military during Partition deals with an examination of the institutional integrity and structural cohesiveness of the military, while also discussing the 'military' involvement of ex-soldiers in the Partition violence that ensued in Punjab.[75] Daniel Marston, contends that the operational experiences of the Indian Army in the campaigns of the Second World War equipped it with crucial elements of professionalism and self-assessment, without which most other armies would have broken down had they been pressed at once to oversee an event like Partition while also having to simultaneously divide itself to serve two new nations.[76]

However, the military's involvement in overseeing Partition did not prevent it from being completely isolated from communal pressures, as was revealed in a study by Wilkinson and Jha on the ethnic cleansing and 'co-ethnic immigration' during Partition.[77] Partition severely tested the limited infrastructural capabilities of the State in handling domestic crises, and the role that material insufficiencies (in

[73] B. Prasad (ed.), *Official History of the Indian Armed Forces in the Second World War, 1939–1945: India and the War* (New Delhi: Combined Inter-Services Historical Section, 1966).

[74] Pradeep Barua, *Gentlemen of the Raj: The Indian Army Officer Corps, 1817–1949* (Westport, CT: Praeger, 2003).

[75] Indivar Kamtekar, 'The Military Ingredient of Communal Violence in Punjab, 1947', in *Partition and Post-colonial South Asia: A Reader*, ed. Tan Tai Yong and G. Kudaisya, pp. 196–200 (Oxon and New York: Routledge, 2008).

[76] Daniel Marston, *The Indian Army and the End of the Raj* (Cambridge: Cambridge University Press, 2014).

[77] Steven Wilkinson and Saumitra Jha, 'Does Combat Experience Foster Organizational Skill? Evidence from Ethnic Cleansing during the Partition of South Asia', *American Political Science Review* vol. 106, no. 4 (2012): 883–907.

the security apparatus) played in determining the security of certain areas was palpable.[78]

Nonetheless, some crucial linkages were also developed. The establishment of the Military Evacuation Organisation (MEO)—set up to aid and provide safety to displaced refugees, also highlighted by Joya Chatterji in her analysis of international migration regimes concerning South Asians since 1947[79]—is an example of the inter-institutional linkages that were developed during Partition to mitigate the logistical challenges arising out of the large-scale transfer of populations. However, these linkages were more visible in the western border regions of the subcontinent. The successive waves of refugee migration from east Bengal, like in the case of the 'Jirat refugees',[80] were often undertaken in hurried and violent circumstances, unprotected from persecution and dispossession of their property, highlighting the uneven nature of the security apparatus in the subcontinent at the time of Partition.[81]

The disproportionate aggregation of the military and security apparatus in the northwest occurred due to the 'political entrenchment' of the civil–military bureaucratic lobby in Punjab, as shown by Tan Tai Yong and Gyanesh Kudaisya.[82] Not surprisingly, the bulk of the defence

[78] See, for instance, Yasmin Khan, *The Great Partition: The Making of India and Pakistan* (New Haven and London: Yale University Press, 2007), pp. 117, 144. Khan highlights the woefully inadequate security apparatus in districts of northwestern India like Gurgaon and Mathura, where the police and the military functioned despite severely limited resources.

[79] Joya Chatterji, 'From Imperial Subjects to National Citizens: South Asians and the International Migration Regime since 1947', in *The Handbook of the South Asian Diaspora*, ed. Joya Chatterji and David Washbrook, pp. 183–97 (Abingdon, Oxon and New York: Routledge, 2013), p. 187.

[80] Joya Chatterji, '"Dispersal" and the Failure of Rehabilitation: Refugee Camp-Dwellers and Squatters in West Bengal', *Modern Asian Studies* vol. 41, no. 5 (2007): 995–1032, pp. 1008–9.

[81] The MEO was set up on 1 September 1947. However, its area of operations remained centred on the western border, where it ran some of the largest refugee camps, like those in Kurukshetra, which was placed under its control in October 1947. See, V. Longer, *Red Coats to Olive Green: A History of the Indian Army, 1600–1947* (Delhi: Allied Publishers, 1974), pp. 282–3.

[82] Tan Tai Yong and Gyanesh Kudaisya, *The Aftermath of Partition in South Asia* (London: Routledge, 2001).

architecture of the subcontinent also appeared along this geo-strategic corridor of the Punjab and southern riverine tracts of Balochistan and Sindh provinces, making use of the considerable scale of resources in order to deliver rudimentary military training to their earliest princely clients, and expanding gradually in the mid-twentieth century to include wards of the Indian military personnel (discussed in detail in Chapter 1).

Steven Wilkinson's latest work lays emphasis on an important set of ideas relating to regimental restructuring and political control as integral elements in the 'de-politicization' of the Indian Army.[83] Wilkinson's formidable quantitative data highlighting the continuing patterns of military organization and recruitment before and after 1947 undergirds the importance of 'reform' as an important metaphor in the political processes of the State in the twentieth century. Wilkinson's work opens the door for an exciting new range of scholarship that can be generated to understand the inner civil–political dynamic that has existed in India since 1947. His remarkable study on the post-1947 organizational overhaul of the Indian Armed Forces helps provide an intellectual ecosystem of ideas to study the Indian military's other interconnected aspects on educational and institutional reform.

Indianization of the military, to reiterate, did not end once the armed forces had been filled with a large number of Indian ranks. The expansion in the numbers of Indian officers engendered a continuing engagement of the State with training and feeder institutions on policy issues relating to military education, institutional affiliation, the cadets' performance, and learning outcomes. Thus, 'institutional Indianization' went hand in hand with 'officer Indianization', and this necessitated undertaking a series of periodic administrative measures to make these institutions respond to the changing dynamics of the relations between officers and the State.[84]

---

[83] Steven I. Wilkinson, *Army and Nation: The Military and Indian Democracy since Independence* (Cambridge, MA, and London: Harvard University Press, 2015).

[84] See Report in *The Civil and Military Gazette*, 2 April 1932. In the course of the debate in the legislative assembly, Capt. Sher Muhammad Khan, in response to a legislative motion, remarked that Indianization was not a 'mathematical' issue, but deserved to be scrutinized through the lens of making available the required training and experience for officers that could make them 'competent' to be 'generals'.

Military institutions emerged in the wake of significant political events in the subcontinent. Many of these institutions, which were established, expanded, or scaled down as a result of the consequences of wartime events like changed training procedures or demobilization, caused the State apparatus to penetrate deeply into matters of military institutional administration. This mirrors the penetration of the State into Indian society as remarked by Indivar Kamtekar[85] and military institutions, therefore, illuminate the operational, tactical, and other 'wartime imaginings' [86] of social and economic policies in the subcontinent.

FRAMEWORKS OF MILITARY INSTITUTIONAL STUDIES: GLOBAL CONTEXTS

The literature on military training academies outside of India has been shaped by multiple disciplinary approaches and contexts, not all of which are directly related to the aims of this book. An overview of the broad currents in the existing historiography, however, is helpful to situate the Indian case. Across several instances, the military academies in the case of the Indian historiography are studied only indirectly, often through situating the officer in the context of a 'managerial profession',[87] with scant references to the institutional context in which professionalization takes place.[88] The main aim of much of this literature has been to assess civil–military balance in the countries

---

[85] Indivar Kamtekar, 'A Different War Dance: State and Class in India, 1939–1945', *Past and Present* vol. 176, no. 1 (2002): 187–221.

[86] Benjamin Zachariah, 'The Creativity of Destruction: Wartime Imaginings of Development and Social Policy, c. 1942–1946', in *The World in the World Wars*, ed. H. Liebau, K. Bromber, K. Lange, D. Hamzah, and R. Ahuja, pp. 547–78 (Leiden and Boston: Brill, 2010).

[87] Jacques van Doorn, *The Soldier and Social Change* (London and BH, California: SAGE, 1975), p. 39

[88] Scholarship produced by those such as Giuseppe Caforio has looked at the patterns of professionalization displayed at 'military academies', but with the aims of quantifying the impact of socialization on officer's political and social attitudes, including career motivations. See Giuseppe Caforio, 'Military Officer Education', in *Handbook of the Sociology of the Military*, ed. Giuseppe Caforio, pp. 255–78 (New York: Springer, 2006).

that were decolonized after the Second World War, emerging as 'new States'.[89]

The new States, therefore, came to be studied closely during and after decolonization, and especially so during the years of the Cold War. Thus, strategic interest paved the way for a deeper engagement with the militaries of these countries. The term 'new States' was not always necessarily used to define decolonized territories, but also countries that had begun to be seen as important players in the aftermath of the Second World War. While South and Southeast Asia, as well as Anglophone Africa, remained the focus of military institutional studies, newly created States like Israel or ones like Greece and Hungary (for their proximity to the erstwhile Soviet sphere of influence) continued to appear as fertile grounds for military institutional research. Of course, Russian military systems, too, have also continued to attract scholarly attention. Garthoff's characterization of the process of professionalization of Russian officers in terms of a 'new traditionalism', and his analysis of the development of stratified 'castes' within the military mirroring its pre-revolutionary make-up[90] signifies the resonance of older organizational models in the more recent assessments of military structures.

In 1964, William Frank Gutteridge set out to assess the power of military institutions in newly independent States including India.[91] Gutteridge used elements from sociology to highlight the paradox faced by their armed forces, which were colonial in origin and customs, through a modernized 'civil service', which was radically different in composition and conception from the former. This organizational difference provided him the research axis to base his comparative analysis on examining the legitimacy and agency enjoyed by the military in a post-colonial context.[92]

[89] Morris Janowitz, *The Military in the Political Development of New Nations: An Essay in Comparative Analysis* (Chicago and London: University of Chicago Press, 1964).

[90] Raymond L. Garthoff, 'The Military in Russia, 1861–1965', in *Armed Forces and Society*, ed. Jacques van Doorn, pp. 240–56 (The Hague, Paris: Mouton, 1968), p. 251.

[91] William F. Gutteridge, *Military Institutions and Power in the New States*, (Essex: Pall Mall, 1964)

[92] Gutteridge, *Military Institutions and Power in the New States*, p. 15

Gutteridge also pointed out that merely having national training academies in place was not enough to have a disciplined fighting force. He exemplified the case of Sudan, where officers educated at the elite Gordon College, Khartoum, as well as for short periods in British military training schools, were the ones who eventually overthrew the government in 1958,[93] the same year when Gen. Ayub Khan took power in Pakistan. This led Gutteridge to contend that treating 'military development historically as separate from more general political trends' can evidently have grievous consequences, and that the 'history of an Imperial force has a bearing on the development of the national army which succeeds it'.[94] This was also amply evident in the ways post-Independence academies in India came to share certain key organizational elements from the institutions that were set up before Independence, encapsulating much of the organizational continuities which 'outweighed' discontinuities in the law and order apparatus in the immediate years after 1947.[95]

Interestingly, in order to correct the 'anomalies' in the civil–military architecture of the 'new States', Gutteridge advocated a greater involvement of the armed forces in the country's nascent sociopolitical 'public sphere', which was also on display in post-Independence India when the first Indian commander-in-chief echoed the Indian prime minister in seeking a more 'social' role for the military to divest it of its colonial occupational sensibilities.[96] This social 'undertaking' was evident in the ways in which the military had conducted refugee evacuation operations during Partition in the Punjab. However, the use of force in order to maintain public order could also sometimes evoke

---

[93] Gutteridge, *Military Institutions and Power in the New States*, p. 21.

[94] Gutteridge, *Military Institutions and Power in the New States*, p. 21.

[95] Yasmin Khan, 'The Ending of an Empire: From Imagined Communities to Nation States in India and Pakistan', *The Round Table: The Commonwealth Journal of International Affairs* vol. 97, no. 398 (2008): 695–704.

[96] Report in *The Hindustan Times*, 25 January 1949. In his first press conference in January 1949, Gen. Cariappa, as the new commander-in-chief, explained to the media as to 'what kind of publicity would help the people's army of free India'. Cariappa highlighted the various achievements of the Indian Army which projected the organization as a 'social' rather than a 'destructive' force.

memories of colonial traits, which, as Khilnani has pointed out, the Indian nationalists had struggled against the Raj.[97]

Emil Nagy, writing in the late 1960s, shed light on the effect that 'mass communication exercises' came to have on soldiers' military socialization.[98] Nagy focusses on the multiple ways in which military education was conceived across Hungarian military spaces. Perlmutter, in his analysis of the military–educational practices of the Israeli army, has echoed this by characterizing the military's political and military institutional frameworks as an 'instrument of nation-building'.[99]

The sociologist Morris Janowitz has studied military organization and its links with nationalism by drawing out the nineteenth- and twentieth-century forms of nationalist revolutionary ideologies in forging a distinct armed military culture across Europe and America.[100] Janowitz attempted—in contrast to the focus on 'new States'—to turn back the lens on the West by claiming that military institutions were of central importance in fashioning the type of nation-states that emerged in western Europe and USA. Foregrounding the linkages between the military service and the 'political concept of citizenship', Janowitz opined that military service functioned as 'an essential and necessary contribution toward political institutions'.[101] The link between political formations and military structures may also hold clues for the Indian subcontinent. This is because in the wake of military Indianization and recruitment in India, several ideas

[97] Sunil Khilnani, *The Idea of India* (New Delhi: Penguin, 2003), pp. 32–3.

[98] Emil Nagy, 'The Role of Mass Communication in the Political Socialisation of the Hungarian Armed Forces', in *The Military and Problem of Legitimacy*, ed. Gwyn Harries-Jenkins and Jacques van Doorn, pp. 95–112 (London and BH, California: SAGE Studies in International Sociology, 1976).

[99] Amos Perlmutter, 'Israel: The Routinized Revolutionary Army', in *The Military and Politics in Modern Times: On Professionals, Praetorians, and Revolutionary Soldiers*, pp. 251–80 (New Haven and London: Yale University Press, 1977), p. 253.

[100] Morris Janowitz, 'Military Institutions and Citizenship in Western Societies', in *The Military and Problem of Legitimacy*, ed. Gwyn Harries-Jenkins and Jacques van Doorn, pp. 77–92 (London and BH, California: SAGE Studies in International Sociology, 1976).

[101] Janowitz, 'Military Institutions and Citizenship in Western Societies', p. 79.

(some inchoate and ill-informed) of 'citizenship' competed with each other in determining recruitment patterns and ideas of eligibility for a career in the military.

One of the other main themes of research on the militaries in former colonies has been the tenuous balance that exists between civilian governance and military influence on the former; accordingly, many studies seek to explain the causal factors and circumstances that determine when and why the scales have tipped in favour of one over the other. A crucial explanatory factor is often located in the troubled legacies of decolonization. Robin Luckham[102] has written about the politicization of the Nigerian military in the decades after Nigeria's independence (late 1960s), which resulted in successive military coups, enabled in part by the vicissitudes of ethnic politics that shaped the ethnic constituencies of the military as well. This resulted in the frequent manipulation of the military to service different political agendas.

Shuja Nawaz[103] echoed some of Luckham's ideas while seeking to explain military's intervention as a perceived 'panacea' for civilian misgovernance in Pakistan, as well as the rather 'wide footprint' the army has had over civilian institutions, thereby skewing the power balance that is at odds with the sensibilities of democratic States. An idea, initially also propounded by the likes of Charles Tilly from within the 'New Institutionalist' school of political and sociological theory. Tilly, writing at a time when 'new military histories' pioneered by Karsten and others were dominating the historiography in the 1970s and 1980s, remarked on the relative ease with which 'military models' were able to fill the sociopolitical vacuum in new States and destabilizing civil–military relations.[104]

---

[102] Robin Luckham, *The Nigerian Military: A Sociological Analysis of Authority and Revolt, 1960–67* (Cambridge: Cambridge University Press, 1971).

[103] Shuja Nawaz, *Crossed Swords: Pakistan, Its Army, and the Wars Within* (Oxford: Oxford University Press, 2008).

[104] Charles Tilly, 'Reflections on the History of European State-Making', in *The Formation of National States in Western Europe*, ed. Charles Tilly, pp. 3–83 (Princeton, London: Princeton University Press, 1975), p. 75. The international structure, as Tilly outlined, exhibited 'tremendous inequalities' of military and economic power, thereby giving the military considerable space to intervene in domestic politics.

SOURCES

This book is based on archival sources in India and the UK. It has made use of the records of the Military Department as well as the records of the War Staff Secretariat in the India Office Records (IOR) Collection administered by the British Library (BL) in London, UK. Additionally, private papers of senior Indian and British military officers, who witnessed or oversaw the process of Indianization and military institution-building, were also consulted at multiple archival locations across London, Cambridge, Manchester, and New Delhi.

Despite their shortcomings, the memoirs, biographies, and autobiographies of the Indian military officers who served or studied at some of the institutions discussed in this book have also been cited. Although these were written with different agendas in the minds of their authors, they have been a useful source to understand the differences that arose between multiple generations of officers with regard to the newer academies which began to take shape after 1947. Using a mix of KCOs' as well as ICOs' memoirs, these sources (often uncritically used in the larger historiography) offer partial but important glimpses of Indianization through the lens of different classes of these officers. Finally, in addition to the archival sources, I have consulted a wide range of published sources like newspapers, newsletters, and journals to bring out a layered account of military institution-building in India.

CHRONOLOGY

This volume is divided into four chapters, following a broad chronological framework from the early 1900s to 1960s. Each chapter focusses on a single or a set of institutions that emerged in the decades under consideration. However, the main aim of the book is to present a unified narrative in order to demonstrate the shared institutional links between these developments. Therefore, each of the chapters will deal with specific institutions by charting a longer history of the ideas and debates behind their establishment, which will involve a brief review of the decades or years preceding the immediate establishment of the institution under question. The placement of the chapters is also in accordance with the hierarchical training regimens of the military, starting with the feeder schools and concluding with the senior-most military training facility in India today.

LAYOUT

This book covers a broad chronological period, from around 1900 to the 1960s. These sixty years mark the period during which multiple military institutional innovations came about in an eventful domestic and international context. Thus, each of the chapters can be regarded as 'case studies' with a central unifying theme. This central theme is the issue-based exposition of a triangular relationship between these institutions, the armed forces, and the governmental structures, each of whom responded to face and mitigate the administrative challenges associated with Indianization and military institution-building with varying degrees of success and commitment.

The first chapter begins with a survey of the earliest form of institutional architecture that was created before the outbreak of the Great War and put on a firmer footing in its aftermath, in order to provide greater opportunities to young Indian men interested in joining the Indian Army as officers. These initial attempts at providing a platform for future commissions resulted in an inchoate network of royal military colleges and other military schools across north and northwestern India, which were entrusted with the responsibility of training men in order to prepare them for officers' commissions.

The reorganization of this cluster of institutions during the early twentieth century took place at the same time as the domestic political context in India had started to campaign for greater representation for Indians in the Raj's colonial consultative and legislative bodies. This chapter will also set the thematic context for military Indianization by evaluating the changing conceptions and ideas underlying Indianization after the two World Wars. It will also reflect how the official military and governmental thinking on Indianization differed and informed other such colonial State-led efforts in Anglophone Africa.

The second chapter deals with the establishment of and the initial decades in the life of the IMA. Envisaged as the 'Indian Sandhurst', the academy was inaugurated in 1932 and was the first institution that generated a new class of commissioned Indian officers. The IMA, in its early years, grappled with the same administrative and institutional challenges as those of the feeder colleges, highlighting the interdependent nature of institutional expansion and reorganization in the subcontinent. This chapter will shed light on the initial years of its operation where the provisions for joint examinations in India and England, entry for Anglo-Indians, and the IMA's suitability for sons of the princely rulers threatened to erode its legitimacy. The establishment of the IMA also spurred the development of other military institutions in India both on the scale of higher training as well as feeder institutions, chief among them being the NDA.

The third chapter engages substantially with the theme of inter-service training through examining the early decades in the functioning and administration of the NDA, set up in western India in 1949, which later replaced the IMA as the primary entry point for men to acquire inter-service military education and training. This chapter will highlight the post-Independence decades of restructuring the Indian Armed Forces (mainly its division into three service-specific arms: army, navy, and air force), and will also shed light on the ways in which the government envisaged the development of this institution. Central to this analysis would be an examination of the formation of its 'academic' character, thereby amplifying the twin reformatory impulse of institutional Indianization, which was aimed at the twin goals of faster replacement of British officers and continuous assessment of the educational requirements of those Indian officers who would be replacing the former.

The fourth and final chapter looks at the NDC in Delhi that was inaugurated by India's first prime minister, Jawaharlal Nehru, in 1960. It is the last of the military institutional creations designed to meet the training needs of senior-ranking Indian officers. This chapter will contextualize the emergence of the NDC in the changing perceptions, roles, and responsibilities of the Indian Armed Forces. It will dwell at length on the post-Independence cohort of senior Indian military officers that represented the 'constituency' of the NDC and relook at their subsequent assignments, which symbolized a paradigm shift in the mandate of the armed forces, thereby offering a fresh perspective on the post-Independence phase of the military institutional Indianization.

1 Indianization and the Case of the 'Missing Academies' of the Indian Army, c. 1900–45

Indianization of the army's officer cadre was one of the key flash points around which political tensions grew in the early twentieth century. Yet, the larger process, whereby Indians were recruited into the army, was not an exclusively twentieth-century phenomena. It had been carried out ever since the armies of the East India Company gained a foothold in the subcontinent.[1] However, in the assessments of Indianization policies targeted at officers beginning in the early twentieth century, the military training and feeder institutions that emerged around this period have not been fully taken into account.

Indianization, in the late twentieth century, came to be broadly defined as 'the opening of the officer cadre of the Indian army to educated Indians and ending British monopoly over it'.[2] The 'debates

---

[1] Geoffrey Parker, *The Military Revolution: Military Innovation and the Rise of the West, 1500–1800* (Cambridge: Cambridge University Press, 1988), pp. 133–6. Also see, for instance, Richard Holmes, *Sahib: The British Soldier in India, 1750–1914* (London: Harper Collins, 2005), p. 46. Holmes writes about the early Anglo-French rivalries which enabled the rival trade companies from Britain and France to rapidly enlist native troops between 1748 and 1763. These earliest instances of active enlistment by non-Asian military outfits afforded a characteristic identity to the subcontinent's military 'signature' on formations and training procedures.

[2] P.S. Gupta, 'The Debate on Indianisation 1918–39', in *The British Raj and Its Indian Armed Forces, 1857–1939*, ed. P.S. Gupta and A. Deshpande, pp. 228–69 (New Delhi: Oxford University Press, 2002), p. 228.

on Indianization', as they have come to be characterized in literature, have given rise to an impressive amount of scholarship detailing the complex nature of this process, and also revealing how the negotiations between India and Britain on this subject were shaped by the prevailing economic and political circumstances. Yet, there is scarcely any reference made to the manner in which this process was affected by the institutions which were, in large measure, responsible for training and educating men who could replace the British officers.

The aim of this chapter is to outline and examine the Indianization policies from the standpoint of their diverse, regional network of three types of military feeder institutions: the Chief's colleges established in the mid-nineteenth century; the King George's schools set up in the mid-1920s; and lastly, the Lawrence schools, whose expansion in the mid-1920s in order to train students for a career in the military highlighted the inter-institutional nature and sensitivities of military institution-building and reform.[3]

It was this late nineteenth-century network of institutions which laid the groundwork for other, higher commission-awarding institutions to emerge in the subcontinent in the twentieth century that will be discussed in the subsequent chapters. Many of these academies, such as the IMA and the NDA established in 1932 and 1949, respectively, are widely recognized institutions today. However, in trying to locate the genesis of the ways in which the demand for more Indian officers was articulated by politicians, government officials, and others in the twentieth century, it is important to 'excavate' the histories of the 'missing academies', that is, the feeder training institutions that widened and contextualized the discussions surrounding Indianization of the officer cadre of the Indian military in crucial ways.

This chapter is divided into four sections. The first section outlines the political and constitutional context in which the Indianization took place. The second section deals with the analysis of the earliest institutional appearances of military academies in the subcontinent that coincided with the initial phase of the official discussions surrounding Indianization. The third section will 'probe' the familiar narrative on

---

[3] Two other feeder institutions—Prince of Wales Royal Indian Military College and the Kitchener College—will be discussed in the subsequent chapters in the context of other formal officers' academies.

early twentieth-century Indianization, in the light of the findings presented in the previous section. The fourth section relates to the shifts in the Indianization policies in the aftermath of the First and Second World Wars and examines the global contexts in which Indianization policies gained greater resonance in other parts of the Empire as it attempted to introduce similar policies in West Africa.

THE MILITARY AND POLITICAL CONTEXT TO INDIANIZATION: REVIEWING THE LATE NINETEENTH CENTURY

The military and political context to Indianization of the Indian military hosts a number of interconnected developments. Yet, a critical review of that context is essential to point out and explore the 'institutional appearances' that had started to dot the subcontinent at this time in response to the measures forwarded or propounded by colonial officials in India. Starting from the late nineteenth century, a string of difficult colonial military campaigns from the Anglo-Afghan Wars (1839–42, 1878–80, 1919) to the distant Boer wars (1880–1; 1899–1902), had alerted the British to the fact of necessary reforms they would have to undertake with regard to the Indian Army whose military efficiency was central to their security interests in the subcontinent. A steady westward shift in response to the 'Russian threat' to the northwestern frontier of the subcontinent heralded some key organizational and doctrinal changes for the army.[4]

These early attempts to engineer the army in accordance with the strategic and security imperatives had already begun to alter the institutional map of the forces. The gradual shift of security concerns to the northwest of the subcontinent by the end of the nineteenth century widened the functional protocol of the Indian Army from mainly internal policing to frontier defence. This shift was representative of

---

[4] Gautam Sharma, *Indian Army through the Ages* (Bombay: Allied Publishers, 1966), p. 247. Sharma contends that while the Army came to be concentrated more towards the northwest frontier, it involved the abandonment of thirty-four military stations and building of new accommodation for the troops in Punjab. The region was fortified, garrisoned, and connected by means of railroads.

the larger definitive organizational churning that the Indian Army was experiencing in its own doctrine, tactics, and cooperation with civilian authorities, and which would reach its peak in the years between the First and Second World Wars.[5]

The shift of military forces in the subcontinent happened in the late nineteenth century and peaked in the early twentieth century when Lord Roberts, the commander-in-chief of the Indian Army (1885–93), acted on the proposals to unify the three presidency armies into a single whole. The merger eventually took place after his departure in 1895. These 'Presidency armies' were now effectively under central command of the commander-in-chief.[6] Nonetheless, they maintained and developed their respective recruitment areas and acquired their distinctive caste and class 'regimental signatures' in an effort to maintain the 'martial races theory' that had undergirded much of their recruitment policy.[7] While the armies were getting merged into a unified central organization, newer groups like the Sikhs had also been incorporated into this system of military service to sustain and perpetuate this pseudo-scientific 'praxis' of recruitment.[8] The Sikhs, who had been disarmed after the fall of Punjab at the hands of the Company forces in the mid-nineteenth century, had begun to be identified and incorporated into the system resulting in novel modes of organization, chief among them being the Punjab Irregular Frontier Force, formed in 1849 to man the Empire's newest and northwestern promontory into Central Asia.[9]

[5] Srinath Raghavan, 'Protecting the Raj: The Army in India and Internal Security, c. 1919–1939', *Small Wars & Insurgencies* vol. 16, no. 3 (2005): 253–79.

[6] Scheme for the Redistribution of the army in India (Calcutta: GoI, 1904), BL, IOR/L/MIL/17/5/5/1741. See also Scheme for the Redistribution of the army in India and the Preparation of the army in India for War, India Office, 1904, BL, IOR/L/MIL/17/5/1742.

[7] Thomas R. Metcalf, *Ideologies of the Raj*, in *The New Cambridge History of India*, Volume III, Part 4 (Cambridge: Cambridge University Press, 1994), pp. 125–8.

[8] Kaushik Roy, 'Race and Recruitment in the Indian Army: 1880–1918', *Modern Asian Studies* vol. 47, no. 4 (2013): 1310–47.

[9] Tan Tai Yong, *The Garrison State: The Military, Government and Society in Colonial Punjab, 1849–1947* (New Delhi, London: Sage Publications, 2005), p. 37.

In the process of streamlining it for frontier fighting, Lord Kitchener, one of the most influential commanders-in-chief of the Indian Army (1902–9) in this period, set the Indian Army on a long path to modernization by creating a demand for more rigorously trained personnel and abolishing the 'Indian Staff Corps', thereby bringing a uniform military organization under the governor-general. This shifted the recruiting gaze of the Raj inwards and to look for men who could man the highly specialized garrisons along the northwest frontier, which was witnessing a hectic phase of military build-up.[10]

While this new phase of military organization was significant, it fitted incongruously with the ideational coordinates through which this new military architecture was sought to be staffed with. This was incongruous, because, while on the one hand, training of the recruits became more specialized in the regiments, their selection and subsequent careers, on the other hand, rose and fell with the vicissitudes of flawed 'anthropometry' and pseudo-scientific notions of race and caste, which continued to endure in the seemingly modern early twentieth-century military reorganization, in the form of what Gajendra Singh has termed the 'mothballed negatives' of the past.[11]

Nonetheless, the Indian Army had begun to acquire a specialist role for itself, and in this changed organizational mandate, there appeared signs of further institutional reform. The transition from presidency armies to the 'Indian Army' took place just at the time when demands for opening the officer cadre to Indians began to be heard in official governmental circles and stray official memoranda in India. Hence, the Indianization process followed close on the heels of significant organizational change in the Indian Army and its perceived goals and objectives.

An extensive cast of characters who worked from their bases both in India and Britain—whether it was the Viceroy's Council, the Central Legislature, the War Office, or the secretary of state for India in London—spoke about the need to Indianize the army and entered into what has been called as a 'fortuitous partnership' which laid the

---

[10] Sharma, *Indian Army through the Ages*, p. 247.

[11] Gajendra Singh, *The Testimonies of Indian Soldiers and the Two World Wars: Between Self and Sepoy* (London and New York: Bloomsbury Academic, 2014), p. 33.

foundations for Indianization of the officer corps from the late nine-teenth century.[12] Chief among them was Sir George Chesney, military member (formerly military secretary [MS]) of the governor-general's council, who, from 1885 till 1891, tried on four different occasions to convince the military and political officialdom in India and Britain to implement policies that would admit Indians as officers.[13]

Chesney's first attempt to pitch for a credible training architecture for Indians was in 1885 in a minute to the commander-in-chief of India, Gen. Sir Donald Martin Stewart.[14] However, at this stage, Chesney's overall understanding about instituting military Indianization was lim-ited to 'native gentlemen' from the noble houses: 'a class which, perhaps above all others', in Chesney's opinion, 'ought to be carried with us'.[15] 'Martial' ideas of 'gentlemanly suitability' for military service often conflated the former with a preference for wards and scions of the princes and aristocrats, resulting in instituting military measures that were designed to represent only such sections among the Indian classes whom the government deemed fit. Chesney's advocacy of Indianization and the need to rev up the primary institutional architecture to train aspiring officers went hand in hand with the plans to institute channels through which these 'aspiring officers' were to be placed in the army. From 1885 until 1889, Chesney soldiered on with one proposal after other—against considerable odds—explaining his schemes to govern-ments in India and Britain to open the military officer ranks to Indian men, but it resulted in only ad-hoc, limited measures.

[12] Pradeep Barua, *Gentlemen of the Raj: The Indian Army Officer Corps, 1817–1949* (Westport, Connecticut: Praeger, 2003), p. 20.

[13] For details of Chesney's proposals, please see Chandar S. Sundaram, 'Reviving a "Dead Letter": Military Indianization and the Ideology of Anglo-India, 1885–91', in *The British Raj and Its Indian Armed Forces, 1857–1939*, ed. P.S. Gupta and A. Deshpande, pp. 45–97 (New Delhi: Oxford University Press, 2002).

[14] This minute is cited in Despatch to the secretary of state for India, No. 57, 3 August 1917, Sir George Chesney to Gen. Sir Donald Stewart, Minute dated 22 January 1885, paragraph 9, Document page no. 3, BL, IOR/L/MIL/7/19019.

[15] Despatch to the secretary of state for India, No. 57, 3 August 1917, Sir George Chesney to Gen. Sir Donald Stewart, Minute dated 22 January 1885, paragraph 9, Document page no. 3, BL, IOR/L/MIL/7/19019.

This argument for selective, regiment-based Indianization became a dominant feature of subsequent negotiations that took place between the commander-in-chief, the viceroy, and the India Office in the decades between the late 1880s and 1920s, and followed almost a mathematical progression scale in the number of regiments that were to be Indianized, starting from the proposal to Indianize one solitary regiment and ending at the infamous '8 unit scheme' of 1922.[16] These schemes were selective in their implementation of Indianization and were often criticized for their segregationist features.

By 1888, Chesney had become more forceful in his proposals to institute a 'system of military education' in India.[17] Citing instances of the French and American military training establishments (the latter would come to play an important role in the formation of the NDA in 1945), Chesney advocated a self-supporting 'single' military college that could train younger Viceroy's Commissioned Officers (VCOs) as potential replacements for British officers.[18] This proposal structured the place of the 'Academy' on a firmer footing than in the past. Chesney advocated the role of this academy as that of a 'staff college' too, one which could 'round out' the practical experience of the young VCOs who attended it.[19] This short introduction to staff work, in fact, would add on to what was being done at another institution in India—the Roorkee Training School—where a small class of VCOs and Indian NCOs were being given training in 'military surveying' and sketching skills.[20] However, Chesney's proposals were not viewed

---

[16] Anirudh Deshpande, *British Military Policy in India, 1900–1945* (Delhi: Manohar, 2005), p. 98. Additionally, it was decided that from 1926, only Indian officers would be appointed to these eight units, resulting in a gradual Indianization of these units, with perhaps a future phase of Indianization reserved upon administering suitability tests to the Indian officers. For details of the scheme, see Report of Committee Appointed by H.E. the Commander-in-Chief in India, June 1923, BL, IOR/L/MIL/17/5/1779.

[17] Military Education for Natives of India, 23 January 1888, Lord G. Chesney, BL, IOR/L/MIL/17/5/2202.

[18] Military Education for Natives of India, 23 January 1888, Lord G. Chesney, BL, IOR/L/MIL/17/5/2202.

[19] Sundaram, 'Reviving a "Dead Letter"', p. 69.

[20] Military Education for Natives of India, 23 January 1888, Lord G. Chesney, BL, IOR/ L/MIL/17/5/2202.

favourably by the military establishment led by the commander-in-chief, Gen. Roberts.

Finally, in 1890, Chesney 'urged in favour' of the proposals that had emanated from the Punjab government, aiming to provide the Lahore-based Aitchison College—one of the Chiefs' schools—with a military training component in its curriculum.[21] The proposal was to train various classes of students within Aitchison for employment onto higher services within the military: students of 'high rank' could be appointed as second lieutenants; others as *jemadars* (junior officers); and students from native states could be potentially employed as officers of Imperial Service Troops.[22] Chesney also remarked that irrespective of the consideration of whether or not native officers should be raised to higher forms of service, the professional education of native officers' should be advanced.[23] These 1890 proposals, favoured by Chesney to offer military education to prospective officers, hint at the relationship that was sought to be established between technical colleges and military education—an early sign of the later twentieth-century efforts in aligning officers' academies to regular university structures.

One of the earliest academic institutional developments in the subcontinent, during the late nineteenth century, had been the rise of scientific training colleges including medical and engineering schools.[24] This development had an important impact on the early struggles to establish a military network of colleges, particularly the engineering colleges, which had the potential to transfer substantial skills from their own basket to that of the military. Thomason College, in particular, was suggested as a possible site to offer post-graduate technical instruction to the graduates of the IMA after 1932.[25]

---

[21] Cited in GoI (AD) Despatch No. 57 of 1917, 3 August 1917, para. 17, p. 7, BL, IOR/L/MIL/7/19019.

[22] Cited in GoI (AD) Despatch No. 57 of 1917, 3 August 1917, para. 17, p. 7, BL, IOR/L/MIL/7/19019.

[23] Cited in GoI (AD) Despatch No. 57 of 1917, 3 August 1917, para. 17, p. 7, BL, IOR/L/MIL/7/19019.

[24] Anil Seal, *The Emergence of Indian Nationalism: Competition and Collaboration in the Later Nineteenth Century* (Cambridge: Cambridge University Press, 1968), pp. 121–2.

[25] Chapter VIII, Report of the Indian Military College Committee, 15 July 1931, BL, IOR/L/MIL/17/5/1790.

It is easy to see Chesney's failed moves as indicative of British military policy being disfavourably inclined towards issues of Indianization at this time. There are also grounds for supporting such an assertion. Much of the resistance against reform of the Indian Army was based on the experiences of the 1857 mutiny and the worth of any new suggestion was measured against its ability to either foment or finish any further acts of rebellion and subversion by troops. Thus, reform measures instituted in the aftermath of 1857 were always done on an 'experimental' and 'selective' basis designed to prevent the outbreak of an armed revolt.[26] This was evident in not just the implementation of the short-lived 'regiment-based' Indianization policies but also in the management of the feeder network in the subcontinent.

MILITARY FEEDER INSTITUTIONS: CHIEF'S COLLEGES, KING GEORGE'S SCHOOLS, AND LAWRENCE SCHOOLS

Chesney's failed attempts at introducing a more regular and self-sustaining scheme of Indianization did not signal the end of military 'institutionalization' because while he petitioned the government to reconsider their position on Indianization, several feeder military training spaces had already begun to emerge in the subcontinent. These 'missing academies' or feeder institutions resided in the gaps and crevices of the late nineteenth and early twentieth centuries, which have been papered over in the pursuit of explaining the rise of an 'Indian Sandhurst' in the twentieth century. However, it is imperative to revive the story of these early institutional developments because a fuller explanation of the patterns of military institutional reform and Indianization in the period is incomplete without looking at the early inter-institutional links, whose struggles with administration and policies of recruitment and training set the context for the discussion on the establishment and reorganization of the higher military training infrastructure in the subcontinent.

---

[26] See Section I, 'Recommendations of the Indian Army Organization Commission, 1859', in *The Evolution of India and Pakistan: 1858 to 1947, Select Documents*, ed. C.H. Philips, H.L. Singh, and B.N. Pandey (London: Oxford University Press, 1962), pp. 506–7.

These institutions—collectively known as the Chief's colleges—
were established in particular regions of the subcontinent to cater to the
educational requirements of the local princely states. The Rajkumar
College, for instance, was opened in Rajkot (in the modern-day state
of Gujarat) in the late nineteenth century to serve the princes of the
Kathiawar states. Similarly, Mayo College in Ajmer was set up around
the same time to serve the princely states of the Rajputana (now the
modern-day state of Rajasthan). Daly College, set up around the time
of Mayo College as a 'residency school' in Indore to cover states of
the Central India Agency,[27] later figured briefly as the site for training
the first batch of KCIOs in 1919 before the scheme was abandoned.
Aitchison College was erected in 1886 in Lahore to meet the needs of
the Punjab princely families.[28]

It is, therefore, important to see the larger institutional implications
in Chesney's late nineteenth-century proposals. Chesney's suggestions
on the addition of more 'service-specific' training modules at these
aforementioned Chief's colleges, such as Aitchison, brings to light a key
network of military cum preparatory institutions invested in the task
of training and educating a set of students who would be interested in
taking up a military career.[29] The Chief's colleges later played a pivotal
role during the First World War in aiding the Empire's War effort. Their
contribution was mainly in the form of monetary assistance. By 1917,
a 'College War Fund' had come to be maintained at the Mayo College
in Ajmer out of which regular donations were 'placed at the disposal
of the Viceroy'.[30] A small number of its princely graduates also took

---

[27] Comprising modern day Indian states of Madhya Pradesh, Chhattisgarh,
parts of eastern Maharashtra, and Odisha.

[28] Barbara N. Ramusack, *The Indian Princes and Their States* (Cambridge
and New York: Cambridge University Press, 2004), p. 111.

[29] Military Education for Natives of India, 23 January 1888, Lord Chesney,
BL, IOR/L/MIL/17/5/2202.

[30] Report on the Mayo College, Ajmer, Rajputana, 1917–18, Chief's
Colleges: Annual Reports, BL, IOR/L/PS/10/401. Out of the college war
fund maintained by boys, masters, guardians, and subordinate staff of the
college, a special 'donation of rupees 1000 was placed at the disposal of His
Excellency the Viceroy on 4 August 1917, the 3rd anniversary of the declara-
tion of war'. Regular lectures on the War were also being given in all classes
throughout the school.

part in some of the campaigns of the Great War—the numbers and names being recorded in the reports annually since 1914.[31] The reports, therefore, never failed to showcase the colleges as integral elements in the Raj's military framework, testifying to the Colleges 'profoundest interest' in the Great War in which the 'empire was engaged'.[32] This interest, as the reports highlighted, was expressed mainly through their financial and participatory assistance towards the War effort.

However, this apparent optimism in the reports masked a growing and palpable sense of official unease regarding the future status of these institutions. By the early twentieth century, and increasingly after the First World War, the Chief's colleges had actually begun to decline. The reports frequently cited—alongside wartime donations and lists of its graduates enlisting to fight in Europe—a fall in the numbers of incoming students. The Daly College, located in central India, termed 1915–16 as a 'quiet year' owing to the departure of its fourteen students, all of whom withdrew at once.[33] While the report pointed at the increased fees at the College as a possible reason for the sudden withdrawal, there were other more important underlying causes which the report failed to fully take note of.

About half of those who withdrew from Daly College that year immediately sought admission in the nearby administrative and police training facilities of the state, effectively questioning the scope of education that was being imparted at the institution.[34] The Daly report remarked upon the increasing number of its students, also referred to as 'Kumars'—a title arising out of their royal or aristocratic lineage—looking for work outside their states. It also admitted to the fact that

---

[31] Report on the Mayo College, Ajmer, Rajputana, 1914–15, Chief's Colleges: Annual Reports, BL, IOR/L/PS/10/401. Several such reports never failed to highlight the number of Princes and noblemen who took part in the First World War campaigns.

[32] Report on the Mayo College, Ajmer, Rajputana, 1914–15, Chief's Colleges: Annual Reports, BL, IOR/L/PS/10/401.

[33] Report on the Working of the Daly College for 1915–16, in Chief's Colleges: Annual Report, BL, IOR/L/PS/10/401. During the year 1915–16, fourteen Kumars left the college and nine Kumars joined the college, so the total number fell to fifty-five.

[34] Report on the Working of the Daly College for 1915–16, in Chief's Colleges: Annual Report, BL, IOR/L/PS/10/401.

it was not always 'easy or possible' for a *durbar* (royal court) to find suitable employment for one its Kumars just at the time when that Kumar leaves the Daly college.[35] While the report acknowledged the diversification of employment opportunities among its graduates as a step 'in the right direction', it failed to see the causal links between the students looking out for 'other' vocational opportunities and the inability of the college itself to facilitate the aspirational changes in employment choices among its students.

The problem of attracting students was not confined to just the Daly College. A year before the Daly report was tabled, Mayo College at Ajmer, yet another Chief's College, was reporting large-scale withdrawals among its students.[36] The number of withdrawals at Mayo was higher than Daly: a total of thirty-four students from the senior form had decided to leave the institution. This was a direct challenge to the institutional legitimacy of Mayo as more than two-thirds of those who had left hailed from its core constituency, that is, Rajputana.[37] More importantly, the institutions that the students joined upon leaving Mayo College were indicative of how the changed landscape of education in India was casting a long shadow on the educational programmes at the Chief's colleges and their relative position vis-à-vis other emerging institutions. Many of those who chose to leave Mayo joined other civilian or more regular military formations. Some of the more notable ones like the prince of Alwar joined the Government College in Ajmer, while Abdul Khan from the principality of Tonk decided to enrol at the Mohammedan Anglo Oriental College in Aligarh.[38] Kanwar Shumsher Jang of Nepal proceeded to join the Imperial Forest College at Dehradun—the site of another formal feeder college that was to come up in 1922–3.

[35] Report on the Working of the Daly College for 1915–16, in Chief's Colleges: Annual Report, BL, IOR/L/PS/10/401.

[36] Report on the Mayo College, Ajmer, Rajputana, 1914–15, in Chief's Colleges: Annual Report, BL, IOR/L/PS/10/401.

[37] Rajputana today approximates to the territories included in the modern-day Indian state of Rajasthan.

[38] Report on the Mayo College, Ajmer, Rajputana, 1914–15, in Chief's Colleges: Annual Report, BL, IOR/L/PS/10/401. Several students, as the report listed, went on to join the military departments of the states from which they came from.

Some of the students from the Mayo College had also joined the ICC—a cadre of military service that was formed in 1901. It was created mainly as a vehicle for officer training for the princely and aristocratic set, many of whom were trained at the Chief's colleges. The ICC's failure, like the decline of the Chief's colleges at this time, arose out of the ad hoc and 'experimental' nature of the ways in which military reform was being carried out and which had begun to falter by the 1920s. Chandar Sundaram's work on the corps offers useful insights as to why it ultimately failed to work in the long run.[39] Sundaram contends that one of the reasons for the corps's unpopularity stemmed from its inability to provide substantial career opportunities for its graduates.[40] The princely chiefs' and rulers' growing sense of disaffection with the ICC was more than amply exhibited in the dismal performance of the cadets, and the high attrition rate robbed the ICC of much of its sheen by 1917 when it was disbanded before a brief revival in 1923.[41]

The ICC was otherwise favourably placed in the military institutional framework: a credible link between the Chiefs' Colleges, which were the source for many of ICC's recruits,[42] and a commission in the native forces and the Imperial Service troops ready to absorb the graduates.[43] However, the ICC failed despite these

[39] Chandar S. Sundaram, '"Treated with Scant Attention": The Imperial Cadet Corps, Indian Nobles, and Anglo-Indian Policy, 1897–1917', *The Journal of Military History* vol. 77, no. 1 (2013): 41–70.

[40] Sundaram, '"Treated with Scant Attention"', p. 69

[41] See, Part IV, 'Soldier for the Raj?: Accommodation and Resistance at the Imperial Cadet Corps', in *Reversing the Gaze: Amar Singh's Diary—A Colonial Subject's Narrative of Imperial India*, ed. Susanne H. Rudolph, Lloyd I. Rudolph, and M.S. Kanota, pp. 268–79 (Westview Press, Boulder: 2002). Out of the initial class of twenty-one recruits who entered the ICC in 1902, only four cadets were commissioned in 1905 upon graduation.

[42] Document No. 7, 'Lord Curzon's Memorandum on Commissions for Indians, 4 June 1900', in *The Evolution of India and Pakistan: 1858 to 1947, Select Documents*, ed. C.H. Philips, H.L. Singh, and B.N. Pandey, pp. 518–21 (London: Oxford University Press, 1962), p. 521.

[43] K.M.L. Saxena, *The Military System of India 1850–1900* (New Delhi: Sterling Publishers, 1974), pp. 152–4. The Imperial Service Troops, renamed as the Imperial State Forces after the First World War, were formalized in 1889 when sections of the Indian princely states' forces were converted into the

factors, because it did not extend these commissions to enable the men to command the regular British-staffed regiments that existed in the Indian Army—a central issue that would continue to plague subsequent discussions on officer Indianization. The unpopularity of the ICC coupled with the limited opportunities for officership in the military had considerable implications for the Chief's colleges, who, by their own admission, were struggling to place their graduates onto formal vocational pathways. The disbandment of the ICC, thus, coincided with the decline in student numbers at the feeder colleges illuminating the critical bonds that linked higher military service with its training spaces.

It was clear, then, that the Chief's colleges had not managed to successfully adapt themselves to the changing patterns of educational aspirations among the princes and were struggling to train some of its core clients for whom they were established in the late nineteenth century. The failure was also compounded by the pressures of financial austerity brought about by the First World War that restricted the ability of these colleges to expand and undertake critical structural and systemic reforms that could have stemmed the departure of students in large numbers. The limiting influence of fiscal restraints on institutional reform was evident in the case of another Chief's College—the Aitchison College in Lahore.

The shrinking post-War budgetary allowance had crippled the Aitchison College's operations. By 1920, the college was asking the government to increase its grant over and above its annual subvention in order to undertake 'urgently required improvements'.[44] The college had petitioned the Punjab government in 1920 after which the latter had recommended an additional grant from within the provincial revenues to be made to Aitchison, in an apparent attempt to shore up

---

Imperial Service Troops. Saxena also contends that 'there was no intention on the part of the government to use the Imperial Service Troops as an integral portion of its regular divisions'.

[44] Letter to Montagu, Secretary of State for India from GoI comprising Chelmsford, C.C. Monroe, W.H. Vincent, Muhammad Shafi, W.M. Hailey, T.H. Holland, A.P Muddiman, 13 May 1920, Chief's Colleges: Annual Reports, BL, IOR/L/PS/10/401.

its financial strength—a rare measure for which approval had to be secured from the secretary of state's office in London.[45]

However, the dire situation of 1920 was not solely attributable to post–War austerity. The central government had, as early as in 1906, started making arrangements for providing financial packages to these institutions to stimulate their growth and aid their reform but the colleges were found wanting.[46] Declining student numbers, combined with annual budgetary cuts before the First World War, had resulted in a severe shortage of staff at institutions. For instance, even before the 1920 fiscal emergency at Aitchison, the institution was already demanding the government to review its functioning. Demands to augment its teaching staff by 'appointing additional masters' at a 'net extra cost to Indian revenues of Rs 32,000 a year' while also seeking a reorganization of the 'Indian Educational Service' to serve Aitchison College were being made almost at the same time as the aforementioned 'mass withdrawals' were taking place at Daly and Mayo.[47] The reversal in the growth curve of the Chief's colleges was accelerated during the years of the First World War and accentuated the volatility of institutional functioning in this period. Aitchison College illustrates

---

[45] Letter to Montagu, Secretary of State for India from GoI comprising Chelmsford, C.C. Monroe, W.H. Vincent, Muhammad Shafi, W.M. Hailey, T.H. Holland, A.P. Muddiman, 13 May 1920, Chief's Colleges: Annual Reports, BL, IOR/L/PS/10/401.

[46] Letter to Montagu, Secretary of State for India from GoI comprising Chelmsford, C.C. Monroe, W.H. Vincent, Muhammad Shafi, W.M. Hailey, T.H. Holland, A.P. Muddiman, 13 May 1920, Chief's Colleges: Annual Reports, BL, IOR/L/PS/10/401. The letter charts out the longer history of financial support that was being extended to the Chief's colleges. As per the letter, in a despatch dated 30 August 1906, Lord Minto's government explained the financial result of the reforms which had been introduced to the Chief's colleges at Ajmer, Lahore, and Rajkot, recommending that an annual subvention of Rs 21,634 and an additional grant of Rs 12,000 should be made to the Aitchison College in Lahore. The subvention was subsequently increased by Rs 6,366 a year as a result of the representations contained in the despatches from Lord Hardinge's government in July 1913 and September 1914.

[47] Memorandum from GoI to Secretary of State for India, Marquess of Crewe, 10 July 1913, Chief's Colleges: Annual Reports, BL, IOR/L/PS/10/401.

TABLE 1.1   Abstract of Receipts and Expenditure in Recent Years at the Aitchison College, Lahore

	1914–15	1915–16	1916–17	1917–18	1918–19
Receipts	138,285	153,919	159,104	163,105	175,043
Expenditure	136,893	155,807	161,733	165,885	170,960
Balance	+1,387 [*sic*]	−1,888	−2,629	−2,780	+4,083

Source: Adapted from Chief's Colleges: Annual Report, BL, IOR/L/PS/10/401.

the impact of this inherent volatility on the financial position of such institutions as reflected in Table 1.1.

A combination of academic and vocational dissonance with newer emerging sites of training and learning as well as fiscal imprudence had marred the functioning of the Aitchison institution. Aitchison's declining stature was at best a reflection of the changing institutional landscape in India—a recurring feature in the patterns of military institutionalization in the subsequent decades.

To address the problems of the Chief's colleges, a set of reforms were proposed in 1920 to establish a new institutional network to fill the gap that was created by these ailing institutions. These reforms were aimed at establishing a new set of institutions called King George Royal Indian Military Colleges (henceforth King George's schools) that could provide facilities for higher 'degree-awarding studies along special lines' for which the 'Princes had looked in vain'.[48] While one of these institutions—a 'higher' Chief's College, proposed to be set up in Delhi and intended to 'provide an all-India perspective for Princes'— never materialized, it served what Barbara Ramusack has termed as the 'stepping stone' towards the Chamber of Princes.[49] However, in terms of the military institutional landscape, this was also a 'stepping stone' towards the development of other military feeder schools at this time.

The emergence of the King George's schools, initially along India's northwestern fringe between 1925 and 1930, and some of which now

[48] Report on the Mayo College, Ajmer, Rajputana, 1914–15, containing a News Report in the Times Educational Supplement, dated 10 December 1921, in 'The Chief's Colleges', Chief's Colleges: Annual Reports, BL, IOR/L/PS/10/401.

[49] Ramusack, *The Indian Princes and Their States*, p. 111.

continue albeit in a different form, namely, the '*Rashtriya*[50] Indian Military College', were meant to fill the gap that had been created as a result of the inadequate educational and training programme delivered at the Chief's colleges and to win back its constituents who were beginning to leave for other institutions.[51] The King George's schools were different from the earlier network of feeder spaces of the late nineteenth century in one key aspect. While the Chief's colleges were mainly geared to provide education to the princes, in the wake of the early twentieth-century transformation and expansion of the Indian Army in response to Lord Kitchener's military reforms, a need was felt to widen the institutional remit of feeder training spaces. The King George's schools, therefore, were the earliest military feeder institutions that were mandated to include the children of the Raj's emerging military constituencies, such as the VCOs and Anglo-Indians, in order to provide them with a 'cheap' and 'comprehensive education'.[52]

The King George's schools came under the direct administration of the commander-in-chief of the Indian Army and the capital expenditure for the schools was borne out of the 'King Emperor's Patriotic Fund'—a fund that was created out of the wartime endowments from the Indian princes to the British monarch.[53] A share of the seats were

---

[50] '*Rashtriya*' is roughly translatable as 'National'.

[51] Regulations for King George's Royal Indian Military Schools, Jhelum, Jullundur, and Ajmer, 1933 and 1939, BL, IOR/L/MIL/17/5/2303. These schools were set up in the years between 1925 and 1930, and the object of education was to: 'to enable the boys to find a career in their fathers' regiments or corps.' Two additional schools were opened after the Second World War in southern India (in Bangalore and Belgaum).

[52] 'Appendix I, Lord Rawlinson's Last Speech in the Legislative Assembly: Reviewing His Military Policy, March 4, 1925', in *The Life of General Lord Rawlinson of Trent: From His Journals and Letters*, ed. Maj. Gen. Sir Frederick Maurice, pp. 343–52 (London: Cassell, 1928), p. 350.

[53] 'King George's Royal Indian Military Schools' (Lecture by Capt. T.H.L. Stebbing, MC, MA, AEC, Commandant, KGRIM School, Jalandhar), *The Journal of the United Service Institution of India, January 1936*, vol. LXVI, no. 282, consulted from: Subject File 15, B.S. Moonje Papers, Nehru Memorial Museum and Library Archives (NMML Archives), New Delhi. The 'King Emperor's Patriotic Fund' was at the personal disposal of the King and was started in July 1918. It was decided that the fund should be invested, and its

reserved for the sons of the soldiers of the Indian States Forces (ISF; the armed constabularies of the princely states), the Frontier Corps, as well as other irregular northwest-based militias.[54] The apportioning of seats within different frontier-based militias at these schools signified the strategic importance that was attached to the defence of the northwest frontier of the subcontinent, and also attested to the need to constantly co-opt the differentiated and growing constituency of military personnel of the early twentieth century in the evolving military institutional architecture of the Raj.

The Lawrence School network, although not formally in the category of military feeder schools, was an important institutional development that provided the first signs of the inter-institutional nature of military reform in India. It was founded in the latter part of the nineteenth century in northern and southern parts of India, and initially catered exclusively to the wards of British army personnel.[55] However, by the mid-1920s, the syllabus and the Lawrence 'constituency' had shifted considerably to include 'Anglo-Indians',[56] and a more regular military component had been added to the curriculum, to the extent that the southern Lawrence School at Lovedale (situated in the present-day Indian state of Tamil Nadu, neighbouring the Indian Army's Staff College) was designated as the 'Lawrence Memorial Royal Military School, Lovedale' upon receiving a royal ascent in 1925, signifying the change in its institutional mandate and aims of education.[57]

income devoted to the relief of Indian sufferers with claims based on the War. In 1920, the fund contained approximately Rs 1,000,000.

[54] Regulations for King George's Royal Indian Military Schools, Jhelum, Jullundur, and Ajmer, 1933 and 1939, BL, IOR/L/MIL/17/5/2303.

[55] Hugh Gantzer and Colleen Gantzer, *Never Give In: A History of the One Hundred and Twenty Five Years of The Lawrence School* (Lovedale, Madras: Orient Longman, 1984), p. 47. Gantzer suggests that the Lawrence Asylum at Ootacamund (southern India) was formed during 1858 in honour of the memory of Sir Henry Lawrence, KCB, by whom the establishment at some Hill Station, within the Madras Presidency, of an institution similar to the Lawrence Asylum at Sanawar, had been suggested.

[56] Precise meaning and reference not specified in the Lawrence School records. It could have been used to denote children of Eurasian extraction.

[57] Annual Reports of the Lawrence Memorial Royal Military School, Lovedale, Nilgiris, BL, IOR/L/MIL/17/5/2299.

The Lawrence schools, increasingly after 1925, prepared students for careers mainly in the military. Since 1933—a year after the IMA's inauguration in 1932—the annual reports of the institutions suggested that at least 20–30 per cent of the intake each year, upon graduation, proceeded to join the military.[58] These schools, thus, had begun to forge robust institutional links with other officer-training and feeder schools in the subcontinent, highlighting that the institutional matrix for facilitating the entry of suitably trained candidates for the military had begun to take shape as early as 1925. The Lawrence schools—not formally designated as feeder institutions—retained a widely cosmopolitan ambience of educators and those who were educated, but the crystallization of its links with higher military training institutions is hard to miss. The links between the Lawrence schools and the military were most evident when the former were exposed to the fluctuating demands of recruitment in the latter during the course of the Second World War.

The annual reports of the Lawrence Schools at Sanawar[59] (north India) and Lovedale[60] (south India) reflected the anxieties associated with waves of demobilization that appeared imminent after the conclusion of the Second World War and its impact on the students graduating out of their portals. The reports testify to the immediate impact

[58] See, for instance, Annual Report of the Lawrence Royal Military School, Sanawar, 1 April 1935 to 31 March 1936, 1933–4, BL, IOR/ L/ MIL/17/5/2300.

[59] Sanawar enjoys the distinction of being one of the oldest schools in the British Empire to carry 'colours'. This distinction was granted in 1853 when 'colours' were presented by the then-viceroy, the Earl of Dalhousie. New 'colours' were presented by His Royal Highness The Prince of Wales on behalf of the king-emperor and the Lawrence family at Dehradun on the 13 March 1922. See Rules of the Lawrence Royal Military School, Sanawar, 1941 (1935, Simla: GoI Press), BL, IOR/L/MIL/17/5/2301.

[60] The Lovedale institution was opened in 1858 but underwent significant changes in its composition thereafter. In 1871, the existing 'military orphanage asylums' of male and female children in Madras were merged with the institution, and was designated as the 'Lawrence Memorial School'. See Annexure F, Rules regarding the Constitution and Working of the School Preamble, Annual Reports of the Lawrence Memorial Royal Military School, Lovedale, Nilgiris, 73rd Report, 1932–33, BL, IOR L/MIL/17/5/2299.

of and inter-institutional 'sensitivities' associated with a downturn in military recruitment for institutions that were geared or realigned towards supplying, in large measure, a growing clientele for military service. For instance, the drafters of the Lawrence reports for Lovedale remarked that it will be 'problematical' when, in the aftermath of the 'Japanese war ... it will still be possible for the boys to enter services as easily as they do now' and that the 'the question of careers for those at school-leaving age will quite likely become acute'.[61] The question of unemployment after graduating from a military college became even more acute since the schools had started admitting Anglo-Indian students from the initial decades of the twentieth century, and the non-availability of a military employment option, the report suggested, would considerably affect the chances of such students 'who would find it difficult to find employment outside this country.'[62]

The problem of finding suitable employment guarantees for the Anglo-Indian students continued to be gloomy and even reached higher levels of the government like the quartermaster general's branch, signalling the reach of these schools within the official establishment of the Raj. As early as 1935–6, efforts were underway to get the Anglo-Indian students some 'employment'. The Lawrence Reports do not specify what form of employment they were assigned to, but even after substantive efforts by the school, the report concluded that 'two boys presenting grave problems' were still left 'on our hands', hinting at the struggles through which these schools tried to place some of their graduates into mainstream vocational channels.[63] The 'Indian Sandhurst' or the IMA, which had begun to function in 1932, also faced similar problems in placing the Anglo-Indians within their portal highlighting the persistent and recurring struggles of training, educating and placing the graduates of these institutions within the realm of higher military services. Thus, the 'school' and the 'academy' had developed close links in the process of officering the Indian Army and

[61] Annual Reports of the Lawrence Memorial Royal Military School, Lovedale, Nilgiris, BL, IOR/L/MIL/17/5/2299.

[62] Annual Reports of the Lawrence Memorial Royal Military School, Lovedale, Nilgiris, BL, IOR/L/MIL/17/5/2299.

[63] Annual Report of the Lawrence Royal Military School, Sanawar, 1 April 1935 to 31 March 1936, 1933–4, BL, IOR/ L/MIL/17/5/2300.

a turn in the fortunes of one institutional space was now beginning to have an impact on the other.

The institutional links between the higher military institutions of the twentieth century with the lower feeder colleges were strengthened further after the inauguration of the feeder college known as the Prince of Wales Royal Indian Military College in Dehradun in 1921.[64] It was the precursor to the 'Indian Sandhurst', which came up at the same place a decade later in 1932 in Dehradun in northern India. This college played an instrumental role in the training and education of candidates who were interested in joining Sandhurst, which, after 1919, had started to reserve ten seats annually for Indians. Later, in 1925, when the Skeen Committee was appointed to study the feasibility of establishing an 'Indian Sandhurst', it looked to these feeder colleges as 'supporting institutions' in training and educating candidates for the Indian Sandhurst. The 1925 committee's report recommended comprehensive reform measures for these feeder colleges aimed at building and augmenting their capacity to supply not just prospective cadets for a military academy but also suitably educated graduates who wished to pursue non-military careers.

Thus, the Indian military landscape had acquired a complex, multi-tiered structure of military training and feeder institutions by the early twentieth century. The Chief's colleges, the King George's schools, as well as the Lawrence Schools, together with the Prince of Wales Royal Indian Military College,[65] symbolized the earliest institutional expressions of the Indianization policies that were forwarded by colonial officials in the late nineteenth century. These feeder institutions were the first coordinates plotted on the map of the Indian military, decades before the 'Indian Sandhurst' appeared on the horizon in 1932. Moreover, these 'missing' military academies were the first to contend with educating and training different groups of candidates for military service. In mitigating the challenges associated with training

---

[64] A published account of the Prince of Wales Royal Indian Military College—Arun Prakash, *The Young Warriors: A History of the Rashtriya Indian Military College, Dehra Dun* (Dehradun: RIMC, 2004)—offers a mainly chronological overview of the development of this institution.

[65] For a more detailed analysis of the Prince of Wales Royal Indian Military College, please see Chapter 2.

this varied military constituency of the Raj, there were early hints of the future struggles that the more familiar but understudied officers' academies would have to undertake, changing the meanings and scope of Indianization.

PROBING THE 'FAMILIAR' EARLY TWENTIETH-CENTURY NARRATIVE ON MILITARY INSTITUTIONS

The political rhetoric of the early twentieth century ensured that military issues continued to resonate with the larger aims of the nationalist movement. However, the process through which nationalist leaders appropriated issues of military reform and institution-building was less than 'united' and deviated from the prevalent narrative that portrayed military Indianization as a campaign led by a unified Indian leadership railing against colonial machinations that were preventing India from acquiring a credible hold over its defence architecture. Opinions regarding Indianization and military institution-building sprang from diverse and often contradictory strands within Indian politics and which lent their influence on military policies in unique ways. The fact that a considerable number of Indian leaders, policy officials, and academicians frequently came together to discuss and plan the institutional growth chart for the military should not be mistaken for any kind of a definitive political 'unity' on military issues at this time.

The beginning of a political discussion which formally included Indian leaders on the question of commissioning Indians as officers can be traced back to 1917 when Edwin Montagu, the secretary of state for India (1917–22), remarked in the House of Commons in August 1917 as having 'removed the bar which has hitherto precluded the admission of Indians to Commissioned rank in His Majesty's Army'.[66] Delivered a year before the First World War ended, the statement underlined the

---

[66] Cited in, Sundaram, 'Reviving a "Dead Letter"', p. 46. This oft-repeated remark in the literature on Indianization carries important implications. It sought to bring the various classes of ICOs within the ambit of a King's Commission and also redressed the grievances associated with the ceremonial and dysfunctional ICC.

colonial policy to expand Indian forces to meet wartime needs. This included expanding the commissioned officer ranks in the army.

This statement was supplemented with constitutional provisions that were announced for India as part of the Montagu–Chelmsford Reforms of 1919 and later subsumed under the Government of India Act of 1919. The Act reformed provincial and central legislative councils; widened the ambit of constitutional negotiations; and multiplied the consultative channels through which Indian leaders could discuss issues of political and constitutional reform, not least the issue of 'military reform', taken up by them actively only after the conclusion of the First World War. However, the gradual widening of consultative structures on defence did not mean that military issues were now under popular legislation. Even until 1946, when constitutional proposals were forwarded for the Indian Union by the visiting cabinet mission from Britain, matters relating to defence continued to be limited to official deliberation at the 'centre', that is, the executive seat of government at the viceroy's office.[67]

This constitutional and political context was made clearer in the subsequent years when the controversial Indian Statutory Commission visited India in 1928. Commonly referred to as the 'Simon Commission', it regarded, among other political measures, the process of Indianization as a 'task of greatest possible difficulty'.[68] The protracted tussle to define the constitutional status of India, and within it, that of the military, characterized the nature of negotiations on Indianization in the early twentieth century.

The opening years of the twentieth century were notable for the marked 'convergence' of two policy objectives regarding military Indianization at this time. These two objectives were acquiring more

[67] Effectively, then, defence remained a 'reserved subject'. For details of the preliminary notes on the Cabinet Mission's Plans on Defence, please see, B. Shiva Rao (ed.), *The Framing of India's Constitution: Select Documents*, Volume 2, pp. 694–9 (New Delhi: The Indian Institute of Public Administration, 1966).

[68] 'The Simon Commission on Army Recruitment, 1930', in *The Evolution of India and Pakistan: 1858 to 1947, Select Documents*, ed. C.H. Philips, H.L. Singh, and B.N. Pandey, pp. 532–4 (London: Oxford University Press, 1962), p. 533. The report contended that the 'peaceful unity' of a 'self-governing' India would be at a great risk if it relied solely upon troops drawn from certain selected areas.

Indian officers and establishing an indigenous architecture to sustain a regular inflow of Indians into the army. The convergence of the two demands relating to Indianization into a single policy objective transformed, significantly, the nature of the constitutional relationship between India and Britain on matters of military reform. The importance of the requirement of establishing an indigenous higher military training institution was portrayed as a necessary condition accompanying the grant of dominion status to India. For where else—as leaders, soldiers, and ordinary people were increasingly beginning to realize in the early twentieth century—could one have academies for one's officers, but in a dominion?[69] The grant of dominion status, therefore, at least in the early years of the twentieth century, presented to Indian leaders a cover under which an 'Indian' defence architecture could be persuasively argued for.

One of the prominent Indian leaders to take up Indianization actively at this time was Sir Sivaswamy Aiyar, member of the Central Legislative Assembly (CLA), and politically, the successor to Chesney's 'ginger-group tactics' on Indianization. Aiyar's resolutions, numbering a total of fifteen, moved in 1921 in response to the recommendations of the army in India Committee Report also known as the Esher Committee (1920), were enshrined into a formal Assembly resolution, and are the most cogent expression of interest by an Indian politician on the subject of military Indianization.[70] His proposals included reserving a percentage of King's commissions to Indian subjects and emphasising the need for an Indian military

---

[69] This was argued in a prize-winning essay written by a student at the Prince of Wales Royal Indian Military College, Dehradun. The student, writing in 1933, drew an astute comparison between Canada and India on the broad principles of a federation and concluded that it was 'only a matter of time before the control of the Indian Army passes into the hands of the Indians', since it was 'natural on the part of the Indians to want their army controlled by themselves as is done in the Dominions'. See Magazine Issue, September 1933 of the Prince of Wales Royal Indian Military College Journal, BL, IOR/L/MIL/17/5/2286.

[70] Report of the Committee Appointed to Consider the Report of the Esher Committee, 21 March 1921, CLA Debates, BL, IOR/V/9/49 (Microfilm), 1st Assembly, 1st Session, 11–29 March 1921, Volume 1.

training institution. Aiyar's consistent efforts resulted in a significant milestone in military institutionalization as the government agreed to set up a preparatory school—Prince of Wales Military College at Dehradun—to provide training to those who were interested in competing for the ten reserved vacancies at Sandhurst[71] (these vacancies were authorized in 1918 and later expanded in 1925–6). Several other initiatives proposed by Aiyar with regard to Indianization were stonewalled, but it resulted in the formation of alternative committees by the government which were set up to review the issue of Indianization afresh.[72]

Twentieth-century negotiations on military Indianization often regarded military reform as a delivery of 'rewards' that had been promised to India after the First World War. Aiyar, as one of the several Indian leaders in the Assembly, was often quick to put the government in a spot to justify the delay in delivering that reward.[73] Thus, a sustained focus on viewing military reform as a result of post-War entitlements caused the Indian leaders to overlook the earlier institutions that had been set up towards providing military training to Indians. By neglecting these older developments, political campaigns at this time gave the impression of a partisan debate on Indianization policies and ironed out the complex institutional processes through which more Indians were trained as officers.

Aiyar's subsequent interventions on Indianization policies also did not fully take into account the experiences of the late nineteenth century in institutional reform that had resulted in the enunciation of slow, experimental, and cautious proposals on military reorganization,

---

[71] Inauguration of the 2nd session of the state and legislative assemblies, Speech by Viceroy, CLA Debates, BL, IOR/V/9/50 (Microfilm), 1st Assembly, 2nd Session, 1–30 September 1921, Volume 2.

[72] For instance, the Shea Committee was instituted by the commander-in-chief of the Indian Army and was headed by Lt Gen. Shea, acting chief of the GS. The committee's report recommended steps towards Indianization of the Indian Army through institutional features, primarily the 'unit system' as well as accepting the demand for an 'Indian' academy. See Shea Committee Report, BL, IOR/L/MIL/17/5/1778.

[73] 'No. 69, Aiyar's response to the Skeen Committee Report', in *A Great Liberal: Speeches and Writings of Sir P.S. Sivaswamy Aiyar*, ed. K.A. Nilkanta Sastri, pp. 429–30 (Bombay: Allied Publishers, 1965).

'buried in the pigeon holes' of the government.[74] Aiyar's interventions portray a state of inaction and indifference exhibited by the governments in India and Britain to accelerate Indianization. According to his views expressed in reaction to the 1925 Skeen Committee Report, rapid Indianization was 'dependent' on the formation and expansion of a military training institution in India; he contrasted his views with the 'exponents' of imperial policy who restricted commissions to Indians due to 'insufficient supply' of suitable candidates.[75]

The tensions articulated in the above remarks illustrate that the administrative struggles of the feeder institutions were never adequately factored in while leaders like Aiyar articulated their position on Indianization. A brief review of the feeder institutions and their struggles would have sensitized Aiyar (and indeed sections of Indian political opinion) to the 'slow' and 'experimental' nature of reforms that were being proposed in 1925 for the setting up of higher officers' academies. What seemed to them to be a 'slow' start to Indianization, after a protracted struggle to open up the military to Indian officers, was in fact a result of the fall-outs that were witnessed with the earlier generation of military institutions like the Chief's colleges in the subcontinent, and in whose faltering performance the idea of setting up another academy may have been approached with caution. Of course, this is not to suggest that Indian political opinion such as those belonging to the likes of Aiyar were all misguided, but it is important to highlight that political interventions based on which they campaigned for a faster rate of Indianization were not informed upon by the prior institutional, administrative, and educational experiences in preparing diverse groups of Indian men for officership. That many of the earliest administrative challenges that arose in the IMA were principally of the same nature that had plagued the functioning of the feeder schools was proof of the interdependent nature of military Indianization. Problems encountered in one type of institution had a subsequent impact on other forms of military training institutions. These roadblocks significantly impacted the rate of Indianization and also sharply questioned the fierce rhetorical pitch of Indian political opinion on the subject

---

[74] Remarks on the 'Indian Sandhurst Committee Report', in *A Great Liberal*, p. 392.

[75] Remarks on the 'Indian Sandhurst Committee Report', p. 396.

of military Indianization. As newly formed nationalist parties and legislative factions jockeyed for influence, military reform and institution-building acquired a new lease of life. Nonetheless, the efforts to campaign and establish those institutions were informed upon by a multitude of dissensions and conflicts of opinions.

The demands for rapid Indianization emanated from disparate legislative groupings of Indian leaders, who drove the campaign forward with different aims and motivations and which were made more evident in the negotiations that were to take place in 1931 on the establishment of the IMA. What allowed Indian politicians to devise a common 'strategy' with respect to Indianization (but who could not forge a united 'alliance' of any sort on Indianization policy) was due to what P.S. Gupta has termed as the effective 'floor coordination' at the CLA.[76] Gupta outlines that by 1924, the 'Swaraj Party'—a faction of the Congress leaders led by Motilal Nehru and Chittaranjan Das that entered electoral politics after breaking away from Gandhi-led non-cooperation tactics in 1922—had garnered forty-one of the 101 seats to be filled by elections in the reorganized CLA. Another cluster of seventeen members grouped themselves under the leadership of M.A. Jinnah as the 'Independent Party'.[77] Although not dealt with in greater detail by Gupta, an instrumental role was also played by the 'Liberals' and the 'Responsivist Co-operators' groups in the CLA that attempted to forge, in association with other political factions, a common strategy with regard to pressing the government on implementing Indianization.[78]

This political re-grouping on the floor of the CLA's house gave way to a 'constitutional tussle' in 1925, which momentarily brought Indian leaders (including Aiyar) in a united political contest with the government over the issue of Indianization—a process which was now identified chiefly with the cause of establishing an 'Indian Sandhurst'.

---

[76] P.S. Gupta, 'The Debate on Indianisation 1918–39 ', in *The British Raj and Its Indian Armed Forces, 1857–1939*', ed. P.S. Gupta and A. Deshpande, pp. 228–69 (New Delhi: Oxford University Press, 2002), pp. 230–3.

[77] Gupta, 'The Debate on Indianisation 1918–39'.

[78] Srinath Raghavan, 'Liberal Thought and Colonial Military Institutions', in *India's Grand Strategy: History, Theory, Cases*, ed. Kanti Bajpai, Saira Basit, and V. Krishnappa, pp. 86–109 (New Delhi: Routledge, 2014).

Claims, therefore, of any unity of opinion among Indian leaders on the Indianization issue after the First World War stem mainly from this political re-grouping of Indian leaders. Thus, the electoral and constitutional reforms had considerably transformed the membership in the CLA so as to allow a loosely grouped oppositional sections to take shape which lost no time in dissecting both the political and military aspects of Indianization, but they did so in fragmented and multiple voices, which were often uninformed about the workings of the larger military institutional apparatus.

Besides these multiple political voices and agendas guiding military Indianization, certain other developing international contexts also shaped these policies. The years after the First World War reflected constant shifts in the terms and scope of those policies. Identifying these shifts is central to understanding the ways in which the underlying principles governing Indianization shifted gears periodically to shape this process not just in India but also in other parts of the British Empire.

SHIFTS IN THE TERMS OF INDIANIZATION POLICIES AND ITS INTERNATIONAL IMPLICATIONS

This section aims to highlight the changes in the meanings that have constituted Indianization in the twentieth century. These changes will be traced through a comparison of post-War 'demobilization' schemes after 1918 and 1945 to highlight their impact on the Indian military's institution-building processes, foregrounding the conflicts relating to the service regulations of ICOs at this time. In the aftermath of the two World Wars, the discourse on Indianization shifted, and incorporated two major themes. The first was related to devising a method for sustainable Indianization of the officer ranks in the face of large-scale demobilization and post-War fiscal austerity. This second theme related to post-War fiscal austerity and its international implications for military institution-building in the British colonies such as India and parts of colonial Africa. It showed that Indianization was shaped not just by legislative debates but other more significant economic and transnational factors operating upon institution-building processes in India. Additionally, this section examines the international implications of Indianization as the British Empire attempted to introduce similar policies in parts of West Africa further highlighting the 'diffusionist' nature of colonial military policies.

'Reform' and 'Review' in Military Institution-Building

The enunciation of constitutional goals for India was first outlined in 1919 after the conclusion of the First World War in the form of the Montagu–Chelmsford Reforms, which fostered the emergence of an inchoate group of Indian politicians to discuss the policy of Indianization in the CLA. However, the years leading up to the Second World War and after mark a distinct change in the relationship between India and Britain. This was because any offers of awarding dominion status to India that had dictated specifically matters of military reform before 1930 were now deemed unacceptable to a wide section of Indian political opinion, paving the way for demands hinged at full independence from colonial rule.[79] This changed relationship had ramifications on issues of military reorganization in the subcontinent and was also symptomatic of the underlying changes in the ideas and policies constituting Indianization.

While institutional reform remained a pressing need for the political and military contenders of this period, institutional 'review' on the other hand—of existing military facilities and establishments—acquired a tight grip in New Delhi and London after the Great War and well until the Second World War. This involved relocating or downsizing existing smaller training centres in India like the regional centres for military troops' education.[80] However, in the aftermath of the devastating Allied losses in the early stages of the Second World War, there was a momentary shift in expanding the military infrastructure seeking a dramatic increase in the number of trained officers. The official governmental attention was focussed on 'modernisation of the British element of the Army in India' but it was also tempered by the consciousness that any 'attempt to maintain

---

[79] S.R. Mehrotra, *India and the Commonwealth: 1885–1929* (London: George Allen and Unwin, 1965), pp. 236–7.

[80] 'India's War Effort': Expansion of the Armed Forces, Memorandum by the Secretary of State for India, 30 January 1942, British Cabinet Office Papers, Volume II, NMML Archives, New Delhi.

modernised British forces in India, at the expense of the Indian tax-payer' while leaving the Indian Army 'unmodernised' would give rise to 'political difficulties'.[81]

These 'political difficulties' manifested in the incidents of 'political protest' by military personnel in the years of the Second World War in 1945–6, testifying to the 'social intricacies' of the national movement that is often seen as the progenitor of substantive military Indianization.[82] These protests went on to define a new conception of Indianization that included demands for not just more Indians in the armed forces, but also addressing the structural, occupational, and educational needs of those Indians that were being used for Indianizing the military.[83] This twin feature of Indianization would characterize the processes of the formation and expansion of the higher military academies after 1945 in a unique manner by setting the context for the implementation of measures that would closely align officers' academies with civilian structures of learning, redefining, yet again, the aims and objectives of this century-long process of including commissioned Indian officers.

The financial austerity and budgetary constraints after the two World Wars meant that official military policy was concerned with laying off a significant section of those who, in the struggles and debates of the previous decades, had come to embody the 'Indian' element in Indianization: the VCOs as well as other commissioned officers. Indianization, which had been as much about recruiting more and

[81] Report of the Modernization Committee 1938, Army HQ India, BL, IOR/L/MIL/17/5/1801. Among the many military institutions examined in this report, the Staff College was not affected, while other infantry schools, signal schools, education schools, and the chemical warfare school as well as the Chemical Defence Research Establishment were sought to be relocated.

[82] Anirudh Deshpande, 'Sailors and the Crowd: Popular Protest in Karachi, 1946', *Indian Economic and Social History Review* vol. 26, no. 1 (1989): 1–28.

[83] The most notable example of this protest was the RIN mutiny in Bombay in 1946, which started on the pretext of a service-related grievance, but then spread across other naval establishments near Bombay and even Karachi. See 3/1 Records 1943, Folder Concerning India: Extract from India Command, Fortnightly Security Intelligence Summary No. 5, 1 March 1946, 71/21/3, Lt Gen. F Tuker Papers, Imperial War Museum Archives (IWM Archives), London.

more Indians, was also now about demobilizing a major section of their ranks. The negotiations on Indianization, therefore, sat uneasily with the determined cutbacks in defence spending that were implemented after 1918 and also 1945. This reduced expenditure had an impact on military recruitment, and posed a 'paradox' as to how the putative rates and methods of Indianization were to continue against stark fiscal odds. However, in these waves of military demobilization, there were finer differences in the manner in which the First and the Second World Wars impacted military Indianization policies and the development of military institutions.

The First World War discourse on military reform attempted to redress the concerns arising out of the selective and experimental measures of Indianization. However, in doing so, it was responsible in the playing out of much larger systemic concerns relating to the future occupational role of Indians in the Indian Army. The stage, therefore, was set for the intensification and complication of the Indianization issue involving a host of related aspects. 'Operational contexts' associated with Indianization, for instance, relayed official concerns about accommodating more Indian units in international combat theatres onto a broader platform. Driven by the need to augment British units in the Middle East, some of the consequences of including more Indian troops in the forces were more sociological than operational, and ended up in mixing wartime tensions with racial ones.

The fears relating to the exploitation of Indian Muslims fighting alongside the British by the Turkish forces in order to affect morale, was often 'perceived with danger' by officials in India and Britain.[84] Terms of service and 'field conduct' attracted official attention from London during the Indianization of the expeditionary forces of the Great War. While concerns regarding the indoctrination of Indian Muslim soldiers were unfounded, apprehensions about troop loyalty remained. This acquired urgency in the wake of multiple 'desertions' by troops, especially the Pathan soldiers, whose enlistment took place as part of a larger historical 'contractual relationship' forged by the Indian Army in the northwest. Thus, any breaches in the terms of service or

---

[84] James E. Kitchen, 'The Indianisation of the Egyptian Expeditionary Force: Palestine 1918', in *The Indian Army in the Two World Wars*, ed. Kaushik Roy, pp. 165–90 (Leiden: Brill, 2012), p. 175.

treatment of personnel from the northwest were occasionally met with desertion, sharply reflecting the contested nature of cultural modes through which the Raj's several military constituencies were co-opted in the military system.[85]

The Indian experience of the Great War, especially the dispiriting campaign in Mesopotamia[86]and the criticism of the Indian Army operations during the Third Anglo-Afghan War of 1919, led to the institution of the 'Army in India Committee', also known as the Esher Committee of the Army in India Committee Report of 1919–20 which threatened to cause a rift between the governments in Delhi and London.[87] Jeffery has pointed out that the Esher Committee recommendations caused significant unease in several official quarters.[88] He ascertains that the report was guided by War Office concerns to establish a firm hold over Indian Military affairs through a preponderant influence of the British Imperial GS upon the GoI. This was thought to link up imperial affairs closely with Indian defence (a matter that was to recur in 1928 Simon Commission issue amidst huge protest), but the Indian government saw differently, mainly because the Indian military had begun to appreciate a far more autonomous operational role for itself after 1918. In doing so, the Indian military was trying to move away from its 'control-centre' in Britain. This spirit of moving away from the operational nucleus in London was also symbolized in the formation of the Indian Army's Staff College as an institution for delivering instruction for middle-ranking junior officers.

The huge contribution of Indian forces to the First World War campaigns placed it in a commanding position in the Empire as far as manpower was concerned, and the Indian government by virtue of this human resource, wanted a certain degree of autonomy on the issues

---

[85] Dennis Showalter, 'The Indianisation of the Egyptian Expeditionary Force, 1917–18: An Imperial Turning Point', in *The Indian Army in the Two World Wars*, ed. Kaushik Roy, pp. 145–63 (Leiden: Brill, 2012), p. 153.

[86] Nikolas Gardner, 'Morale of the Indian Army in the Mesopotamia Campaign: 1914–17', in *The Indian Army in the Two World Wars*, ed. Kaushik Roy, pp. 393–417 (Leiden: Brill, 2012).

[87] This was different from the Esher Report of 1904 for the 'British Army'.

[88] Keith Jeffery, 'An English Barrack in the Oriental Seas? India in the Aftermath of the First World War', *Modern Asian Studies* vol. 15, no. 3 (1981): 369–86.

of policy, strategy, and deployment of these large military reserves. The Esher Committee suggested a 'reform of the military organisation in India in the context of Indian political conditions and infrastructure'[89] but it did not provide the instruments through which these reforms could be instituted. To counter the political unrest in India relating to post-War conditions of service and economic instability, it sought to bring the military ever closer to civilian authority for an effective adjudication on these issues. Attempts to alleviate the post-War economic misery of the Indian Army did not endear the financially strapped Indian government to any sort of reform that called for further spending of minimal resources at this time.[90] Thus, the parallel waves of reform and downsizing the Indian military, apparent in the Esher Committee Report, set the register for the subsequent decade in which military institutions were discussed.

Talk of 'institutional' review also continued alongside retrenchment and fiscal cuts. Thus, even though the Military Requirements Committee, set up in 1921, had recommended the establishment of an Indian military college (as well as the formation of feeder residential schools), the report did not provide an adequate basis for this institution to emerge. The report's main contents were focussed on examining the fiscal and budgetary constraints on the military in India.[91] This found expression in the successor to the 1921 Military Requirements Committee, known as the Shea Committee of 1922.[92] The Shea Committee proposed a three-stage plan for Indianization, which would theoretically Indianize the army in thirty-five to forty years beginning with a proportionate regiments–based Indianization within the different 'arms'.[93] This eventually took the form of the invidious

[89] Deshpande, *British Military Policy in India,* p. 44.

[90] Deshpande, *British Military Policy in India*, p. 71. Grants to moulvis and religious instructors were also postponed. The formation of an Indian Corps of Clerks supposed to supply clerks to the establishments of commands, districts, and staff officers was also ruled out.

[91] Proceedings of the Committee appointed by the Governor-General-in-Council to examine the military requirements of India, (Simla: GoI Press, 1921), BL, IOR/L/MIL/17/5/1773, Part II, pp. 18–19.

[92] Shea Committee Report, BL, IOR/L/MIL/17/5/1778.

[93] Arms, in this case, would mean the different services within the military, comprising both regimental affiliations as well as service-specific formations.

'Eight Unit Scheme', later rescinded by the Jacob Committee that was appointed in 1923 by the new commander-in-chief in India, Lt Gen. Alexander Cobb. The Shea Committee suggested a key reform which was earlier put forward by the George Chesney almost half a century ago in 1879 that pointed towards the establishment of an Indian military college that could train young men for prospective commissions.

However, the report of the Indian Retrenchment Committee (IRC) in 1923 poured cold water over any hopes of reform that were generated in the committees that were appointed before. This IRC, set up under the chairmanship of Lord Inchcape, noted that the cost of training establishments had increased 'enormously' since 1913–14 and concluded that the provision for training and educational establishments should be reduced by Rs 742,450.[94] Similarly, for the feeder schools, the committee could not agree to any 'justifications' for the employment of a large staff across these establishments and recommended a 'freeze' on their provisions at Rs. 3,300,000, starting from 1923–4.[95]

These restrictions were instrumental in the decline of the feeder network as successive waves of financial neglect crippled their administration, leading to a consistent downfall in student numbers that necessitated a further round of institutional overhaul, mirroring the patterns that were witnessed in the years after the Second World War. 'Demobilization' became an even more dominant paradigm in the campaign for a 'leaner military' after 1944–5. Demobilization, undoubtedly, worked in the broader context of a streamlining of Indian defence, and had come to be accepted as a natural outcome of restructuring the force which had been facing a steady decline in its annual budgetary allocations since 1920–1. This steady decline in fiscal allocations for the military had an impact on impeding crucial modernization schemes (which also included plans for setting up training institutions in India)

---

[94] Report of the Indian Retrenchment Committee, 1922–3, Her Majesty's Stationery Office [HMSO], 1923. BL, IOR/L/MIL/17/5/1781. See under 'Educational and Training Establishments', pp. 17–18.

[95] Report of the Indian Retrenchment Committee, 1922–3, HMSO: 1923. BL, IOR/L/MIL/17/5/1781. See under 'Army Education', pp. 19–20. An exception was made in the case of the King George's schools and the Prince of Wales Royal Indian Military College at Dehradun.

TABLE 1.2   Army Education: Staff Employed and Expenditure Incurred

	1913–14		1922–3	
	No.	Total Cost (Rs.)	No.	Total Cost (Rs.)
Supervising and Inspecting Staff	7	104,000	63	341,300
British Army School of Education	—	Nil	83	184,200
Indian Army School of Education	—	Nil	65	126,000
Garrison Regimental and Detachment Schools for British Troops	243	322,000	524	1,612,000
Garrison Regimental and Detachment Schools for Indian Troops	6	Nil	579	444,000
Lawrence Military Schools	50	169,000	184	399,900
Prince of Wales Royal Indian Military College	—	Nil	47	111,300
King George's Schools	—	Nil	—	20,000
Language Rewards	—	295,000	—	300,000
Miscellaneous	3	193,000	1	253,300
Total	309	1,211,000	1,546	3,792,000
Less Receipts	—	40,000	—	67,000
TOTAL	—	1,171,000	—	3,725,000

Source: Report of the Indian Retrenchment Committee, 1922–3, Her Majesty's Stationery Office [HMSO]: 1923. BL, IOR/L/MIL/17/5/1781, p. 19.

for the army, and it was in this context that the Chatfield Committee visited India to suggest further fiscal reforms in 1938.[96]

Officer Indianization acquired a new degree of urgency after the Second World War. While demobilization after the First World War

[96] The Chatfield Committee Report, also known as the Secret Report of the expert Committee on the Defence of India 1938–9, was instituted to study the state of Indian defence in the latter half of the 1930s and forward recommendations on the same.

affected mainly soldiers, non-commissioned ranks and other commissioned ranks like the VCOs, the wave of retrenchment after the Second World War was all encompassing as it involved ICOs, including those of the IMA as well as Emergency Commissioned Officers (ECOs) who were also briefly trained at officers' academies. Indians as commissioned officers were a category of military personnel who had debuted only two decades earlier. Their impending disbandment raised urgent existential questions on the policy of Indianization itself.

Demobilization after 1945 and its impact on the military institutional architecture needs to be analysed in terms of what Yasmin Khan has referred to as the process of 'segmented reconstruction'.[97] Towards the end of the Second World War, the Indian government and the military started drafting plans for demobilizing troops and distributing 'state largesse' through a selective, though, 'technocratic and apolitical' process of distribution that relied on old loyalist networks of military clientele.[98] Khan's assessment and characterization of such policies also helps in contextualizing the impact of Indian demobilization on military educational schemes after 1945, which led to the development and application of a range of 'segmented' institutional features focussing on extending and accentuating the 'technocratic' aspect of military education at the academies, both in Britain and India.

The features which shaped the development of major officers' academies and other training spaces grew out of a similar institutional review of British military facilities after 1944–5. The challenges relating to the implementation of demobilization schemes in India were remarkably similar to the developments in Britain. For instance, in a note detailing the 'Post-Armistice Educational Scheme' for demobilized British soldiers, the War Office in London struggled to determine the exact vocational composition of the army so as to devise a uniform educational policy for its personnel.[99] In pondering over the benefits of offering a

[97] Yasmin Khan, *The Raj at War: A People's History of India's Second World War*, pp. 226–7 (Gurgaon: Random House India, 2015).

[98] Khan, *The Raj at War*, pp. 226–7.

[99] 'Address on Post Armistice Educational Scheme', August 1944, Brig. Noel Joseph Chamberlain Papers, Liddell Hart Centre for Military Archives, King's College London, UK. The report questioned War Office estimations of the British Army being comprised those from retail, clerical, and distributive sectors. It also posed questions on the nature of demobilization schemes as

'vocation-based' versus 'technical' education, the War Office reflected the ad-hoc nature of policies that were attempted in the wake of this large-scale retrenchment of the forces, many among whom possessed different skills and propensities for any one uniform educational scheme to work. Nonetheless, certain important institutional elements such as the Army Schools of Education were created at this time, and their important role in reorganizing military education underlined the discussions surrounding the efficacy of demobilization schemes in Britain.[100]

The background to the whole scheme of educating the demobilized officer, soldier, and auxiliary, as remarked by the secretary of state for war in the House of Commons in July 1944, was the desire that they (the demobilized personnel) leave the Army with 'increased understanding of those problems of citizenship of which every member of a vital democracy should have knowledge' about.[101] These 'problems of citizenship', outlined by the secretary, were linked with educational provisions and the skills with which the demobilized soldiers and officers would be equipped to negotiate their way in the civilian workplace. This feature of educating the military personnel before they were released necessitated the development of an inter-institutional network in which the Army Educational Corps played a key role in the staffing of nodal educational schools across Britain and overseas.[102] Thus, in

---

being partial towards technical apprenticeships as opposed to other 'general' educational schemes centred on vocational imperatives.

[100] See 'Memorandum on the General Structure of Army Education After the War', 1A, Gen. Sir Ronald Forbes Adam Papers, Liddell Hart Centre for Military Archives, King's College London, UK.

[101] Statement by the Secretary of State for War in the House of Commons, 25 July 1944, Brig. Noel Joseph Chamberlain Papers, Liddell Hart Centre for Military Archives, King's College London, UK.

[102] Chapter VII on Education, 3/13, Gen. Sir Ronald Forbes Adam Papers, Liddell Hart Centre for Military Archives, King's College London, UK. Several educational centres known as the Army Schools of Education opened up alongside formal military institutions in Europe and the Middle East, offering modules on agriculture and building for the West and East African soldiers stationed there. This pattern was also adopted in India. Also see Note on 'Army Education and Army Bureau of Current Affairs (ABCA), 3/4/5, Gen. Sir Ronald Forbes Adam Papers, Liddell Hart Centre for Military Archives, King's College London, UK.

making use of the 'unrivalled opportunity' to succeed in the 'greatest endeavour for Adult education',[103] British authorities advocated a close collaboration between the universities, the adult education organizations and civilian education schemes as a central feature of its wartime army-education proposals.[104]

The efforts to organize an institutional basis to rehabilitate demobilized ranks in Britain tallied with those in India, though institutional mechanisms in India were developed only in the 1940s, later than they appeared in Britain. These efforts provided the basis for the planning of other higher inter-service academies, where discussions surrounding the precise nature of military education for Indian officers were intimately tied to the questions of the validity of existing academic protocols in the larger non-military civilian spaces of higher education. These questions represented an early sign of the future patterns of development and management of officer education schemes in India.

In a report of the Army School of Education (ASE), set up to monitor and implement educational schemes in India, the need for the 'continued instruction of prospective VCOs, NCOs and technical experts' was reiterated.'[105] This report was significant because it offered proposals to institute a network of preliminary training for 'highly skilled specialists' within the confines of a military unit and commission instructors for delivering this training. It resulted in laying out certain proposals in 1944 to set up the Military College of Science in India that, apart from maintaining 'a close liaison with research, development, scientific training and similar establishments and organisations', would 'nominate members of its staff to serve on service committees concerned with armaments and warlike stores; or to act as advisors or

[103] 'Address on Post Armistice Educational Scheme', August 1944, Brig. Noel Joseph Chamberlain Papers, Liddell Hart Centre for Military Archives, King's College London, UK.

[104] This collaborative feature was part of the larger process of social transformation and the 'construction' of the wartime conceptions of British citizenship during the Second World War, as has been analysed by the historian Sonya Rose. See Sonya O. Rose, *Which People's War?: National Identity and Citizenship in Britain, 1939–1945* (Oxford and New York: Oxford University Press, 2003), p. 21.

[105] Report of the Army School of Education, September 1939–July 1940, 601/1416/WD, History Division, Ministry of Defence, GoI, New Delhi.

consultants'.[106] The idea behind this proposal, the report mentioned, was to develop a 'nucleus' of highly trained educational experts on whose basis the post-War educational training schemes could be established in India.[107]

Thus, demobilization had decisively reshaped the contours of the Indianization policy by injecting the themes of educational reorganization of Indian military personnel into the narrative. This transformation in the Indianization policy grew out of the post–Second World War context which stemmed from the shared institutional practices of military reorganization in India and Britain.

The questions of demobilizing a large force 'could not have been answered easily', for as Deshpande points out, the aspirational changes between the generations of the First and the Second World Wars were different and that led them to approach demobilization differently. Therefore, post-1945 schemes of resettlement of demobilized personnel relied heavily on development and industrialization channels through which it 'might be possible to absorb those who did not want to return to their previous occupations'.[108] These channels, though, were limited and not equally available for everyone.[109] Military institutional

---

[106] Appendix to the War Office Letter, 43/MCS/1023 (MT8), 18 October 1944, BL, IOR/L/WS/1/761. One of the main aims of this college was to train commissioned officers and NCOs and others to 'fit them for employment on technical staffs, in technical appointments in the Ministry of Supply, in appointments of the staffs of armament firms, or in similar appointments elsewhere.'

[107] Appendix to the War Office Letter, 43/MCS/1023 (MT8), 18 October 1944, BL, IOR/L/WS/1/761.

[108] Anirudh Deshpande, 'Hopes and Disillusionment: Recruitment, Demobilisation and the Emergence of Discontent in the Indian Armed Forces after the Second World War', *Indian Economic and Social History Review* vol. 33, no. 2 (1996): 175–207, p. 196.

[109] Deshpande, 'Hopes and Disillusionment', p. 196. The problem with the VCOs and the NCOs was even more acute, since most would have wanted to stay in the organization, while the tradesmen and technicians within the ranks would have 'clamoured for quick demobilisation' to look for opportunities elsewhere. This trend of non-agricultural preference for resettlement was faintly visible even after the First World War, when the Esher Committee Report of 1920 encountered the economic and educational demands made

practices after 1945, therefore, tended to address this anomaly by offering a technocratic component of education to its officers so as to avoid
replicating the earlier conditions of demobilization and retrenchment
that rendered a large force helpless in evolving non-civilian workplaces
inhabited by skilled and competitive labour force.

Understanding 'Africanization'

Indianization during the course of the decades from the 1880s to 1930s
transformed from a mere legislative assembly debate and acquired the
characteristics of a major policy issue for the governments in India
and Britain. It also began to be held up as a source for extending
similar reforms in other parts of the Empire reflecting the critical
global implications of military reorganization in India. A memorandum circulated in the mid-1940s in London gave rise to the possibility of its application to parts of Anglophone Africa,[110] signalling
the international effects of officer Indianization on the empire. The
Africanization campaign was to peak in the latter part of the twentieth
century when India helped Ethiopia set up its own Officers' Training
Academy in 1958, symbolizing the decades-long international and
inter-institutional policy network that Indianization had helped generate during the Second World War.[111]

The Royal West African Frontier Force as well as the King's African
Rifles were chosen to be 'Africanized' in the post-War period by the
Colonial Office—the department created in Whitehall to deal with the
British Empire's colonies in southwestern Africa. The King's African

---

by the VCOs and NCOs (discussed earlier in this section). Also, while recruitment in the aftermath of the Great War was not a cause for concern, newer
lucrative openings for various trades in the East Asian markets had begun to
provide alternative employment avenues for soldiers causing the Raj to invest
more heavily into recruitment drives.

[110] Letter from Col W. Rolleston, Liaison Officer, Colonial Office to Lt
Col M.M. Stevenson, India Office, Whitehall, 1 June 1943, File: 'Indianisation
and Africanisation', BL, IOR/L/WS/1/1366.

[111] File No. 11: Speech delivered on the occasion of the first graduation
parade of the Halessalesi I Military Academy, Ethiopia, October 1960, Gen.
Thimayya Papers, NMML Archives, New Delhi, India.

Rifles and the Royal West African Frontier Force were part of the small colonial armies that were 'rapidly expanded' in the wake of the Second World War campaigns in the Africa, Middle East, and Southeast Asia.[112] Their active participation in the War effort was one of the key reasons as to why local African military formations were first chosen for accommodating African officers.

Even though proposals for the mobilization of African armies outside imperial defence were advocated after the First World War, it took the events of the Second World War and the shortage of British manpower for a change to occur in the policies of the Colonial Office.[113] Interactions between the Colonial Office and Whitehall during the Second World War, therefore, portray a picture of careful deliberation on the issue of Africanization. It involved a wholesale examination of Indianization measures, including issues of commissions, sources of recruits, and their potential placement in a regiment, which had been implemented in the subcontinent to study the applicability of such policies on what, was, admittedly, a smaller scale of experiment in Africa.[114]

A questionnaire sent along with a letter by the liaison officer of the Colonial Office to the India Office in 1943 formed the basis on which the contours of the West African policy on officer recruitment came to be discussed.[115] Negotiations on securing an Africanized

---

[112] David Killingray, 'Labour Mobilisation in British Colonial Africa for the War Effort, 1939–46', in *Africa and the Second World War*, ed. D. Killingray and R. Rathbone, pp 68–96 (Basingstoke: Macmillan, 1986), p. 68. An analysis of military mobilization in southwestern Africa, particularly Botswana has been provided in a richly detailed account in Ashley Jackson, *Botswana 1939–1945: An African Country at War* (Oxford: Clarendon Press; Oxford University Press, 1999), pp. 31–56.

[113] David Killingray, 'The Idea of a British Imperial African Army', *The Journal of African History* vol. 20, no. 3 (1979): 421–36.

[114] Killingray, 'The Idea of a British Imperial African Army'. Although the African forces were reduced due to post-War budgetary constraints, Killingray points out that demands for creating an African military force as an imperial force continued to be made, albeit with little or no support forthcoming.

[115] See Letter from Col W. Rolleston, Liaison Officer, Colonial Office to Lt Col M.M. Stevenson, India Office, Whitehall, 3 July 1943, File: 'Indianisation and Africanisation', BL, IOR/L/WS/1/1366.

officer corps also included discussing and planning for an educational infrastructure that could sustain Africanization on a long-term basis. This was to be accomplished by reviewing the 'full and frank story' of how the 'Indianisation system evolved' so that the West African military authorities could avoid the mistakes of the Indian experiment.[116]

By 1952, only nine African officers had come to hold the 'Queen's Commission'—equivalent to the King's Commission of the previous decades—in the territory formerly known as Gold Coast (now Ghana) and were mainly commissioned in the Royal West African Frontier Force.[117] This was paltry compared to the numbers in India, but in other crucial ways, the nature of Africanization bore similarities with the Indian model. These similarities were most evident in the pre-cadet training and formal training procedures that Ghana adopted during the Second World War and pointed towards the structured, institutional approach taken to increase recruitment from universities and feeder colleges. The increased recruitment, in turn, provided the basis for further institutional reform of feeder training networks, leading, interestingly, to the articulation of the demand for an 'African' Sandhurst.[118] Moreover, the prospect of higher training of these commissioned officers also necessitated discussions surrounding their staff training, mirroring developments that took place in India almost three decades ago, and reflected the stark similarities that existed in military institution-building processes between India and West Africa.

The parallel set of reforms being undertaken in India and West Africa have been examined by David Killingray, whose work on the African soldiers during the Second World War draws out the early struggles in

---

[116] Letter from Col W. Rolleston, Liaison Officer, Colonial Office to Lt Col M.M. Stevenson, India Office, Whitehall, 1 June 1943. 'Indianisation and Africanisation', BL, IOR/L/WS/1/1366.

[117] An address given to the Gold Coast Press by Brig. W.S. Ritchie OBE, Commander, Gold Coast District on Wednesday 3 December 1952, at Gold Coast District HQ, WIGG/3/6, George Edward Cecil, Baron Wigg Papers, Special Collections, London School of Economics and Political Science (LSE) Library, UK.

[118] An address given to the Gold Coast Press by Brig. W.S. Ritchie OBE, Commander, Gold Coast District on Wednesday 3 December 1952, at Gold Coast District HQ, WIGG/3/6, George Edward Cecil, Baron Wigg Papers, Special Collections, LSE Library, UK.

opening the officer ranks in the West African Forces to African men. Killingray refers to the deep racial prejudices with which colonial military policies operated in Africa—factors that significantly impacted not just recruitment but also official and social perceptions surrounding African mobilization and demobilization.[119] Challenges such as interrogating African officers' behaviour in the mess reflected the similarities with which Indianization policies—apart from the numerical replacement—had to contend with the reconceptualization of military spaces once more Indian officers started to gain commissions.[120]

The instrumental shift in the military policy pursued in the subcontinent was not the fact that the Indian Army became staffed with a higher number of officers by the mid-twentieth century, but the fact that by the time India was coerced to join the Second World War, the terms of Indianization had widened to incorporate the precise method through which Indian officers would be commissioned, their powers of command and the duration of their services, and the value of their training-cum-educational attainments while in service. All of these issues had become integral to the process and definition of Indianization of the military.

As this chapter has outlined, the earliest proposals to structurally modify the Indian military were forwarded towards the latter part of the nineteenth century, which was responsible for the establishment of a relatively dense network of training and feeder institutions that formed the bedrock for the more visible and publicized architecture of military academies that began to be set up in the twentieth century. A staid focus on the campaign for an 'Indian Sandhurst' has erased the important continuities that Indian military institutionalization had come to embody with the decades of the late nineteenth century. This chapter has aimed to shed light on this crucial link, and by doing so, it has challenged the prevailing understanding and the 'historical imaginings' of the concept of military Indianization in two fundamental ways.

---

[119] Frank Furedi, 'The Demobilised African Soldier and the Blow to White Prestige', in *Guardians of Empire: The Armed Forces of the Colonial Powers c. 1700–1964*, ed. D. Killingray and D. Omissi, pp. 179–97 (Manchester and New York: Manchester University Press, 1999).

[120] David Killingray, *Fighting for Britain: African Soldiers in the Second World War* (London: James Currey, 2010), pp. 84–5.

First, it shifts the gaze away from the constitutional and political encounters of the 'Indianization campaign' to get more Indian officers. It does so by looking at the ways in which specific policies were designed by the government in collaboration with the military to make the latter more representative and structurally flexible in response to the geo-strategic considerations at the turn of the early twentieth century. By shifting the lens to the precise institutional developments that determined patterns of Indianization, it is possible to draw out a larger history of the ways in which the Indian military was sought to be refashioned by the colonial government before the issue became a selling point in the emerging political rhetoric of the early twentieth-century nationalist movement. Fixing the attention on the institutional development of the military's academies also gives a holistic view of the historical and interlinked development of Indianization: a process that developed upwards from the regional, district-level networking between military schools, moved on to the setting up of senior feeder colleges, and then leading on to the arrival of a commission-awarding academy in 1932.

Second, Indianization is often understood as a mechanistic process of a gradual, often contested replacement of British officers with Indian men. This is a narrow and deterministic reading of an important process which had profound structural, organizational, and political consequences. A vice-like grip on the more obvious, politically combative element of the Indianization discussions favours only a particular view to be forwarded—one that portrays the process as a contest between two opposing sides of a partisan campaign.

The chronological and spatial foci of Indianization suggests otherwise, and highlights a more layered understanding of the process—one that goes beyond the 'replacement' narrative to underscore the critical administrative issues that were encountered once the indigenous military institutions began to be set up. Once an institutional frame was in place, the Indianization debate also began to expand in scope and content. No longer was 'replacement of the British officers' the sole concern. It included a host of institution-specific concerns which posed a hurdle in achieving the targeted rate of Indianization that was being championed in the assembly and politico-executive circles of the Raj. Thus, a steady focus on the institutional developments within the Indian military mirrors the changing conceptions of Indianization itself and it broadens the debate on what has constituted Indianization ever since the first signs of a training architecture began to emerge in the Indian subcontinent.

The vocabulary of Indianization and institution-building had changed by the time the first commission-awarding training academy was inaugurated in 1932. From a discussion on 'how' and 'where' to secure more Indians to serve as officers, the years leading to the Second World War had shifted the goalposts to the questions of 'how many' and 'what' kind of Indians will get the opportunity to stay on as officers and what measures would then have to be undertaken to maintain the rate of Indianization—an issue, which by the time the 'Indian Sandhurst' was set up in 1932, was already more than half-a-century old.

2 The 'Indian Sandhurst'
1925–45*

The IMA was the first flagship officers' training academy set up in the Indian subcontinent that had the powers to award commissions to Indians desirous of becoming officers. Known informally as the 'Indian Sandhurst', after the British Royal Military Academy at Sandhurst, the IMA quickly acquired an important status in the years immediately after its inauguration in 1932, and is one of the few officers' training academies that feature, with a limited degree of detail, in the literature on Indian military institutions.

The emergence of the IMA transformed the discussions and negotiations on Indianization by including newer categories of assessment. Such categories included the politics surrounding commissions, thus altering the terms of the debate from demanding 'more Indian officers' to asking 'what class of officers'[1] would be required now to sustain

---

* An earlier and different version of this chapter was presented at a symposium, Re-newing the Military History of Colonial India, 21–2 August 2013, at the University of Greenwich and published as Vipul Dutta, 'War and Indian Military Institutions: The Emergence of the Indian Military Academy', in *Culture, Conflict and the Military in Colonial South Asia*, ed. Kaushik Roy and Gavin Rand, pp. 239–57 (Oxon, New York: Routledge, 2018). I am grateful to Dr Gavin Rand and Professor Kaushik Roy for their thoughtful comments.

[1] Much like the 'class company' regiments of the late nineteenth-century Indian Army, which grouped together bands of men from similar provinces or castes in various battalions. The 'class' being referred to here would be an indication of the economic and/or ethnic background of the cadets in question.

Indianization. The emergence of IMA also raised newer questions about the nature of cadet recruitment, generating new debates on the class and ethnicity of the cadets who were deemed suitable (or otherwise) to enter the IMA. Additionally, the more grounded and seemingly banal administrative realities of running the IMA foregrounded important questions on the nature of military institutional reform and its impact on the Indianization of the military and its occupational diversification. This included struggles arising out of training a differentially schooled group of cadets and also taking steps to ensure that the IMA retained its appeal among the group that had campaigned most vociferously for it—the princes.

The IMA did not emerge in isolation but grew out of the early twentieth-century cluster of military training feeder institutions discussed in the previous chapter. However, this crucial organizational link is overlooked in the literature that views the IMA as essentially a by-product of the nationalist movement in India. The role of Indian politicians in the discussions surrounding the IMA, during and after the Round Table Conferences (RTCs) in London from 1930 to 1931, is undeniable. Nonetheless, in assigning a sizeable share of credit for the IMA's emergence to the Indian political leadership, a larger institutional history of the IMA—one which can offer insights into how officer Indianization progressed from the late nineteenth to the early twentieth century—runs the risk of being ignored.

LAYING THE GROUNDWORK: THE SKEEN COMMITTEE REPORT OF 1925–6

While negotiations for an increased number of Indian officers continued after the First World War, the early years of the twentieth century in Indian military reform ought to be remembered for the first steps that were taken to secure a commission-awarding institution for Indians. These first steps laid the groundwork for the subsequent establishment of the IMA in the form of the Skeen Committee, also known as the Indian Sandhurst Committee of 1925–6.[2]

---

[2] The Skeen Committee was appointed in June 1925 under the chairmanship of its namesake, Lt Gen. Sir Andrew Skeen, KCB, KCIE, CMG, chief of the GS, India. Its members were: Pandit Motilal Nehru, member of Legislative

The report submitted by this committee is an important site to locate the early organizational configurations of the IMA, for it recommended an enhancement of the post–First World War offerings of Indianization. The report recommended doubling the number of vacancies reserved for Indians at Sandhurst to twenty from the initial ten seats which were offered to Indians immediately after the Great War. It also recommended to 'progressively' increasing the number of vacancies at the British military institutions until such time as a 'military college on the lines of Sandhurst is established in India'.[3] However, beyond this mathematical expansion in seats, the report outlined some key policy proposals that transformed the character of Indianization. It was the first cogent expression of the need to modify, adapt and synchronize Indianization policies with a view towards the parallel development of the occupational and educational profile of the officers who were required to replace British officers.

The Skeen Committee was also notable for its membership.[4] The committee had on board a distinguished selection of politicians,

---

Assembly (MLA); M.A. Jinnah, MLA; Honourble Sardar Jogendra Singh, minister of agriculture, Punjab government; Phiroze Sethna, member of the Council of State; Diwan Bahadur Ramachandra Rao, MLA; Nawab Sir Sahibzada Abdul Qaiyum, KCIE, MLA; Sub. Maj. and Hon. Capt. Hira Singh, Sardar Bahadur, member of the British Empire (MBE), MLA, late 16th Rajputs; Dr Ziauddin Ahmed, CIE, MLC, pro-vice chancellor, Aligarh Muslim University; Capt. J.N. Banerjee, Bar-at-Law; Maj. Thakur Zorawar Singh, MC, chief secretary, Council of Administration, Bhavnagar State, (representing the Indian States); Ris. Maj. and Hon. Capt. Haji Gul Mawaz Khan, late 18th Lancers; Maj. Bala Sahib Dafle, Seventh Rajput Regiment; and Mr E. Burdon, CSI, CIE, ICS, secretary to the GoI in the Army Department. Pandit Motilal Nehru tendered his resignation as a member of the committee on 11 March 1926. See Report of the Indian Sandhurst Committee, BL, IOR/L/MIL/17/5/1783.

The Skeen Committee bore implications for future phases of military institution-building in India. See Vipul Dutta, 'Educating Future Generals: An Indian Defence University and Educational Reform', *Economic and Political Weekly* vol. 53, no. 32 (2018): 47–54.

[3] Report of the Indian Sandhurst Committee, 14 November 1926, BL, IOR/L/MIL/17/5/1783.

[4] P.S. Gupta, 'The Debate on Indianisation 1918–39', in *The British Raj and its Indian Armed Forces, 1857–1939*, ed. P.S. Gupta and A. Deshpande, pp. 228–69

officers, and educationists, but the fact that it brought, albeit briefly, two prominent Indian political leaders together—Motilal Nehru and M.A. Jinnah—was symbolic of one of those few occasions on which the two leaders worked towards a common objective. While Motilal Nehru resigned from the committee early on, the representation from two important leaders to examine issues of military reform reflected the priority that the latter was accorded. The committee also had on board leaders like Moonje who were side-lined in the committee but went on to play a larger role in the 1931 Chetwode Committee that was appointed later.

The Skeen Committee deserves scrutiny in its own right, for it was one of the first comprehensive attempts to seriously consider the prospect of establishing an Indian officers training academy. It also lays bare the global context surrounding the formation of the IMA, for it was the first time that the committee members were given the opportunity to study existing military institutions in England, France, Canada, and the United States Military Academy at West Point, the last of which was later to become the institutional model for the NDA, set up in 1949 in western India.[5] These tours were undertaken by a sub-committee comprising M.A. Jinnah; Phiroze Sethna, member of the Council of State; and Maj. Thakur Zorawar Singh, chief secretary of Bhavnagar state.

The Skeen Report deliberated upon augmenting and improving the quality of Indian cadets for entry into Sandhurst and other military institutions in Britain. The committee was instituted to recommend a precise and uniform method of selection of cadets from what was seen to be an unusually large and differentially trained pool of Indian candidates. This ever-widening pool of Indian candidates posed a challenge for greater Indianization as it complicated efforts to devise a uniform standard for determining 'suitability' for commissions. In addition to this feature, the report also dealt with certain other associated issues related to training like student funding and administration—issues that

---

(New Delhi: Oxford University Press, 2002), pp. 243–5. Gupta pointed out the ways in which the political membership of the Skeen Committee served as an instrument to balance out the numbers of 'supporters' and 'opposers' of the government's view on the subject.

[5] Discussed in Chapter 3.

later played an important role in the organization of the IMA and other academies.

The Skeen Report was notable in flagging important issues of recruitment, such as the definitions of an 'ideal cadet' in terms of his academic qualifications, and also for reflecting upon the interlinkages between university spaces and military institutions to forge a more suitably trained cadet for officership. While issues such as educational qualifications posed a problem in ascertaining which Indian candidate was suitable for an officers' commission at Sandhurst, the nature of these problems stood magnified if an Indian officers' academy was to come up in the foreseeable future in India. It was this possibility of having an Indian academy that informed the Skeen Committee's main recommendations.

In its visit to the United States Military Academy at West Point, the committee took special note of the diversified sources of recruitment for candidates looking to acquire officers' commissions. It noted the fact that university graduates were also given the opportunity to enter the academy—a point on which the committee lobbied the Army Council in London to a great extent. This was also taken up actively by the 1931 Chetwode Committee which recommended putting into place structures that could facilitate the entry of suitable candidates from universities and from within the ranks for a career as an officer in the military.[6]

In addition to USA, the recruitment system prevailing at the Canadian military college at Kingston, also found special favour with the Skeen Committee. The Canadian model of issuing 'vacancies to each province each year according to its population' by a selection board of the defence headquarters appealed to the Indian polity's own evolving federal set up, after the Montagu–Chelmsford Reforms of 1919 had introduced bicameral provincial legislatures affording a degree of authority to the provinces in key issues of administration.

---

[6] The 1931 Chetwode Committee referred specifically to the Skeen Committee's tour of the United States Military Academy at West Point and noted the relatively small percentage of its cadets being sourced through nomination and the 'equal opportunity' afforded to men from the ranks and other services who wanted to join the military. See Report of the Indian Military College Committee, 15 July 1931, BL, IOR/L/MIL/17/5/1790, p. 55.

The Canadian system of recruitment had to be necessitated in India, the committee noted, 'in view of the provinces being soon converted into autonomous federating units of the Central Federal Government', and that without such a system, it would be 'impossible to create a really national army' in India.[7]

The study tours of military institutions abroad helped catalyse the inter-linkage between the processes of Indianization' and nationalization of the armed forces. This is because studying foreign academies in detail helped the members to effectively design the contours of a prospective Indian military academy along a country-wide basis of representation and institutional ethos much like other academies that were functioning as per their regional or national conditions. The institutional element was hard to miss in these visits, as the committee did not choose to visit only military offices and defence headquarters, which would have been a more usual choice to study and examine recruitment policies, but instead toured actual foreign officers' academies to study the administrative challenges of acquiring and training prospective officers.

The Skeen Committee report, therefore, was instituted on the underlying principle of institutionalization of officer recruitment. This institutionalization did not just mean a seamless introduction of an officers' academy, since it obviously took decades to set up one in 1932 after a sustained phase of negotiations in the face of post-War demobilization and budgetary constraints. Instead, it meant a gradual forging of feeder instructional network of institutions that could supply a sufficiently trained set of Indian men eligible for earning officers' commissions. A sizeable number of Indian candidates trained at these reorganized feeder institutions would then, it was hoped, provide the justification for the case of establishing an officers' academy in the subcontinent.

[7] Report of the Indian Military College Committee, 15 July 1931, BL, IOR/L/MIL/17/5/1790, p. 56. The 1931 report makes several references to the Skeen Report, particularly in the context of developing a 'national army' in India. The 1931 report concluded that the 'system of nominations' would not be acceptable to the states as they would not tolerate the perpetuation of 'Army monopolies' in favour of a few so-called martial classes as it 'perpetuated the myth of an artificial distinction of martial and non-martial classes' and 'propagates the poison of communalism in the body politic of India.'

Therefore, the recommendations forwarded by the Skeen Committee for the purposes of increasing the number and academic credentials of suitable candidates for an officers' commission had a distinct institutional element to it. After studying officer recruitment practices in North America and Britain, the committee offered suggestions on improving the recruitment processes by focussing its attention on augmenting the capacities and capabilities of the feeder training networks in India, specifically, the Prince of Wales Royal Indian Military College.

The Prince of Wales Royal Indian Military College was one of the many such feeder institutions that had emerged not just to train and supply an annual cohort of Indian men desirous of joining Sandhurst as potential KCOs, but also to circumvent the problem of an 'undesirably large' numbers of failed cadets at Sandhurst.[8] The Skeen Report noted that the Prince of Wales Royal Indian Military College was the only institution run along the lines of English Public School, where an avowed effort was made to 'supply the wants mentioned in the system of education' desirable at British military institutions.[9] This system of education was the set of principles and qualities that the Skeen Committee was interested in having imparted to the Indian cadets bound for Sandhurst, for it believed that the 'lack of leadership' and the 'willingness to accept responsibility' placed the Indian cadet as a 'foreign' and 'inferior element' among the British cadets in England.[10] The committee seemed to have implicitly acknowledged that the lack of such qualities could also have been expressions of sociocultural dissimilarities in the conduct of Indian and British cadets, for it noted that such an adverse assessment of cadet behaviour would also hold true for 'British cadets were they to train among Indian men

[8] Superintendent Government Printing, India, *The Army in India and Its Evolution: Including an Account of the Establishment of the Royal Air Force in India* (Calcutta, 1924), p. 161 (number of failed cadets unspecified).

[9] Indian Sandhurst Committee: Report of the Sub-committee which visited Military Educational Institutions in England and Other Countries, BL, IOR/L/MIL/17/5/1786.

[10] Indian Sandhurst Committee: Report of the Sub-committee which visited Military Educational Institutions in England and Other Countries, BL, IOR/L/MIL/17/5/1786.

in India'.[11] However, the whole prospect of asking British personnel to undertake training and monitoring its results in India appeared moot due to the absence of any officers' training academy in the subcontinent. The Skeen Report recommended the expansion and upgradation in the facilities of the Prince of Wales Royal Indian Military College and the introduction of a curriculum that could make it compatible with university authorities to allow a broader acceptability of the Prince of Wales Royal Indian Military College graduates at both higher military institutions as well as other networks of civilian employment.[12] It also recommended the formation of sister colleges across India and to begin imparting training to prospective navy and air force cadets signalling the impeding trifurcation of the Indian military into service-specific autonomous armed wings.[13]

The Prince of Wales Royal Indian Military College did not institute a college diploma in its curriculum in accordance with the Skeen recommendations until 1934, but when it did, it marked a profound shift in its stature.[14] The upgradation of the educational curriculum at the Prince of Wales Royal Indian Military College made it a formal academy in its own right—a site at which graduates of the other regional but underperforming junior Chief's colleges could go to undertake an advanced training and education in pursuit of an officers'

[11] Indian Sandhurst Committee: Report of the Sub-committee which visited Military Educational Institutions in England and Other Countries, BL, IOR/L/MIL/17/5/1786.

[12] Report of the Indian Sandhurst Committee, 14 November 1926, BL, IOR/L/MIL/17/5/1783.

[13] Report of the Indian Sandhurst Committee, 14 November 1926, BL, IOR/L/MIL/17/5/1783. The suggestions for introducing navy and air force curriculum was unique, especially because the two arms were relatively slow to develop in India, partly due to the highly technical nature of the services, as well as the budgetary constraints which had stunted reform in the aftermath of the Great War. This trifurcation into naval and air wings did not happen until after Independence came to India.

[14] Prince of Wales Royal Military College, Dehra Dun (Manual), BL, IOR/L/MIL/17/5/2283. To meet the requirements of candidates who were unsuccessful in this examination the need was felt for a college diploma, which would be recognized by the universities as equivalent to their matriculation or entrance examination, but it was not acted upon immediately.

commission.[15] This cycle of institutional reconfiguration of Indian feeder colleges around a central modified 'model' institution would replicate itself repeatedly over the next decades, after its first appearance in the early twentieth century as discussed in the previous chapter in the assessment of Chief's colleges. The cycle was noticeable again when the IMA opened in 1932 and several regional schools and colleges were upgraded and reformed to provide a better class of trained cadets for the IMA.

The Skeen Report went further to suggest that it was precisely these inadequate institutional conditions for training that necessitated the rapid establishment of an Indian college since the sooner a new institution was set up, 'the sooner [would] it establish its own traditions' and networks of liaison with local authorities to rev up the recruitment process, all this while saving up on the 'holiday expenses of the Indian cadets' that they incurred in sailing to and from England and paying up for their training there.[16] Thus, in seeking to lower the 'holiday expenses'[17] and the unnecessary anxiety of an 'Indian parent to send his son to a foreign institution at an impressionable age', the Skeen Report managed to establish the basis on which future negotiations for higher institutional reform could take place. The report was instrumental in portraying the necessity of having an 'Indian institution' as a solution for the twin Indian problems of cadet recruitment and education.

The Skeen Report was significant in one additional aspect. The report was instrumental in extending the scope of employment of

[15] Regulations for the Prince of Wales Royal Indian Military College, 1934, BL, IOR/L/MIL/17/5/2285.

[16] Indian Sandhurst Committee: Report of the Sub-committee which visited Military Educational Institutions in England and Other Countries 1926, BL, IOR/L/MIL/17/5/1786.

[17] On a note related to 'expenses', the Skeen Committee also laid down a blueprint for the 1931 committee to work out the details of student fee and expenses at the IMA. In a survey of the French Military Academy at St. Cyr, the Skeen Committee found that the education of cadets, provided they agree to serve a minimum of ten years, was free. In Canada, the cost of educating the cadet was substantially lower than a regular university education (USD 1,450), while in USA, the whole education was found to be subsidized by the State. See Report of the Indian Military College Committee, 15 July 1931, BL, IOR/L/MIL/17/5/1790, p. 64.

Indians in the higher ranks of the Indian Army. In addition to the extension in the number of seats reserved for Indians at Sandhurst, it sought to introduce vacancies at other British military academies at Woolwich and Cranwell (training facilities for the Royal Air Force [RAF]) so as to provide a complement of Indian officers who could then serve as KCOs in not just limited regiments but also in the technical, artillery, engineering and motorized air arms of the army—services which were sparsely populated by Indians at the time.[18] Introducing the 'technical' element in military training was also proposed by George Chesney in 1898,[19] who strove hard to persuade the viceroy to offer courses of technical interests to prospective Indian officers in order to upgrade the skill set of the late nineteenth-century Indian Army, but this approach was ad-hoc. It was the Skeen Report that enshrined some of the most fundamental principles of the late nineteenth-century official efforts to Indianize the army along with a parallel development and upgradation of the occupational profile of the men.

The development of Indianization along with the parallel enhancement of the skills and role-profiles of prospective Indian officers was a trend that would get accentuated with the emergence of the post-Independence Indian officers' academies like the NDA, the Staff College, and the NDC. Nonetheless, its expression as a policy resolution through the offices of a consultative committee in 1925–6 signalled the beginning of an important institutional trajectory for the Indian military and its officers.

The Skeen Committee attempted to reify and sharpen this skill-based upgradation of the Indianization aspirants by tying the 'university' and the 'academy' together. Its report offered important ideas for accelerating the pace of Indianization by focussing its attention on university trained graduates who had the skills, the sensibilities, as well as the academic backing to pursue rigorous officer-training

---

[18] Recommendations of the GoI on the Report of the Indian Sandhurst Committee, BL, IOR/L/MIL/17/5/1787. The committee also put forward the case for a progressive increase of reserved seats at the British academies beyond the current five per cent of the total reserved to unreserved seat ration at Sandhurst and Woolwich. This was not agreed to by the Army Council, nor was it viewed favourably by the Indian government.

[19] Discussed in Chapter 1.

courses and who could then replace the British officers at a faster rate than before, with an accompanying ease of being able to function and sustain in their professional capacities as officers. In all the countries that the committee visited, except France, it was struck by the availability of alternative mechanisms for entry of men into the academies and viewed the universities in India and abroad as potential sites for increased recruitment of prospective Indian officers who held the key to both a faster and professional system of Indianization.[20]

This solved—in the committee's view—the problem of the quality of cadets, as university graduates could be expected to bear a 'wider outlook and broader general education.' The Officers' Training Corps (OTC), that is, the university-based part-time system of imparting military training to students aspiring to join the territorial or regular army was a model that was sought to be emulated in India.[21] Besides, attempts to lobby the government to allow greater access to Indian undergraduates to join the OTC abroad was aimed to encourage men who wanted to join the army at a later age by instituting a system of 'antedates', thereby putting them on the same level of seniority as their counterparts from Sandhurst who had joined the academy immediately after their matriculation.[22]

Even though a definite date for the establishment of the 'Indian Sandhurst' could not be established, leading many to regard the Skeen

---

[20] Indian Sandhurst Committee: Report of the Sub-committee which visited Military Educational Institutions in England and Other Countries 1926, BL, IOR/L/MIL/17/5/1786.

[21] Sarvepalli Gopal, *Jawaharlal Nehru: A Biography, Volume I: 1889–1947* (New Delhi: Oxford University Press, 2012). Nehru, while studying in England, had also shown interest in the Officers' Training Corps at Harrow (Gopal, *Jawaharlal Nehru*, p. 19). Later at Cambridge, he even applied for admission into the 'University Mounted Infantry' (Gopal, *Jawaharlal Nehru*, p. 25).

[22] Indian membership of the Officers' Training Corps at universities like Cambridge had followed a chequered path. Indians were initially accepted for ancillary medical work during the First World War and then later in 1937, it was again proposed to open the membership to foreigners including Indians. The proposal did not seem to have been accepted. See Hew Strachan, *History of The Cambridge University Officer Training Corps* (Tunbridge Wells: Midas Books, 1976), p. 156.

Committee as a failure,[23] the report paved the way for further debates on the future organizational anatomy of the 'Indian Sandhurst' by probing the role of the princes and the relative status of a future Indian officers' academy vis-à-vis the British officer academies. The report advocated reserving a share of the seats for men from the State Forces, a measure that was also endorsed by the 1931 Chetwode Report, provided that the men from the princely states underwent the same course of training as the VCOs. Besides, it also asked the princely states to fund the training of these cadets as they were ultimately to be posted to the units of the Imperial States Forces, setting in motion a long battle of different motivations, ideas, and agendas that came to govern the establishment and functioning of the 'Indian Sandhurst'.[24]

These were to later become issues of considerable importance in the wake of the emergence of the IMA when the seats reserved for the forces of the princely states were not being adequately filled, reflecting in part the princes' predilection for commissions earned at Sandhurst or Woolwich. This preference for 'foreign' academies reflected the fluid institutional space that would be inhabited by the IMA in the years after its inauguration, aided in part by the Skeen and Chetwode Committees themselves, which kept the route to other kinds of officer commissions half open.[25]

ESTABLISHMENT OF THE IMA: THE CHETWODE COMMITTEE REPORT AND CONFLICTS OF CONVICTION

Since the 1870s, the British Army in India, that is, the organization staffed by British military personnel deployed in India, had come to be

[23] Report in the Civil and Military Gazette, 10 March 1928.

[24] Report of the Indian Sandhurst Committee, 1925–6, BL, IOR/L/MIL/17/5/1784.

[25] Indian Sandhurst Committee: Report of the Sub-committee which visited Military Educational Institutions in England and Other Countries 1926, BL, IOR/L/MIL/17/5/1786. The Skeen Report suggested that 'there may be a tendency, prejudicial to the service as a whole, for those who have been trained at the older and more expensive college to look down on those who have been trained at then newer institution'.

maintained in part by the 'Cardwell System', which stipulated that an equal number of troops were required to be maintained in Britain as those sent overseas, so that 'regular drafts from the former could replace the latter on overseas service'.[26] By withdrawing garrisons from self-governing colonies and reducing troop commitments, Britain hoped, at the turn of the twentieth century, to signal the colonies that they were to be increasingly responsible for their own security and that any future combat engagements would demand a greater contribution from colonial troops.

This contribution was duly asked for in late nineteenth- and early twentieth-century conflicts in not just China (Boxer Rebellion of 1900)[27] and the Boer Wars (1899–1902), but also more directly in the First World War (1914–18), where Indian troops formed one of the largest overseas military contingent to fight the war of their colonial rulers. After the Great War and the mitigation of the 'Russian threat' in the 1920s, the notion steadily grew that India should contribute to the general defence of the Empire in a more coherent and systematic way than in the previous century.[28] However, India's assuming a greater share of imperial commitments was dependent upon having a modernized and professional fighting force so that it

---

[26] Brian Bond, *British Military Policy between the Two World Wars* (Oxford: Oxford University Press, 1980), p. 99. The Cardwell Reforms were the brain-child of Edward Cardwell, secretary of state for war, 1868–74, and were aimed at the reorganization of the British Army after the Crimean War (1853–6). The reforms were part of the larger strategy through which a sizeable expeditionary force could be formed during an emergency.

[27] Susanne H. Rudolph and Lloyd I. Rudolph, 'Part II—The Jodhpur Lancers in China: Imperial Soldiers or Coolies of the Raj?', in *Reversing the Gaze: Amar Singh's Diary—A Colonial Subject's Narrative of Imperial India*, ed. Susanne H. Rudolph, Lloyd I. Rudolph, and M.S. Kanota, pp. 125–64 (Boulder: Westview Press, 2002). The Boxer Rebellion in particular exhibited the first signs of a developing, albeit difficult relationship between the British and Indian troops on account of the inferior status of Indians within the Army.

[28] Brian Bond, *British Military Policy between the Two World Wars* (Oxford: Oxford University Press, 1980), p. 102. According to the author, the whole period of the inter-War years could be viewed in terms of the gradual reconciliation of these discordant views of the Indian Army's priorities—traditional frontier defence or broader imperial commitments.

could effectively partake in the task of maintaining the defence and security of the Raj.

The principle of greater responsibility for defence and security falling onto the colony came to be formally enshrined in the proposals of a defence sub-committee that was constituted during the RTC convened in 1931 in London. The RTC was announced to assuage the political bickering that had erupted in response to the 'Simon Commission' that had come to India to monitor and review the working of the 1919 Reforms—the same constitutional proposals that had attempted to initiate a set of reforms for the Indian Army—immortalized in the Indianization debates conducted by Sivaswamy Aiyar among others. The defence sub-committee of 1931 was mandated to look into the question of setting up an Indian officers' training academy. This was a momentous occasion as it led directly to the formation of the Indian Military College Committee or the 'Chetwode Committee' under the chairmanship of Lord Chetwode, the commander-in-chief of the Indian Army, which recommended the establishment of an 'Indian Sandhurst'.[29]

The recommendations of the 1931 report were iconic: It resulted in the formation of the IMA, an institution that continues to function in its capacity as an officers' training academy to the present day. Yet, in its efforts to draft measures for the Indian Sandhurst, the committee reflected the contested and contradictory nature of Indianization. Consisting of members from different occupational and ideational

---

[29] The Chetwode Committee of 1931 comprised the following:

Officials: chief of general staff; adjutant general in India; secretary to the GoI in the Army Dept; deputy MS, Army HQ, Sir George Anderson, Kt., CIE, director of Public Instruction, Punjab; Khan Bahadur Sharbat Khan, CIE.

Non-Official Members: Sir Abdur Rahim, KCSI, Kt, MLA; Sir P.S. Sivaswamy Aiyar, KCSI, CIE; Rao Bahadur Chaudhri Chhotu Ram, MLC; Lt Col HA.J. Gidney (later Sir Henry Gidney), MLA; Dr B.S. Moonje; S.N. Mukarji, Esq, principal of St. Stephen's College, Delhi; Capt. Sher Mohammad Khan, MBE, MLA; Lt Narain Singh Bahadur, MC, IDSM.

Members from Indian States: Maj. Gen. Rao Raja Ganpat Rao Raghunath Rajwade, CBE, inspector general of Gwalior Army; Col Lachhman Singh, QMG, Patiala State Forces; Lt Col Mirza Kader Beg, Sardar Bahadur, Commandant, 1st Hyderabad IS Lancers.

persuasions, the report signalled that any future discussion of military institutional reform would have to contend with the wide-ranging motivations, agendas, and ideologies of all those who were interested in the project to Indianize the military.

The discussions surrounding the establishment of the IMA also laid the basis—as it did in the case of other academies—for an overhaul of the administrative and functional basis of the subsidiary feeder institutions in the subcontinent, validating my argument that institutional reform and its Indianization was a multi-tiered process. It was not easily explainable through a reductionist approach by identifying the 'winners' and the 'losers' in the battle to secure an Indian academy, but instead pointed towards the long-term developments in the run up towards the establishment of higher military institutions.

The 1931 report forms the immediate context to the IMA's establishment. However, the Skeen Report of 1926—not all of whose recommendations were accepted by the government—also makes a recurring appearance in the former. The 1931 report testified to the presence of considerable dissent among members who repeatedly invalidated the claims of any 'unity in Indian opinion' on military Indianization at this time. The differences among the members were highlighted in Gen. Chetwode's covering minute of the 1931 report, which suggested a deep rift among members and also between committee members and the government over the interpretation of the 'terms of reference' on the basis of which the committee was to proceed.[30] The 'minutes of dissent' that were forwarded by certain members of the committee frame the debate around the IMA along two important axes.

First, it undergirds the constitutional and intergovernmental hierarchy within which the IMA question was discussed. It was apparent that the terms of reference for the committee were set by the governments in India and Britain and were not supposed to be tampered with, thereby limiting the role of members over adjudicating on important associated matters relating to IMA's administration. Second, it also exposed the disunity that existed among Indian members on matters of military reform and Indianization—an early sign of a fractured and complicated process through which the IMA emerged.

[30] Report of the Indian Military College Committee, 15 July 1931, BL, IOR/L/MIL/17/5/1790, p. 31.

It also highlighted a conflicted terrain, as questions of security and the 'class' of recruits got interwoven with the administrative issues of the IMA. This necessarily meant a clash of interests, for security and Indianization were seen to be the preserve of the government, while the committee was only entrusted with the question of setting up the IMA, bearing a largely 'consultative' role. However, the early years of the twentieth century, during which several military reform committees were set up, signified that the two ostensibly distinct issues— Indianization and the campaign for an academy in India—could not be examined separately. It took the inauguration of the IMA for the colonial government to fully understand that both the above issues were tied to each other more firmly than was earlier thought, and any attempt to halt or accelerate Indianization had an immediate impact on the existing as well as imminent plans for setting up military institutions.

A strong protest against the ostensibly symbolic role of the 1931 Chetwode Committee was registered in a minute by P.S. Sivaswamy Aiyar, the Indian liberal who, on earlier occasions, had played a key role in the constitutional negotiations surrounding Indianization from the 1920s. Aiyar criticized the role played by the commander-in-chief in restricting the committee's task to mere 'technical details of the military'.[31] Aiyar's trenchant criticism stemmed from the fact that the committee's role in taking a broad view of Indianization was being disregarded by the government. To the Indian politician, the 1931 Chetwode Committee seemed to be an extension of the previous decades' brainstorming on how to acquire a more 'Indian' military. It was in this spirit, Aiyar suggested, that all the reports of the previous committees appointed to look into military Indianization (Military Requirements Committee [1921] and the Shea Committee [1922]) should be handed over to the Chetwode Committee members for their examination.[32]

[31] Minute by Sir P.S. Sivaswamy Aiyar and Maj. Gen. Raja Ganpat Rao Raghunath Rao Rajwade. In the Report of the Indian Military College Committee, 15 July 1931, BL, IOR/L/MIL/17/5/1790, pp. 76–7.

[32] Minute by Sir P.S. Sivaswamy Aiyar and Maj. Gen. Raja Ganpat Rao Raghunath Rao Rajwade. In the Report of the Indian Military College Committee, 15 July 1931, BL, IOR/L/MIL/17/5/1790, pp. 76–7.

This demand was made to review the earlier plans of Indianization that had been discussed before, so that newer plans could be drafted in the light of the findings of the older reports. One main area in which this comparison was especially sought was the study of number of vacancies that were to be allotted to the IMA, and, by implication, a sign of the government's attitude towards greater Indianization of the officer cadre. The members were eager to discuss the number of proposed vacancies at the IMA, which, much to the consternation of Aiyar and other Indian leaders, had been fixed at sixty seats. B.S. Moonje, another Indian member of the committee, added ballast to this tirade by asserting the unquestionable authority of the 1931 Chetwode Committee in deciding the annual intake of the academy.[33] Moonje also questioned the relative position of the 1931 Expert Committee vis-à-vis the Indian government and wanted to seek a clear confirmation of the precise role and mandate of the expert committee members invited to draft proposals for an Indian officers academy. Members like Moonje and Aiyar took strong exception to the fact that an initial complement of sixty cadets taken in annually by the IMA would not only slow down the process of Indianization significantly, but that this number also sat at odds with what previous Indianization reports had suggested.

The issue of vacancies had great resonance in the debate because it was multi-tiered. At one level was the obvious fight over greater numbers for Indian cadets to be trained as officers. At another level, the debate took into account how the annual intake was to be structured, that is, who and which 'classes' of cadets were to be admitted or nominated. Parallel to this debate was the discussion surrounding the 'sectional quotas' for cadets from the provinces and its impact on the intake levels for the new academy. Moonje and Aiyar stated that there existed various ways in which the vacancies at the IMA could have been calculated by the government, but a fixed number, arbitrarily allocated, threatened to freeze the intake of Indian men for several years to the detriment of the Indian military.

---

[33] Minute by B.S. Moonje. In the Report of the Indian Military College Committee, 15 July 1931, BL, IOR/L/MIL/17/5/1790, pp. 44–74. See also Anirudh Deshpande, *British Military Policy in India, 1900–1945: Colonial Constraints and Declining Power* (New Delhi: Manohar, 2005), pp. 104–112.

Moonje pointed out the ways in which the IMA's intake was calculated in the past based on the recommendations of the Shea Committee
(1921–2), which suggested a phased Indianization programme stretch-
ing over three decades. The committee had vaguely recommended
the establishment of an Indian military college and estimated that
the complete Indianization of the Indian Army was possible within
a thirty-year period.[34] Based on this data, Moonje arrived at a higher
complement, that is, ranging between 100 and 120 as the annual IMA
intake of cadets. This figure, he remarked, stood justified to provide a
'substantial increase' in the rate of Indianization. Another committee,
which was in cold storage by the time the Chetwode Report was tabled
in 1931, was the Indian Military Requirements Committee of 1921. It
suggested that '25% of the India Army cadetships at Sandhurst should
be thrown open to Indian youths', and with a progressive increase of
2.5 per cent in the cadetships annually, it would have resulted in equal
proportion of British and Indian officers entering the Indian Army in
a period of ten years.[35]

These calculations of Indianization rates rested on the fact that about
7,000 British officer ranks needed to be replaced for full Indianization
to be realized, and in accomplishing this task, a phased process of

[34] Cited in The Report of the Indian Military College Committee, 15 July
1931, BL, IOR/L/MIL/17/5/1790, pp. 50–1. The Shea Committee recommended the average annual output of an Indian Academy to be: (*i*) 81 cadets
during the first period of Indianization of fourteen years; (*ii*) 182 cadets during
the second phase of nine years; and (*iii*) cadets ranging between 88 and 106 in
number during the third period of seven years. The numbers did not include
the Indian State Forces, which were fixed at thirty.

If the Shea Committee recommended the above output for Indianization
to be complete within thirty years, Moonje deduced that the intake must be
higher still, taking into the account the rate of wastage among the first period
officers at 3 per cent per annum and inferred that the Shea committee recommended the following figures for intake for the proposed academy: (*a*) 81 plus
3, that is, 84 cadets during the first period of Indianization of fourteen years,
(*ii*) 182 plus 6, that is, 188 cadets during the second period of nine years; and
(*iii*) proportionate increase over a number ranging between 88 and 106 in the
third period over seven years.

[35] The Report of the Indian Military College Committee, 15 July 1931,
BL, IOR/L/MIL/17/5/1790, pp. 50–1.

three decades would have to pass.[36] In addition to this, the Shea Committee had also recommended about 3,000 officer commissions to be officered solely by 'outsiders' (that is, non-ranks and non-VCO candidates), which, Moonje asserted, meant that the average intake of outsiders would be about 111 cadets per year.[37] These quantitative exercises convinced the 1931 committee, and certainly Moonje and Aiyar in particular, that the government was 'disingenuous' in awarding vacancies to the IMA so as to halt the pace of Indianization.

Nevertheless, Moonje's interventions in the debate regarding vacancies at the IMA reflected more than an avid interest in the 'Indian Sandhurst'. Just a year later, in 1932, he would be busy setting up his own feeder training institution to the IMA in central India for which he had made quite a robust use of his official contacts in New

[36] The Report of the Indian Military College Committee, 15 July 1931, BL, IOR/L/MIL/17/5/1790, pp. 50–1.

[37] Cited in The Report of the Indian Military College Committee, 15 July 1931, BL, IOR/L/MIL/17/5/1790, p. 53. The number of 111 cadets was arrived at in the following way: For intake of cadets other than those classed as army cadets according to the scheme of Indianization recommended by the Shea Committee, the scheme provided the following:

1. During the first seven years of Indianization, two-thirds of the King's commissions be reserved for the Indian officers holding the viceroy's commission;
2. During the remaining twenty-three years, half of the King's commissions would be reserved for the above; and
3. The rest would be thrown open to competition from outsiders (that is, non-army cadets).

On the basis of the aforementioned formula, the 1931 Expert Committee arrived at the following numbers for outsiders coming into the academy:

1. For the first period of fourteen years of Indianization, the rate of intake to be 34 per annum;
2. For the second period of nine years, the rate of intake to be 141 per annum; and
3. For the third period of seven years, the rate of intake to be 228 per annum.

Thus, 34×14 plus 141×9 plus 228×7 makes the total for the three periods to be 3,381 commissions for outsiders, which, on an average rate, comes down to 111 cadets per annum.

Delhi.[38] Moonje was desirous of establishing and organizing schools for imparting 'elementary military education' to 'Hindu youths' under the aegis of the 'The Central Hindu Military Education Society', established in Nagpur in central India, and which later gravitated towards imparting military education to prospective police constables as well.[39] His ideas for a military school were born as a result of his travels to Europe and Britain, where the model of a 'public school', found favour with his early plans to develop—with suitable modifications—a similar facility 'to suit the Indian situation and particularly the social and economic conditions of the Hindus' for whom the school was primarily meant to cater.[40]

He sought to fulfil this by staffing this institution (known as the Bhonsala Military School) by appointing officers and instructors from the Prince of Wales Royal Indian Military College and other feeder institutions. The precise educational aims of this institution were unclear, and while it did enjoy limited support from some of Moonje's colleagues like P.S. Aiyar,[41] the proposal to employ officers from the King George's schools was not received enthusiastically by the commander-in-chief.[42]

After having debated the issue of vacancies at IMA, which remained at sixty, whatever unity that existed among the Indian members on

[38] Subject File 32, Letter from B.S. Moonje to Chetwode, Commander-in-Chief, Indian Army, 31 March 1932, B.S. Moonje Papers, NMML Archives, New Delhi, India.

[39] Subject File 24, Report of 'The Central Hindu Military Education Society' (HQ Nagpur), B.S. Moonje Papers, NMML Archives, New Delhi, India.

[40] Subject File 26, Report of the Progress of the work of the Society from 1 January 1935 to 15 August 1936, Conception of the Idea of the Military School, B.S. Moonje Papers, NMML Archives, New Delhi, India.

[41] Letter from Sir P.S. Sivaswamy Aiyar (Madras), 22 February 1936, Subject File 26, Correspondence with Philip Chetwode and local rulers concerning the establishment and location of Bhonsla Military School, Nasik. B.S. Moonje Papers, NMML, Delhi. Aiyar expressed some concerns to Moonje regarding the institutional viability of the school. Despite its stated aims of imparting a 'military education', Aiyar expressed doubts about the precise nature of education that Moonje had in mind.

[42] Subject File 24, Chetwode's letter to Moonje, 29 April 1932, B.S. Moonje Papers, NMML Archives, New Delhi, India.

the 1931 Chetwode Committee ended at this point. From here on, substantive issues relating to the IMA's organizational details divided the members into various positions. This resulted in multiple points of contact between the government (which also did not speak in one voice) and the committee members who were already penning their points of dissent for inclusion into the official report. Like the process of Indianization itself, subsequent conflicts arose partly in response to differences in interpretation of clauses outlined in previous reports on Indianization, and partly out of the discontent of the Indianization policy itself. This disunity was also on display in the discussions surrounding the examination provisions of the IMA.

The IMA was required to admit cadets based on a written examination and this soon lent itself to a controversy regarding the distribution of vacancies between 'nominated' cadets, that is, those who had been selected from within the ranks of the Indian Army,[43] and 'competitive' cadets, the ones who passed the entrance test. This time, the objections were raised by S.N. Mukarji, member of the 1931 committee and principal of the Delhi-based St. Stephen's College. Mukarji broke ranks with his colleagues and questioned the wisdom in allotting as much as thirty vacancies (out of a total of sixty) for army cadets, that is, nominations from within the ranks of the Indian Army.[44]

Mukarji's intervention flagged up an important issue for debate. As per the proposed regulation of the 1931 Chetwode Committee Report, the commander-in-chief had to select thirty army cadets into the IMA, a policy that Mukarji found untenable, since in the last '3 or 4 years', he contended, 'only two persons from the Indian army were considered fit for nomination for Sandhurst'.[45] The whole policy to 'recruit new men of a higher type into the Army by offering them the bait of an early nomination to a course at the IMA' was unacceptable

[43] These cadets were also known as the 'Y' cadets. These were mainly men from the non-commissioned ranks of the Indian Army, who, upon demonstrating a reasonable level of education, could be chosen for further training as officers. The criteria were often based on being able to successfully pass the Army Special Certificate of Education.

[44] Minute by S.N. Mukarji, Report of the Indian Military College Committee, 15 July 1931, BL, IOR/L/MIL/17/5/1790, p. 41.

[45] Minute by S.N. Mukarji, Report of the Indian Military College Committee, 15 July 1931, BL, IOR/L/MIL/17/5/1790, p. 41.

because, as Mukarji remarked: '[M]en of the proper standard for King's Commissioned ranks are not forthcoming in the existing army.'[46] Mukarji was speaking to concerns that had first led to the creation of the Skeen Committee, which was tasked to recommend measures to improve the quality of the cadets selected for Sandhurst, many of whom were failing to complete their courses.

His reservations against nominations was also rooted in the principle of making the army a 'competitive' avenue for entry and employment, and remarked that the majority (70 per cent was his estimate) of those who gained admission into the British academies were from the 'enlisted classes',[47] who proceeded to England not through the route of a nomination but an examination. This, according to him, was enough to convince those (unnamed in the official report) who feared that by opening the IMA by way of competition, the officer ranks would be 'swamped by members of the non-enlisted classes', revealing the potency of elitist prejudices that dictated officer entry channels in India.[48]

This was an unusual argument to posit. Competitive examinations had only recently been introduced as far as military recruitment for prospective officers was concerned, and in the case of post-Independence academies like the NDA, established in 1949, entry selection through examinations caused widespread resentment, not so much because the 'non-enlisted classes' were 'feared' to have excelled at them, but because the whole system seemed unpredictable and unreasonable to many who took these examinations. Thus, for Mukarji to suggest that enlisted classes be convinced to enter through the competitive route seemed rather progressive.

For a brief moment, it appeared as though the establishment of the IMA had awakened the possibility of what C.J. Dewey termed the 'institutional replacement' of the obsolete regimes of recruitment principles on which institutions had stood, signifying a move 'from

[46] Minute by S.N. Mukarji, Report of the Indian Military College Committee, 15 July 1931, BL, IOR/L/MIL/17/5/1790, p. 41.

[47] Referring to either upper class candidates or those with traditional, lineage-based links with military service like the aristocrats, or both.

[48] Minute by S.N. Mukarji, Report of the Indian Military College Committee, 15 July 1931, BL, IOR/L/MIL/17/5/1790, p. 41.

patronage to competitive examination'.[49] However, this replacement was not fully apparent in the case of the IMA. The planning for a new institution and insistence on competitive examinations as a mode of entry only gave a momentary glimpse of heralding more equitable practices of acquiring officers' commissions. In reality, this sentiment coexisted with a large body of opinion that favoured a status quo-ist approach on maintaining the traditional networks of recruitment channels into military service. Mukarji himself provided a quick turn-around in his views to exemplify the 'institutional obsolescence' that was associated with the discussions surrounding IMA's recruitment strategies in 1931.

Mukarji's subsequent line of reasoning dealt with how a high proportion of nominated army cadets could mark a dent in the efficiency of the Indian Army. His questionable premise that the efficiency of the British Army rested on its officers' public-school education led him to believe that having in the army 'as many as 50 per cent of the cadets for the military college ... from the Indian army ranks, which can hardly boast of having recruits from among the Dehra Dun college boys or from any other institution of a similar type' was not in the organization's best interest. Training these army cadets would be an uphill task and their set habits 'at the age of 23 to 25 years' would be an impediment in the face of teaching them powers of 'leadership and initiative'. Mukarji doubted whether men of this age (or class?) could ever be made to 'acquire traits of character which young lads in institutions like the Prince of Wales' College can acquire before they come to the military college'. It appears that Mukarji had merely substituted the 'martial race theory' with a theory of class snobbery.[50]

This episode was not unconnected to the 'new Indianization' plans that Aiyar had objected to in his minute in the 1931 report, many of which splintered Indian officership into other class-based groups. For

[49] C.J. Dewey, 'The Education of a Ruling Caste: The Indian Civil Service in the Era of Competitive Examination', *The English Historical Review* vol. 88, no. 347 (1973): 262–85.

[50] Minute by S.N. Mukarji, Report of the Indian Military College Committee, 15 July 1931, BL, IOR/L/MIL/17/5/1790, p. 43. Mukarji, later in his note, advocated as a temporary measure to keep nominated vacancies at one-third of the total, eventually whittling it down to one-fifth of the total intake.

instance, regulations put forward by the commander-in-chief, such as the proposals to post newly commissioned KCIOs in units mainly to replace the VCOs, stirred a hornet's nest. These regulations appeared to suggest the imminent disbandment of an important cadre of the VCOs. Aiyar, in his dissenting note, associated the removal of VCOs with earlier segregationist schemes that were pursued to divide the Indian Army along class lines.[51]

The VCOs were often targeted in the Indianization debates, and their removal was invariably perceived to be the most convenient 'first step' that was advocated by the government in response to the demands for placing newly commissioned Indian officers in units in greater numbers.[52] The elimination of the VCO cadre was also suggested by the 1922 Shea Committee, but it was ignored. However, their issue continued to dominate the post–Second World War demobilization discourse, when calls to disband the VCO cadre were becoming louder—this time from the VCOs themselves, who complained about the disparities in their status and service entitlements with respect to their British counterparts, that is, the warrant officers (WOs).[53]

Later, the graduates of the IMA were also sought to first replace the VCOs and then proceed to replace the British officers, thus taking a considerable amount of time for Indianization to proceed. Moreover, the precise meaning of a viceroy's commission remained controversial since it was often conflated with the dominion's commission of Australia and Canada, suggesting parity with a King's commission, whereas in reality the two were quite different in status. Upon IMA's inauguration

[51] Minute by S.N. Mukarji, Report of the Indian Military College Committee, 15 July 1931, BL, IOR/L/MIL/17/5/1790, p. 101.

[52] Replacing the VCOs with ICOs of the IMA risked introducing a new form of segregation in the Indian Army, thereby undoing the efforts of the past decades in trying to Indianize the army along the principle of equality among Indian and British officers.

[53] Note by Brig. K.M. Cariappa on the VCO Rank to H.E. Gen. Sir Claude J.E. Auchinleck, Commander-in-Chief India, Reorganisation Committee India, 5 November 1945, Cariappa Papers, National Archives of India [NAI], New Delhi, India. Cariappa suggested that the VCO rank remain, terming it 'as an economical and yet an efficient rank', which provided an incentive to a very large number of young Indian 'other ranks' with limited educational qualifications to work up to.

in 1932, a discussion on the nomenclature of the commission that was
to be awarded to cadets was settled on the ICO, which was signed by
the governor-general. This was done to ensure that the graduates of the
IMA held a superior status to those of the VCOs (and also implying
that the ICO was not equivalent to the King's Commission).[54]

A section of the seats at the IMA were also reserved for the princes
and cadets from the State Forces, and this generated another significant
and tense round of negotiations among members. The Indian princely
states occupied an ambivalent space and legitimacy in the eyes of the
1931 committee. The lukewarm participation of the princes in the
IMA discussions was in stark contrast to the generosity with which
they favoured the welfare of prospective cadets bound for England. By
1928, a sizeable share of scholarships, bursaries, or grants awarded to
cadets who had been selected to go to Sandhurst or Woolwich were
supported by Indian princes.[55] The committee, perhaps taking note of
this sponsorship and concurring with the Skeen proposals earlier, did
not see it appropriate to ask the princes to contribute any funds towards
the establishment of the college or its maintenance, but decreed that
the expenses of the cadets from their State Forces should be borne by
the states and not the central government.[56]

The aforementioned position was an unusual one to adopt, and apart
from the dissenting members (Moonje, Gidney, Rajwade, Lachhman
Singh, and Narain Singh), the proposal sat at odds with the substantial
financial support the princely states had traditionally extended to the
Raj and specifically to the feeder schools, whose endowment, in addition to funds for scholarships and bursaries, drew largely from the royal
treasuries of these states. States' support to feeder institutions was made
possible partly as a result of the wartime expansion of the princely

---

[54] Collection 430/89, Form of commission for officers graduating from
Indian Military Academy, Dehradun, India, and for officers of Indian Air Force,
BL, IOR/L/MIL/7/19124.

[55] Provisional Regulations Respecting Admission of Indian Gentlemen
to the RMA, Woolwich, the RMC Sandhurst and the RAF Cadet College,
Cranwell, 1928, BL, IOR/L/MIL/17/5/2290.

[56] Chapter VI, Provisional Regulations Respecting Admission of Indian
Gentlemen to the RMA, Woolwich, the RMC Sandhurst and the RAF Cadet
College, Cranwell, p. 16, 1928, BL, IOR/L/MIL/17/5/2290.

'investment portfolios' arising out of the interest payments on British war loans.[57] Thus, it could not have been possible to run the feeder schools without a great degree of royal munificence, and because the feeder schools' fate was tied to the fate of the IMA, ignoring the princes could have been a costly mistake.

This was not to be, as quite a few princes themselves came to view the IMA as a 'lesser' institution compared to its British counterparts. Even after 1932, when the IMA was in place, some of the princes continued to train and aspire for Sandhurst, calling into question the sincerity with which the case for the 'Indian Sandhurst' was being championed by the them. Moreover, the cadets belonging to the State Forces (those who did not belong to aristocratic families) performed poorly in the IMA, thereby, downgrading the importance of the princes in the theatre of twentieth-century military reform.

As one of its last recommendations, the 1931 committee reiterated that the control of the Dehradun College was to be retained with the military and the curriculum to be suitably adjusted so as to enable its graduates to earn qualifications which would render them suitable for civilian employment too. This need to tie the obvious military aspect of educational institutions with civilian institutions in order to make available a broad spectrum of employment and further education opportunities to its graduates remained a dominant motif of subsequent military institutionalization practices in the decades that were to follow.

THE COMPLEX CONSTITUENCY OF THE IMA: CADETS, 'CLASS', AND 'CITIZENSHIP'

Although conceptualized as a space where the question of Indianization could be resolved according to British authorities' terms and conditions, which were frequently qualified by others, the IMA was as much a cause for resentment among Indians as it was to Britain in subsequent years. Questions over inclusion of cadets as well as their assessment and commissions were the axes along which some major issues developed and embroiled all the stakeholders involved with the creation of the IMA.

---

[57] Cited in Hew Strachan, *Financing the First World War* (Oxford and New York: Oxford University Press, 2004), p. 219.

Taking stock of the contingent nature of military reform in the previous decades, some members of the 1931 committee alleged that 'it was plainly' put to them that the 'officering of the Indian Army with Indians' was an 'experiment' and what was being proposed (the academy) 'should suffice for the purpose'.[58] The members warned the government that any 'experimental' nature of institutional innovation, such as in the case of the IMA, would be rejected by the Indian public, and only a definite policy of Indianization secured in the context of an 'Indian Sandhurst' would be acceptable. The IMA's inauguration, therefore, signified a brief sense of 'finality' for military institutional policy as well as for the people campaigning for it. Its establishment was seen as having successfully sold the idea of Indianization to the British by the Indian leaders. This euphoria, however, as this section will demonstrate, was short-lived.

In its early years, the IMA drew candidates through joint examinations in India and London. However, the idea of joint examinations did not deliver any parity to candidates or their chances of selection. Where the Indian examination threw itself open to candidates from all over the country, the London examination was seen as an adjunctive exercise to the main examination in India. Whitehall made frequent demands to close down the London examination and to make travel to India a mandatory requirement for taking the examination.[59] Notwithstanding the official reason that the London examination drew a smaller number of candidates and was thus disproportionately expensive, the antipathy towards the examination went deeper. Whitehall saw the practice of examining candidates in Britain as a measure that would potentially open the field not only to Indians and Anglo-Indians with British domicile, but also

> All Indians and Anglo-Indians with extra-Asiatic domiciles who are British subjects ... if the examination were to be abolished in the future and we had in the meantime made provision for the examination in this country of this sort of candidate, we might be ... in an awkward

[58] Minute by Abdur Rahim, Rai Bahadur Chaudhri Chhotu Ram, and Mr S.N. Mukarji, Report of the Indian Military College Committee, 15 July 1931, BL, IOR/L/MIL/17/5/1790.

[59] Letter from L.W. Homan to J.A. Simpson (Military Department, Whitehall), BL, IOR/L/MIL/7/19127.

position. For the candidates in question might then regard themselves as having a reserved right to be examined, and the Government of India might raise objections to opening the examination in India to this sort of candidate.[60]

Opening the field of entry to candidates with 'non-Indian domiciles' would have been troublesome in the wake of the limited number of vacancies in the IMA, which, despite ongoing debates about the quality of the intake, was unable to provide seats for most cadets who took the entrance examination. The problem of greater inclusion was not just India's alone as the above quote seems to suggest. Britain was also uneasy at the prospect of granting entry to these candidates. By allowing Anglo-Indians to train at Sandhurst or Woolwich, Britain would then have had to 'formally' open its gates to all classes of individuals, including the princes, most of whom were clamouring to enter Sandhurst instead of the IMA. Such a development would have rung hollow not only with the nationalist leaders, but would also have negated the tenuous trope of a 'national institution' with which the IMA was beginning to be portrayed in India by the government.

The case of the Anglo-Indians (living in India and abroad), here referring principally to persons of Eurasian parentage, provides a ringside view of the ways in which the IMA tried to alter its entry channels for cadets belonging to various classes, highlighting the enduring presence and potency of 'race' and ethnicity' in a supposedly modern institution for military training. The whole question of conducting joint examinations for the IMA hinged on the Anglo-Indians and where they could be accommodated. In a dramatic reversal, when the GoI forwarded the radical proposal to scrap the London examination in order to focus solely on Indian candidates, Whitehall—alarmed at the prospect of having to absorb such candidates ordinarily resident in Britain—now argued that the Anglo-Indians represented an important source of recruitment for the Indian Army, their small numbers being outweighed by the high percentage of 'successes' in the examinations.[61]

---

[60] Letter from L.W. Homan to J.A. Simpson (Military Department, Whitehall), BL, IOR/L/MIL/7/19127.

[61] Collection 430/88, Minute by Defence Department, p. 256, Indian Military Academy, Dehradun: committee report (1931), arrangements for

In addition to this, Whitehall also outlined the 'obvious advantages of getting into the Indian Army as many boys as possible who have been educated at English schools', and 'so long as that source exists, it seems desirable to use it'.[62] Whitehall stressed the Anglo-Indians' public-school credentials in order to convince the Indian authorities to absorb them. London felt that several Indianization committees in the past had considered public-school education as a desirable element for prospective officers and would therefore see the Anglo-Indian candidates through that lens. Of course, Britain was not willing to accommodate these public school–educated Anglo-Indians in British academies.

The case of the Anglo-Indians and their ambiguous place in military institutional networks first surfaced in the feeder instructional space of the Prince of Wales Royal Indian Military College and the Lawrence Schools, almost a decade before the IMA was set up in 1932.[63] In a memorandum issued by the Anglo-Indian and Domiciled European Association of Calcutta in 1923, the body demanded the inclusion of Anglo-Indians to the Prince of Wales Royal Indian Military College in order to make them eligible for a King's commission. Consequently, the Indian government, in consultation with the War Office in London, was compelled to outline its policy on candidates of 'mixed descent'.[64]

While there was no official restriction on the consideration of Anglo-Indians and other domiciled European communities in India to be included into commissioned ranks; privately, however, officials stated the difficulty, if not the impossibility, 'for the lads of the community particularly those who were coloured and were not prepared

---

simultaneous examination arrangements in England and India, question of dates, etc., BL, IOR/L/MIL/7/19123.

[62] Collection 430/88, Minute by Defence Department, p. 256, Indian Military Academy, Dehradun: committee report (1931), arrangements for simultaneous examination arrangements in England and India, question of dates, etc., BL, IOR/L/MIL/7/19123.

[63] See, for instance, Arun Prakash, *The Young Warriors: A History of the Rashtriya Indian Military College, Dehra Dun* (Dehradun: RIMC. 2004), pp. 213–14.

[64] Question of admission of Anglo-Indians in the Army through the RIMC, Dehradun, BL, IOR/L/MIL/7/13079.

to foreswear their birth' to enter Sandhurst via an examination.[65] The Anglo-Indians occupied a particularly unique position with respect to military institutions as there was no historical precedent according to the government, for their employment as royal 'commissioned' officers. This accentuated their identity sharply along racial lines, even more so when the government, outwardly and hypocritically, remarked that 'colour was not a practical difficulty', despite it keeping the doors for awarding officers' commissions only half-open for 'persons who were not of pure European descent.'[66]

The solution for the Anglo-Indians, the government in London suggested, lay in declaring the Anglo-Indians as 'Indians', thereby, making them eligible to earn a cheap education at the Prince of Wales Royal Indian Military College. The Anglo-Indians, though a limited number, were also eligible to train at the Lawrence Schools, yet in declaring the Anglo-Indians as domiciled 'Indians', the government hoped to send out the message that 'only one avenue to Sandhurst would be open' to them: either the 'competitive examination held in England or nomination and examination in India, under arrangements applicable to Indian candidates, but not both'.[67] This was characteristic official double-speak, as in the words of a government official in the War Office: hopes of making the army a career would 'prove to be illusory for 99% of the youths of the community', as Sandhurst was 'of no practical value' as an avenue to Anglo-Indian lads.[68] Thus, plans to

---

[65] Question of admission of Anglo-Indians in the Army through the RIMC, Dehradun, BL, IOR/L/MIL/7/13079.

[66] Secretary of State-in-Council Draft Minute, 1917, BL, IOR/L/MIL/7/13055. In 1917, in response to a query from the War Office, the secretary of state-in-council had suggested disallowing candidates for commissions in the British Army who were not of pure European descent, barring those who had distinguished themselves in battle. The minute forewarned against opening the commissions to such candidates as it could then open the gates for the 'Eurasians', like the Anglo-Indians.

[67] Question of admission of Anglo-Indians in the Army through the RIMC, Dehradun, BL, IOR/L/MIL/7/13079.

[68] Memorandum from the Anglo-Indian and Domiciled European Association, Calcutta India, BL, IOR/L/MIL/7/13079. An 'Anglo-India Corps' had also been established in 1916 but it was not successful. See Secretary of State-in-Council Draft Minute, 1917, BL, IOR/L/MIL/7/13055.

facilitate the entry of Anglo-Indians into military service were often disingenuous.

The joint examination system was often seen in London as an 'avoidable' task. The examinees like the Anglo-Indians however, were seen in a different light, which in turn made the organization of these joint examinations a necessary exercise, at least for a few years until the mid-1940s when it was disbanded. Nonetheless, the episode highlighted the conflictual impact that Indianization had on minority groups of the Raj. On a larger scale, the position of the Anglo-Indians raised important questions on the nature of the IMA's inclusion priorities, and highlighted the careful recalibration that was undertaken to define who was supposed to be entering its portals and in what number.

Questions of 'citizenship' and 'nationality', as a consequence, formed an interesting backdrop to the discussions surrounding the entry to the IMA. The 1931 report drew the attention to the prospect of the 'recruitment of "non-nationals"' from territories outside the boundaries of India'.[69] Although the official report did not state a firm position on the subject, the additional dissenting notes of some of its members aided in festering the issue further. The members, mainly Abdur Rahim, S.N. Mukarji, and Chhotu Ram, asserted that 'no one who was not a British Indian subject or subject of an Indian state' was eligible under the 'rules of appointment as an officer of the Indian army', thereby signalling, that such 'non-nationals' would not be admitted to the Indian Military College.[70]

The 1931 committee's decision to outline which communities were the 'non-nationals' and, therefore, unfit to enter an Indian military institution poses a big question about the political consciousness (or the lack of it) surrounding the geo-political meanings associated with the Indian dominion as it stood in 1931. How did the members of the 1931 committee draw their inferences on who was or was not 'fit' to be the 'ideal type' for an Indian military academy? To push this even further, what and where was the geographical or political border

---

[69] Report of the Indian Military College Committee, 15 July 1931, BL, IOR/L/MIL/17/5/1790, p. 38.

[70] Report of the Indian Military College Committee, 15 July 1931, BL, IOR/L/MIL/17/5/1790, p. 38. By the committee's own admission, about 17,000 'non-nationals' were already present in the Indian Army.

located in 1931, beyond which a prospective candidate for the IMA was deemed to be unfit on grounds of his 'nationality'? This is not to suggest that any firm or 'tangible' geopolitical realities would have rendered these proposals more credible in determining suitability for the IMA, since the institutionalization and administration of 'border landscapes' itself is a complicated process that continually changes the way people are affected by it.[71]

Yet, the committee, interestingly, advocated these proposals without outlining any precise geographical or political indices through which one was to determine the contours of the 'citizenship' of prospective military cadets. Where the Indian dominion began and ended is a fascinating corollary to the post-colonial questions of how nation–states craft their own citizenship models amid a violent and often messy process of state formation as has been highlighted by Joya Chatterji.[72] Yet in 1931, distinctions between the centre and the regions in the vicinity of a so-called 'border' were still inchoate. Regions such as the northwestern frontier (if this was supposed to be the barrier in the minds of the committee members) were historically the first to be regularly garrisoned in the subcontinent and witnessed the earliest wave of military institution-building in mid-nineteenth century. This military infrastructural development lent a degree of legitimacy to the colonial State's administration of the region. State-centred activities also brought these peripheral regions back it into the 'political' centre of the subcontinent, if not the 'geographical' centre.[73] Exercises to determine suitability for a career in the military complicated the terms on which the Committees discussions were based. In the context of the mid-1930s especially the definitions of territorially bounded forms of belonging were not as coherent or fixed as they became after 1947.[74]

[71] Joya Chatterji, 'The Fashioning of a Frontier: The Radcliffe Line and Bengal's Border Landscape, 1947–1952', *Modern Asian Studies* vol. 33, no. 1 (1999): 185–242.

[72] Joya Chatterji, 'South Asian Histories of Citizenship, 1946–1970', *The Historical Journal* vol. 55. no. 4 (2012): 1049–71.

[73] Chatterji, 'The Fashioning of a Frontier', p. 241.

[74] For an analysis of post-Independence border and state-making attempts, please see Berenice Guyot-Rechard, 'Reordering a Border Space: Relief, Rehabilitation, and Nation-Building in Northeastern India after the 1950 Assam Earthquake', *Modern Asian Studies* vol. 49, no. 4 (2015): 931–62.

Members of the 1931 committee, part of the Raj's colonial establishment politics, attempted to unsuccessfully determine and implant bounded conceptions of identities onto certain groups and communities who had historically inhabited a fluid inter-regional geographical space. This process of casting groups of people and communities into silos of acceptability or non-acceptability for a career in the Indian military was chimerical. Not just the Anglo-Indians, but other groups like the Gurkhas too, in the years after the Second World War, suffered and rejoiced at the hands of these fluctuating protocols of determining 'nationality' so as to regulate entry mechanisms into the military institutions. Setting up an 'Indian Sandhurst' threw up probing questions of nationalism and 'geographical fealty' of prospective cadets, and led the members to contend that it was 'impossible' for them to understand

> how any conceivable national policy could justify us in training and employing men in our Army who owe allegiance to states whose relations with this country, however friendly at present, we cannot always be in a position to control.[75]

Perhaps the members, in a way, were echoing pre-existing conceptions of belonging that had first been advocated in the late nineteenth-century Constitution of India Bill, which linked citizenship to all those who 'were born in India' or naturalization of foreigners.[76] However, in the context of the negotiations surrounding an Indian military academy, the exercise was complicated because questions of 'loyalty' to India attempted to combine security-related concerns with hastily drawn assumptions about racial minorities, which could not easily be fitted into neat boxes of identifiable and domiciled communitarian groups.

The problems in determining eligibility of candidates to train at the IMA only magnified once the institutions started to function in 1932. It struggled to deal with wide-ranging groups of candidates, each of whom bore their own specific problems in the eyes of the military

---

[75] Report of the Indian Military College Committee, 15 July 1931, BL, IOR/L/MIL/17/5/1790, p. 38.

[76] Please see, B. Shiva Rao (ed.), *The Framing of India's Constitution: Select Documents*, Volume 1, pp. 5–14 (New Delhi: The Indian Institute of Public Administration, 1966), p. 6.

authorities in India and Britain. The government, conscious of the unequal and disquieting terms on which recruitment into the Indian Army and the IMA was being carried out, was wary of drawing any comparisons with the Indian Civil Service (ICS). By 1918, the ICS and other public services were being expanded to include Indians in several branches of administration,[77] but the government was careful not to 'rely on analogies from the ICS and IPS examinations to redress anomalies in the IMA exams'.[78] Officials in Whitehall contended that in the 'ICS and the IPS there is no racial distinction as there is in the Indian army now between British officers coming through Sandhurst and Indian officers coming through the IMA'.[79] Whereas for the civil services, its London examination, for a number of years, was the main test with the Indian examination as an annex; for the IMA, in a dramatic twist, the examination in India was now central and the London exam an 'unimportant addition' mainly because of the certain types of candidates in Britain who could not be accommodated in British institutions and for whom the Indian Sandhurst was presented as a 'viable' alternative.[80]

Highlighting the nature of the differences between the civil services and the military in order to justify the differences in their recruitment protocols was grounded in the historical implementation of military Indianization policies, many of which had often proceeded on the basis of a set of cautious and tentative official measures since the late nineteenth century. Until the arrival of the IMA, the whole process of reorganizing the Indian military lacked a sense of purposeful resolve to include more Indian officers, as the policies that were crafted were done so in a chaotic context, mediated by colonial officials, military officers, and Indian leaders, none of whom advanced a unified, coherent

[77] 'Montague–Chelmsford Report on the Indianization of Public Services, 1918', in *The Evolution of India and Pakistan: 1858 to 1947, Select Documents*, ed. C.H. Philips, H.L. Singh, and B.N. Pandey (London: Oxford University Press, 1962), pp. 565–6.

[78] Remarks by J.A. Simpson (Military Department, Whitehall) to L.W. Homan, 3 December 1932, BL, IOR/L/MIL/7/19127.

[79] Remarks by J.A. Simpson (Military Department, Whitehall) to L.W. Homan, 3 December 1932, BL, IOR/L/MIL/7/19127.

[80] Remarks by J.A. Simpson (Military Department, Whitehall) to L.W. Homan, 3 December 1932, BL, IOR/L/MIL/7/19127.

set of principles regarding Indianization. Thus, differences in recruitment methods and underlining the unsuitability of certain groups for
military service were articulated through portraying the functional dissimilarities between the occupational mandates of the military and the
civil service. Claims and 'broad justifications' reiterating the operational
dissimilarities between the army and civil services were patently inac-
curate since the military in India did engage in wide-ranging domestic
campaigns in the subcontinent by actively aiding the civilian structures
and shaping the operational contours of the management of domestic
law and order.[81]

In a lecture delivered at the Imperial Defence College (IDC) in
London in 1931, this was clearly articulated by S.K. Brown when he
remarked that military Indianization could not share the same characteristics as those of the civil services or police mainly because 'the
Army could only be tested in action, the occasions for which were
limited, whereas the Civil and Police services were at the forefront of
mitigating domestic challenges', thereby suggesting that in the former,
only such men could be included as officers 'who enjoyed the complete confidence of officers below and above them'.[82] Conceptions
of 'loyalty' and 'dependability', thus, were purposefully kept nebulous
in order to maintain tight controls on the communities that were
seeking to enter officer ranks, reflecting the operation of class and
race in the domain of military and security affairs. These 'myths' were
perpetuated not just by governments in London and New Delhi but
equally by members and officials connected with devising the admission and management procedures of the IMA, including Indian leaders, many of whom, like Mukarji, represented an establishment-wide
'unease' with including certain groups into the officer cadre of the
Indian military.

The realignments regarding the conception of the 'ideal cadet'
had important consequences for the wider enlistment protocol at the
IMA, and, in fact, presaged key recruitment trends that would evolve
in the years after Independence, in the wake of the renewed military

---

[81] Srinath Raghavan, 'Protecting the Raj: The Army in India and Internal
Security, c. 1919–39', *Small Wars & Insurgencies* vol. 16, no. 3 (2005): 253–79.

[82] Lecture delivered by S.K. Brown to Imperial Defence College (IDC),
Esq, CVO, India Office, Whitehall, 15 October, 1931, BL, IOR/L/MIL/5/857.

institutionalization that took place after 1947.[83] One of the many definitions concerning the 'right type' of cadet for the IMA was related to
associational linkages with revolutionary organizations that were active
in the 1930s and sprang from a radical anti-colonial ideology, directly
threatening the security apparatus of the Raj. Security implications,
thus, converged with recruitment priorities, adding another layer of
'preferability' with regard to incoming cadets.

These layers of 'preferability' of candidates did not stack up in one
direction, but diffused into other contexts calling into question their
sociocultural and occupational backgrounds. The regimens of 'calcu-
lating' suitability did not dictate concerns unilaterally from above but
had to contend and be carefully adapted in view of the messy administrative realities of the IMA, which, despite the fight for vacancies, was
struggling to fill its requisite share of seats with cadets.[84] By 1934, with
the academy in place for two years, candidatures such as those of a certain Mr Sachindranath Sen were considered for entry only after clearing him of all charges of 'sedition' and 'association with a revolutionary
Bengali outfit' through prolonged inquiries into his past.[85] While the

---

[83] Discussed in Chapter 3.

[84] Extracts from 'Editorial', *The Journal of the United Service Institution of
India* vol. LXII, October 1932, No. 269, Slim 4/2, FM Slim Papers, Churchill
Archives Centre, University of Cambridge, UK. The academy opened on 1
October 1932. The first competitive examination for entry took place in July
1932. Fifteen candidates were selected, six of whom were Mahomedan, four
were Hindu, two were Sikh, one was Parsi, one was Indian Christian, and one
was Anglo-Indian.
To these 15 were added another 15 cadets selected from among the non-
commissioned and Indian officers of the Indian Army, and 10 more nominated
by Indian states. The academy, therefore, opened initially with only forty cadets
as opposed to the sixty authorized spaces.

[85] Minute by Military Department, Whitehall, BL, IOR/L/MIL/7/19144.
Several such cases appeared before Whitehall and Delhi, where parents lobbied
to get their sons into British military institutions. See, for instance, Letter from
Mr Chengappa to Lord Burnham, 23 May 1932, BL, IOR/L/MIL/7/19127.
The writer of the letter was distraught over the chances of his son, who,
after failing the medical fitness test, was rejected for entry at Sandhurst. Mr
Chengappa, rueful of the revised entry regulations, 'wondered' if his son could
be sent to Sandhurst by nomination as a 'special case'.

controversy threatened to scotch Sen's (who was otherwise working as an engineer in Bath in England) chances of becoming an officer, Whitehall was also quick to point out to the Indian government, that 'while a taint of sedition was undesirable ... on the other hand recruits are not too easy to get, and it is important not to lose such a promising candidate if it can be avoided'.[86] The episode highlighted the careful balance that had to be struck between rejecting unsuitable candidates, and retaining much-needed ones, for despite the heated discussions on the distribution of vacancies earlier, the IMA was coping with several underperforming cadets, resulting in official embarrassment for the government.

The struggle to fill seats was aided in part by the princely states, who, vociferous in their support for an 'Indian Sandhurst', faltered in keeping up with their other significant commitments to IMA. The steady reduction in the cadet numbers coming in from the states coupled with the preference for commissions earned at British insti-tutions was, in no small measure, responsible in unfairly relegating the IMA's identity as a 'lesser' institution, indicating that the space was meant solely for former ranks to climb higher up the military ladder.

The indifference of the State Forces and the quality of their cadets, some of whom did eventually attend the IMA, also portended serious security issues for the princely states as well as the British. A deficiency in skilled officers meant that the State Forces, administered by the princes under British tutelage and intended to provide a counterbal-ance to the 'Indian Army', would languish. Since many cadets from the State Forces earned commissions into their local formations, it was essential for the government to see them coming in greater numbers. But by the mid-1930s, the whole scheme of 'affording greater support' to the Indian State Forces, initiated in 1921 as a practical sign of 'policy of trust', had broken down owing to the inability or unwillingness of the 'Darbars to maintain efficiency in the units'.[87] The chief reason for sending underperforming states' cadets to IMA, according to the Political Department, was that the princes and chiefs themselves had

---

[86] Minute by Military Department, Whitehall, BL, IOR/L/MIL/7/19144, p. 41.

[87] Minute by Political Department, BL, IOR/L/MIL/7/19145, p. 182.

'failed conspicuously to set an example by sending their own sons to Dehra Dun in favour of an English education and training.'[88] Asserting that abject class bias and racial prejudices forbade many princes to 'associate with the type of British India cadets admitted to the IMA, particularly from the Indian Army ranks', the document's stark conclusion noted that, in fact, 'social distinctions seem to be taken much more seriously by Indians than in modern England and particularly so by the Indian states'.[89] As a solution, it was proposed to refuse recommending the sons of minor princes for Woolwich or Sandhurst 'unless their dynastic salute is of the highest and their personal qualifications exceptional', and to persuade their sons to go to Dehradun instead of England.[90] But 'persuasion' did not amount to an abject 'refusal' to allow the princes to go to England for military training, reflecting again the elitist and class-based context in which regulations worked to perpetuate forms of prejudice among different kinds of groups and communities in India.

Efforts to convince the princes to revert to the IMA continued long after the 1932 regulations 'discouraged' Indians from attending the Royal Military Academy at Sandhurst. Measures were also put in place to make the education of states' cadets at Dehradun as one of the conditions of obtaining increased grants of free equipment to State Forces, but its implementation was not extensively pursued.[91] The episode also confirmed the duplicitous terms with which institutional reform was approached. While keeping the door firmly latched for some of the Raj's subjects, it was kept partially open for certain other classes, thereby creating multiple avenues for a competitive 'bargaining' over commissions and military status.[92]

[88] Minute by Political Department, BL, IOR/L/MIL/7/19145, p. 182. The minute mentions clearly the names of the likes of Raja of Sangli, whose two sons were at the Prince of Wales Royal Indian Military College, later withdrawn to be educated to England. The Maharaja of Rajpipla had secured entrance to Woolwich for his heir-apparent as well.

[89] Minute by Political Department, BL, IOR/L/MIL/7/19145, p. 182.

[90] Minute by Political Department, BL, IOR/L/MIL/7/19145, p. 182.

[91] Minute by Political Department, BL, IOR/L/MIL/7/19145, p. 182.

[92] The practice to reserve a few seats 'unofficially' at Sandhurst for a select group of cadets continued even after Independence—though this was sought to be done 'officially'—where cadets from the dominions

The poor showing of the cadets in the Indian State Forces at IMA posed the risk of eroding the viability of the IMA in the eyes of both the British and the Indians. In regular reports on the general quality of the IMA cadets, published at the end of each term, the states' cadets' performance appeared well behind others. The figures submitted with the report showed their numbers in 1934 to be half their stipulated complement, with only twenty-six out of fifty places taken up by the princely states. Besides, initial returns from the provinces showed no cadets from Bengal, Madras, and only 'small numbers' from Bombay. This skewed representation, in the words of the Political Department, was an 'interesting comment upon the contention of the Indian politician that all educated India' was longing to obtain commissions in the army'.[93]

This state of affairs unsettled the colonial authorities as they feared the spread of this 'indifference to Indian politicians' and thus 'affect their views as regards the method and progress of Indianisation of the regular Indian Army'.[94] The accent was now on promoting 'entry to the IMA as a privilege, and not a condescension as some rulers seem to think',[95] and so a substantial reduction in the number of vacancies allotted to the states' cadets, along with 'stiffening up the entrance qualification still further' by imposing additional English-language tests, was proposed.

The concerns regarding the performance and participation levels of the cadets in the State Forces were not just limited to the IMA. The Staff College and other tactical schools had also begun to report the

---

could be nominated by their governments to attend Sandhurst as part of a Commonwealth training programme. See Army Council Memorandum, D 2505/2, Commonwealth Candidates for Training at the RMA, Sandhurst, BL, IOR/L/MIL/7/13089.

[93] Comments by J.A. Simpson on matters concerning the Second Report on the General Quality of the Cadets at the IMA, BL, IOR/L/MIL/7/19145, 1934–41, p. 179.

[94] Comments by J.D. Coleridge on matters concerning the Second Report on the General Quality of the Cadets at the IMA, BL, IOR/L/MIL/7/19145, 1934–41, p. 179.

[95] Letter from G.R.F. Tottenham, GoI, to Sec., Mil. Dept, with an attached letter in the end, 9 May 1935, BL, IOR/L/MIL/7/19145, 1934–41, p. 148

falling performance outcomes of the State Forces cadets.[96] The annual review reports of the ISF attributed this to a general unfamiliarity with the English language, the medium of instruction at these institutions.[97] A solution was also sought in establishing a pre-officer-training school at Indore for such cadets, but it was not wholly successful in its ability to furnish commission-worthy recruits.[98]

However, at a more fundamental level, the problems faced by the states' cadets pointed towards the larger systemic inadequacies that military Indianization had to contend with. Military academies that were set up to accelerate the pace of training more Indian officers had to put up with the fact of training successive batches of men from wide-ranging sociocultural backgrounds and with experiences in different kinds of military services, not all of which were synonymous with the terms of service and socialization practices found in the Indian Army. Thus, Indianization policies were complicated further in the process of their interaction with the fundamental administrative differences in training a diverse set of men who came forward to replace British officers.

By the mid-1930s, there were major concerns regarding the standards obtained by other recruits who entered upon passing the competitive examination at the IMA. In a 1936 performance report, it was noted that since IMA's inauguration, '8 out of 114 competitive cadets (those who entered upon passing an examination) had been removed as unsatisfactory, whereas 19 out of 121 Indian Army cadets (nominated from within the ranks) were below the mark'.[99] The overall shortfall

[96] The frequency with which the Staff College and other institutions started to report these concerns peaked at around 1944–5.

[97] Annual Review of the Working of the Indian States Forces for the year, 1943–4, BL, IOR/L/WS/1/550.

[98] Annual Review of the Working of the Indian States Forces for the year, 1943–4, BL, IOR/L/WS/1/550. The syllabus of instruction at this school mainly consisted of a 'rigorous physical education and the intensive study of English', in addition to the elementary military subjects. During the period under review, 138 cadets were handled by the school, out of which 126 passed into the Officers Training Schools. However, not all those cadets who passed through the Indore school into Officers Training Schools were 'qualified as fit to hold Commissions at the officers' training school.

[99] Proposals for the improvement of the quality of Indian Army Cadets admitted to the Indian Military Academy, 20 March 1936. Tabled by Mr

in the number of capable cadets filling the seats was a cause for much concern and sat at odds with the political demands for seat expansion. The problem of this shortfall was made more chronic by the differences in the scholastic attainments of the candidates. Educationally, there was a considerable gap between the cadets who trained at feeder institutions like the Prince of Wales Royal Indian Military College and the 'worst Indian army and Indian State Forces Cadets' who entered IMA.[100] While severe competition existed among the open category cadets who entered the IMA—not all of whom passed satisfactorily—via competitive examination, the reserved seats meant for cadets from the State Forces remained largely unfilled or taken up by those who were of a much lower standard than the others, leading to an absence of a margin for selection, resulting in a widely fluctuating batch of cadets for whom devising a common pattern of training and instruction was challenging.[101]

These problems were compounded by other related administrative crises relating to the inclusion of Indian candidates who took their examinations from England, and aside from the practical difficulties of testing them on an Indian syllabus as taught in Indian schools, there were issues of how successful candidates from there would join the academy, and who would bear their travel and living costs while they stayed in India.[102] A common pattern of entrance test was itself

---

Turnbull (Private Secretary to the Permanent Under-Secretary of State, India Office), BL, IOR/L/MIL/7/19155.

[100] Letter from H.I. Macdonald, Army Department, New Delhi, to S.K. Brown, Joint Secretary, Military Department, Whitehall, 1 March 1934, BL, IOR/L/MIL/7/19145.

[101] Letter from Philip Mason, Under Secretary, GoI, to the Secretary, Military Department, India Office, p. 185, 1 March 1934, BL, IOR/L/MIL/7/19145. The cadets from the State Forces were required to pass the same preliminary test as the Indian Army cadets, that is, the Indian Army Special Certificate of Education, with a satisfactory command over 'colloquial English'. There was little competition for State Forces Cadetships as sufficient numbers of these cadets had not been forthcoming.

[102] Letter from Deputy Secretary, GoI, to Secretary, Military Department, 4 April 1932, BL, IOR/L/MIL/7/19123, p. 243. The GoI thought it was impossible to 'expect a successful candidate from England to … reach India in

problematic for the IMA and Public Service Commission authorities in India. The varying quality of IMA's intake included the Anglo-Indians, cadets in the State Forces, Indian candidates born or raised in Britain, as well as cadets drawn from the non-officer ranks. The multi-dimensional sociological challenges associated with Indianization were reflected also in the struggles faced in establishing an acceptable standard of performance among the cadets. Problems in quality of cadets was worrying New Delhi enough to send frequent memoranda to Britain, seeking solutions to the problem as early as 1934, merely two years after the IMA's inauguration.

To address the problem of cadet performance, the government in India offered solutions that brought feeder institutions back into the picture. It was decided to increase the staff of the three King George's schools by the addition of WOs[103] of the Army Education Corps, and by increasing the capacity of the Kitchener College, the sister institution of the Prince of Wales Royal Indian Military College and located at Nowgong in erstwhile Central Provinces, later to become a site for experimental 'inter-service' training.[104] This was also supplemented by detailed plans on the expansion of the Prince of Wales Royal Indian Military College following the recommendations of the Skeen Committee on the same institution almost a decade ago.[105]

The feeder colleges were now to be treated on par with regular degree colleges; the former were sought to be made responsible for imparting a suitable curriculum that could maximize their chances of clearing the IMA examinations.[106] Following this government

---

time to join the Academy by 1st October…. It was for this reason they proposed … that candidates from England should be considered successful and admitted to the second term … and should be counted against the vacancies of that term.'

[103] The WOs were similar in status and precedence to the VCOs in India.

[104] Kitchener College has been discussed in Chapter 3.

[105] Collection 430/95, Expansion of Prince of Wales Royal Indian Military College, Dehradun, 1923–33, BL, IOR/L/MIL/7/19133.

[106] This measure was first recommended by the Skeen Report in 1925–6 but was rejected. It was revived in view of the IMA's problem with training cadets in order to supply a better cohort of educated cadets, highlighting the inter-institutional dependencies on matters of reform.

directive, Indian military schools in Ajmer, Jhelum, and Jalandhar were to be revived, and avenues opened for their cadets to acquire the kind of education which would enable them to gain entry to not only the IMA but also other regular universities if they were unable to clear the IMA examination.[107] The appearance of the IMA, thus, provided the stimulus to upgrade the educational apparatus at these schools. It was decided to standardize the education up to the level of matriculation from the earlier perfunctory curricula of the Punjab civil education code that governed these schools in the northwest.[108] This was done to enable the students to sit for both university entrance examinations as well as the Indian Army Special Certificate of Education. The latter was a mandatory qualification for cadets who were required to be nominated by the commander-in-chief to the IMA, and was especially devised to offer a broad-based education to soldiers and non-commissioned ranks to maximize their chances of gaining officership, failing which it was hoped that the military certificate would enable them to seek livelihoods in civil life.[109]

[107] Situation Report from the Governor of Punjab, 31 July 1937, Memorandum prepared by Committee of Members of both houses of the Central Legislature, BL, IOR/L/MIL/7/19155. A common grouse against IMA's policy of expelling underperforming cadets (even at an advanced level of training) was that it hindered the cadet's chances of getting a place at other universities because of the nature of training received at the academy, which made 'university education' a completely different ball game.

[108] Capt. T.H.L. Stebbing, MC, MA, AEC; Commandant, KGRIM School, Jullundur, 'King George's Royal Indian Military Schools', *The Journal of the United Service Institution of India* vol. LXVI, no. 282 (January 1936), consulted in Subject File 15, B.S. Moonje Papers, NMML Archives, New Delhi, India. The Punjab Civil Code was considered as approximately roughly to Standard III of the English Board of Education Elementary system. Later, the standard of the syllabus was raised to the equivalent of the Punjab Middle School or Vernacular Final Examination, which corresponded approximately to a 'stage slightly beyond the conclusion of the English Primary System.' However, it was soon realized that, if the boys of the King George's schools were to be able to compete with their confrères from the civil world, the standard of their attainments must be again raised to keep progress level with the equivalent product of local schools.

[109] Pamphlets on Educational Training of the Indian Army, 1932, BL, IOR/L/MIL/17/5/2272. The military certificate examinations were a

Aside from the changes within the feeder colleges, the staff at these colleges also came under attack when it was reported that 'a number of junior British officers who had not passed the Staff College examination were holding staff appointments in these colleges'.[110] Pressure to replace 'costlier British instructors with Indians' were accompanied with demands to have more Indians admitted to the Staff College at Quetta and given staff appointments.[111] Thus, in these inter-institutional developments to facilitate Indianization, an accompanying context laid the basis to discuss and campaign for the representation of Indians within the higher military institutional network. The demand for Indian staff officers and other functionaries within these colleges gained a firm hold over policymakers and continued to do so well after Independence.[112]

The institutionalization of military training in the subcontinent, therefore, reflects much more than just the professionalization of military pedagogy. This institutional growth becomes even more apparent in the post-Independence years, where 'newer' protocols of recruitment supplemented by governmental backing resulted in another wave of proposals which sought to widen the ambit of these academies, imbibing them with a reformative spirit not quite dissimilar to the one which sought to refashion the feeder colleges in the previous decades.

---

protocol of testing designed for various non-commissioned classes, but its chief value probably lay in the dissemination of a common language and script, namely, 'Roman-Urdu', which could be used for purposes of instruction, training, and communication.

[110] Press Note, Indian Military Academy: Question of Improvement in Quality of the Candidates, IOR/L/MIL/7/19155, 1936–38.

[111] Press Note, Indian Military Academy: Question of Improvement in Quality of the Candidates, IOR/L/MIL/7/19155, 1936–38.

[112] File 7901-87, POS 287 (Microfilm), Roy Bucher Papers, NAM, London. Gen. Sir Roy Bucher in his farewell note, hoped that the military schools would not be allowed to deteriorate on the pretext of 'financial stringency' and would be made more 'inter-service'. Bucher also envisaged the development of a 'Senior Joint Staff College' as the next step of learning after the Junior Joint Staff College, where both senior officers and nominated civil servants could attend the equivalent of the IDC in the UK. This institution would only emerge in 1960.

However, the changed political landscape after 1947 did not automatically result in a consensus on every issue. While post-Independence governance in India gave credence to revised systems of recruitment that encouraged enlistment from areas beyond the urban centres and 'enlisted classes', the IMA shied away from recruiting men from organizations like the Indian National Army (INA) and gave cold shoulder to the Indian ECOs,[113] many of whom (especially the ECOs) had willingly offered themselves for service earlier.

While the academy functioned continuously during the war years, churning out cadets in tune with the fluctuating demands, it was the years leading up to and during the Second World War that the IMA witnessed a considerable expansion in its institutional presence in the subcontinent. In the eyes of some, it even acquired a considerable degree of legitimacy in India.[114] The multiplicity of courses of varying lengths turned the IMA virtually into a 'factory' of sorts during the Second World War. Although it created flashpoints for future conflicts relating to commissions and demobilization of several cadets trained in these courses, who felt short-changed by the refusal of the authorities to keep their alleged promises of ensuring continued service after the War, the site of the academy as a place for joint wartime training of British and Indian cadets drawn from various backgrounds and levels of education, lent it a certain degree of gravitas it was struggling to acquire in its initial years.

Nonetheless, the problems in training a widely different group of cadets persisted and punctured the IMA's early attempts in asserting its institutional primacy during and after the Second World War.[115]

---

[113] The commission holders came to be known as ECOs as they were recruited during wartime and were trained at the shortened war courses at IMA and other officer-training schools.

[114] B.P.N. Sinha and Sunil Chandra, *Valour and Wisdom: Genesis and Growth of the Indian Military Academy* (New Delhi: Oxford and IBH Publishing, 1992), p. 155. The onset of the Second World War in 1939, soon changed the "complexion of things" in the words of the authors. The steady reduction in the lengths of the courses until 1941 resulted in a sharp, almost six-fold increase in the number of commissioned cadets.

[115] Report of the Director of Military Training (DMT) Gen. Alexander M. Duff, on tour of Southeast Asian Command—India–Middle East–Central Mediterranean Force, 28 June–2 August 1945, BL, IOR/L/WS/1/762.

The IMA's courses were shortened at this time to increase recruitment and an unprecedented expansion of the institution took place. It also hosted British cadets (mainly from the other ranks) for a brief period of time imparting pre-officer training, but found itself facing similar problems of homogenizing a vastly different group of British cadets.[116]

The institutional integrity of the IMA attracted official attention from the government during the 1947 Partition. The IMA was the sole exception among existing military installations in the subcontinent that was not immediately split between India and Pakistan. This was as per the recommendations of Gen. Auchinleck who had been designated as supreme commander of the Indian military to oversee the division of the Indian Armed Forces.[117] However, Sardar Patel, during the negotiations of the Joint Defence Council (JDC), had impressed on the need to split the IMA in order prevent further institutional instability of the armed forces during Partition.[118] The question of the relocation (if any) of the staff of these institutions was an important one. The relocation was not limited to just the training staff but included the entire working force of the Indian armed forces which were also to be

---

[116] Report of the Director of Military Training (DMT) Gen. Alexander M. Duff, on tour of Southeast Asian Command—India–Middle East–Central Mediterranean Force, 28 June–2 August 1945, BL, IOR/L/WS/1/762. One of the main things which a British cadet had to learn at the IMA (or at other officer-training schools) was Urdu. The report stated 'that boys direct out from UK' took some time to get acclimatized sufficiently to embark on the Officer Training School (OTS) Course. For this reason, the GoI was anxious that all the UK cadets should do the full 'Pre-OTS Part II'—a two-month preparatory course on the lines of the British 'Pre-OCTU', that is, the Officer Corps Training Unit, before commencing the Course in India. The report forewarned, that India was prepared to get an 'unlevel' lot of boys, including some who might be found unsuitable as officers as a result of these courses.

[117] MB1/D60/7, Copy of a memorandum from Maj. D.K. Kerkar enclosing a copy of the minutes of Joint Defence Council meeting No 11, 7 October 1947: contemporary copy, Mountbatten Papers Database, Special Collections, University of Southampton, UK.

[118] MB1/D60/7, Copy of a memorandum from Maj. D.K. Kerkar enclosing a copy of the minutes of Joint Defence Council meeting No 11, 7 October 1947: contemporary copy, Mountbatten Papers Database, Special Collections, University of Southampton, UK.

divided.[119] The relatively less disruptive impact of Partition on military training institutions such as the IMA and Staff College testified to the attempts that were made by both sides across India and Pakistan, in the form of institutions like the JDC, to explore opportunities for a rapid and coordinated division of the armed forces training institutions to avoid uncertainty in their administration and functioning.

There is little evidence to show if the same bilateral cooperation was extended to the staff and students of feeder colleges during Partition. However, limited references to these institutions in the proceedings of the JDC as well as the Armed Forces Reconstitution Committee (AFRC)[120] that was appointed to divide military assets and defence stores between India and Pakistan suggests that there were modest discussions on the division and relocation of staff from some of the King George's schools.[121] The nature of the discussion was primarily centred on the 'Trust Funds' that were used in their administration. The AFRC entrusted with the division of critical military assets also took up the matter of the division of military feeder college's resources. The IMA was also sucked into these negotiations as many of these bursaries and funds which were being divided up were also sought to be used for the benefit of the communities that were now being trained at the IMA. However, the division was not just dictated by the need of the two new dominions. Many of the funds endowed by regiments and princely courts insisted on a division that was proportional to the number of classes that made up those regiments or as dictated by the

[119] GB 133 AUC/1230, 'Terms of Reference of the Armed Forces Reconstitution Committee', Auchinleck Papers, John Rylands Special Collections, University of Manchester Library, UK.

[120] The JDC was constituted by a Gazette of India Extraordinary dated 11 August 1947 and the terms of reference of the AFRC were promulgated by the Partition Council on 5 July 1947. Both were set up in order to carry out the reconstitution of the military services into separate forces to serve India and Pakistan.

[121] MB1/D50/1 Copies of agenda items for Joint Defence Council meeting No 13, 3 October 1947—ante 1 November 1947, Mountbatten Papers Database, Special Collections, University of Southampton, UK. The proceedings refer to the King George's School at Ajmer, whose funds went for the upkeep of the education of the 'Jat and Rajput boys', was sought to be transferred to India.

benefactors.[122] Hence, even during the division of monetary assets, the links between the officers' academy and its surrounding cluster of feeder colleges could not be ignored. This relationship was not just defined through ties and networks of fiscal dependence, but in fact signified the structural links that had bound them together and shaped their institutional and administrative relationship to a significant extent.

The IMA comes across as a site for not just the institutionalization of military training within its confines, but also for the development of other institutions that were a part of this matrix of training spaces and were interconnected to each other through vital links of financial, social, military, and human resources. Later in 1949, two years after Independence, the IMA was to undergo a further round of transformation. This resulted in the establishment of an inter-services training wing, later to be known as the NDA, which trained cadets together for the three armed forces, leaving the IMA to train cadets passing out of this new institution solely for commissions in the army.[123] Thus, the evolution of the military training architecture did not just cease with the establishment of the 'Indian Sandhurst' but provided a further and serious push towards thinking about and creating newer institutions to accelerate the military training of Indians.

---

[122] See (vi) A copy of a typescript appendix A, concerning trust funds controlled by the GoI to provide scholarships and so on, in MB1/D50/1, Copies of agenda items for Joint Defence Council meeting No 13, 3 October 1947—ante 1 November 1947, Mountbatten Papers Database, Special Collections, University of Southampton, UK. The division of the 37th Lancers's trust fund, for instance, totalling around Rs 96,700, was suggested to be divided in the ratio of three-fourths Pakistan, one-fourth India. The trust deed 'clearly' showed, the records claim, that 'the fund was to be expended proportionately to the classes enlisted in the 37 Lancers at the time of its disbandment'.

[123] Charles Wright, *Service before Self: A Tribute to the Indian Military Academy before and after Partition* (Eggleston: Raby, 2002). The Armed Forces Academy, in Wright's account, owed its existence largely to the IMA which it absorbed and expanded. The new wing intended to give these young cadets a basic training that was 'mental, cultural and physical which will enable them to proceed to naval, military and air force training centres, according to their aptitude'.

3   The 'Indian West Point'
1945–60

The NDA was conceived and built as an inter-service training academy, one of the first of its kind in South Asia and the newest among a handful in the world. Institutionally, it replaced the earlier IMA, which was inaugurated in 1932, as the primary training school for cadets, and thus became the first step in the ladder for aspirants who would go on to officer the Indian Armed Forces of the modern Indian republic. After 1949, the IMA, as a consequence, became an army-specific training facility for the NDA graduates along with separate naval and air force academies which were established later.[1]

The NDA's emergence in the years after Independence swiftly gave it a distinct 'nationalist' character, and determined, although not entirely, several of its initial methods and processes of functioning, including the selection of cadets. The early years of the academy's functioning brought forth several issues whose nature was not dissimilar to the challenges faced by other older institutions that were established in the subcontinent. Nonetheless, in the drive to seek solutions to

[1] In 1945, a proposal to institute a four-year course at the IMA, Dehradun, for training cadets for regular commissions from January 1947 was not accepted by the government. A two-year course was to begin in January each year until the output from the IMA course became 'related to that from the War Memorial Academy', later known as the NDA. See 'Training of Officers for Regular Commissions in the Indian Army, GHQ India Directive, dated 15 December 1945', in Policy for Provision of officers from the Indian Army, BL, IOR/L/WS/1/789.

those challenges and devising a new institutional identity for this academy, the government and all other military-bureaucratic stakeholders rekindled elements of the Indianization issue of the previous decades.

While the IMA was built in the image of its 'sister concern' in Britain, the NDA story drifted further across the Atlantic, as it was modelled after the United States Military Academy at West Point, following the deliberations of a government-instituted committee in 1945 that travelled across Canada, the UK, and USA. The emergence of the NDA, therefore, is a prism to study the changing character of military policy of this time through the eyes of two different governing systems and historical time scales. The academy was conceived in the Raj but was born in its aftermath. In the years in it was discussed and planned about, it incorporated several elements of its institutional identity from these critical years during which India passed over from being a colony to a dominion, and from a dominion to an independent republic.

This chapter will examine the institutional evolution of the NDA by placing it in a larger international and intellectual context in which it emerged in the latter part of the 1940s. It attempts to move away from hitherto limited understandings of its emergence, some of which see it mainly as an eminent 'national' project. A more critical reading of the available, though limited, sources, including published semi-official accounts of the institution and records of senior officers' visits to foreign military academies, has enabled me to challenge this deeply ingrained assumption.

The larger backdrop behind the germination of the first Indian inter-service academy was anything but 'national'. Formed as a result of the recommendations of an official committee constituted in 1945, it was the result of a widely travelled government-instituted team, which thought about the NDA 'long and hard' before it was formally inaugurated in 1949 in independent India. A closer scrutiny of the NDA's history, therefore, would reveal the more international side to its conception and also illuminate the starkly state-driven or 'establishmentarian' bent in its functioning that became apparent with the march of the subsequent decades of the 1950s and 1960s. An evaluation of the embryonic years of the NDA also represent a converging point for the 'international' and 'national' streams in its formation as both intersected with each other throughout its early years with various counter-intuitive consequences for military institution-building practices.

THE BEGINNING OF INTER-SERVICES TRAINING IN INDIA

The genesis of the idea behind this academy lay in 'War' quite literally. A major chunk of the NDA's financial outlay came in the form of a 'gift' in 1941 from the then-Government of Sudan for building a suitable war memorial to commemorate the gallantry of Indian troops in the North African campaign during the course of the Second World War.[2] It was however, through the efforts of Gen. Auchinleck,[3] who returned to India as commander-in-chief of the Indian Army in 1943, that a more serious approach was adopted into the question of a war memorial, and, more significantly, the form it was to take. Much of the official or semi-official literature pertaining to the NDA at this time connect this moment of Auchinleck's 'second home-coming'[4] to command the Indian Army as the point marking the intellectual birth of the vision behind the NDA.[5] This link, however, as this chapter

---

[2] India's National War Academy, BL, IOR/L/I/202. The money was received by Lord Linlithgow and is believed to be a princely sum of around 'hundred thousand pounds'. The gift was essentially to commemorate the 'exploits of the 4th and 5th divisions of the Indian army in 1941 that saved Abyssinia, Eritrea and Sudan from the Axis menace.'

[3] Address by Auchinleck to the students of the Staff College at Quetta, 2 August 1946, GB 133 AUC/1191, FM Auchinleck Papers, The John Rylands Library (Special Collections), University of Manchester Library, UK. In his address to the Quetta Staff College students, Auchinleck referred to the fact that the 'Indian West Point' would be built to train about 2,500 to 3,000 cadets through the course of over four years, but the real challenge lay in finding the 'right class' of men to come forward for commissions.

[4] Auchinleck was commander-in-chief of the Indian Army twice: once briefly in 1941, and then, in the period of 1943–7.

[5] The literature on the NDA comprises three different volumes published at different times. Among them is the earliest available memorial volume published in 1978, T. Raina, *National Defence Academy: Three Decades of Development, 1949–1978*, Memorial Volume (Pune: The Commandant, NDA, 1978), followed by Raina's another book on the NDA, *Cradle for Leadership, The National Defence Academy, A History: 1949–1996* (New Delhi: Oxford University Press, 1997), and Kishori Lal's *The National Defence Academy* (Pune: Parashuram Process Publishers, 1999).

will show, is instinctive and myopic.[6] The groundwork for an inter-service training school was laid during the course of the Second World War campaigns when a greater need for service cooperation was felt. The massive sweep of the War that knitted together whole continents and oceans into a series of armed conflicts drove the point of combined operations more forcefully, and it earned many supporters, Auchinleck being one of the notable ones in a sea of middle-ranking to senior-ranking functionaries (a group that also later included Lord Mountbatten as one of the key supporters) who actively pursued the idea of opening an inter-service academy in India.[7]

A relatively unnoticed contribution of Auchinleck, however, was in working out and forwarding a set of structural reforms for the Indian Army, which later came to play a key role in the planning of the NDA. As the subsequent sections of this chapter will show, the trifurcation of the Indian Armed Forces into service-specific organizations, each led by its own head, complicated the homogenous, 'army-driven' policies with which the NDA had come to be associated before 1947. The development of separate air force and naval arms thus placed the NDA in differentiated contexts of service-specific training objectives. The division of the Indian Armed Forces was articulated in a committee set up under his (Auchinleck's) chairmanship in 1946 and recommended that the 'constitution of three separate service headquarters each commanded by an independent Commander-in-Chief' was in the best interests of the reorganization of the higher command of the three services.[8] The proposals, however, bore fruit only in the

---

[6] Auchinleck's arrival may have helped push the NDA file further across the bureaucratic corridors, but the idea behind an inter-service academy predated this development.

[7] MB1/D44/6, copy of a paper enclosing a copy of the minutes of Defence Committee meeting No 2, 18 February 1948, Mountbatten Papers Database, Special Collections, University of Southampton, UK. Lord Mountbatten as viceroy had been 'tremendously impressed' by his visit to the IMA at Dehradun and suggested that the NDA first start functioning from Dehradun where he felt the 'correct spirit' was already in existence.

[8] The High Command in India: Report of a Committee set up by H.E. the Commander-in-Chief in India, 1946, Auchinleck Papers, GB 133 AUC/1135, John Rylands Special Collections, University of Manchester. An additional reason why the proposals may not have been implemented was because

post-Independence years when the three services came under the purview of the reorganized Ministry of Defence.

The NDA took shape at a time when ideas of inter-service cooperation had already taken root in military thinking, both in India and Britain. Claims that the NDA became the first training institution that provided such novel methods of training also rest on thin ground, not least in the context of India, where the idea first bore fruit at the level of cadet colleges. This is also attested by a published account of the NDA, but it does not adequately refer to the wide-ranging inter-institutional nature of reform that affected feeder schools at this time.[9] The Kitchener College was one such institution that underwent a series of structural changes and which presaged the larger transformational wave that was to sweep across the Indian military architecture. Kitchener College was established in 1929, and it was part of a wider constellation of preparatory military schools that were set up across the subcontinent to provide training and assistance to younger ranks and NCOs in their efforts to become eligible as officers.[10]

These colleges were part of longer and historic chain of institutions that were opened up across the subcontinent to bolster the nascent Indianization schemes that had been put forward in the closing decades of the nineteenth century. By the 1940s, as a result of a slew of reforms aiming to provide a better pools of trained officers, the Kitchener College, along with several other officers' training schools, started providing, what came to be known as 'pre-commissioned training' to

---

the plan was formulated within the broad framework of a Commonwealth defence arrangement, which did not progress further owing to the political developments in the subcontinent after the Second World War. The prospect of a divided subcontinent sat uncomfortably with the strategic vision associated with a 'united' Commonwealth defence arrangement being advocated by Whitehall. See, for instance, GB 133 AUC/ 1152, Auchinleck Papers, 'A note on the strategic implications of the inclusion of Pakistan in the British Commonwealth'.

[9] T. Raina, *Cradle for Leadership: The National Defence Academy: A History, 1949–1996* (New Delhi: Oxford University Press, 1997), p. 3.

[10] Memorandum of Army Training (India), Individual Training Period, 1929, BL, IOR/L/MIL/17/5/2199.

cadets interested in joining the first full service military academy that existed before the NDA—the IMA.[11]

Auchinleck used the Kitchener College as a 'pilot project' for service-integrated training, transforming it into an Inter-Service Pre-Cadet College (ISPCC) from its primarily preparatory-school moorings. Its ambit was widened further with the inclusion of candidates both from civil life as well as the non-commissioned ranks, who could be trained in the precepts of inter-service military knowledge.[12] In 1931, the same year in which the IMA Committee was set up, a memorandum recommended reforms for the other feeder institutions, the King George's schools specifically, so as to enable these institutions to 'be looked upon as a source of supply of prospective Indian Army Cadets', ensuring a long-term sustainability training model for these institutions as well as deepening ties of their association to major military academies to bolster their institutional legitimacy.[13]

This reorganized role heralded a wave of reforms within the Kitchener College, wherein advanced courses were instituted, aiming to augment the institution's capacity to raise the level of education of its students and enable them to pass the Army Special Certificate examination, an important piece of eligibility criteria for those desirous of earning an officer's commission.[14] These reforms spoke to the nature of early twentieth-century reforms in which institutions like the Lawrence Schools and the Chief's colleges were sought to be organized as a cluster around a major military institution, both for purposes of reform and also to garner greater institutional legitimacy.

This new training protocol was administered under a team that was, at least militarily, quite cosmopolitan, and also played a role in the development of the NDA. One of them was J.T.M. Gibson, who later

[11] These officers' training schools came up in the mid-1940s in Mhow (central India), Belgaum, Bangalore (southwestern India), and Ahmednagar. The schools were responsible, in no small measure, in increasing the officer strength of the Indian Army at this time when there was a need for greater numbers owing to the increased wartime demand for men.

[12] Raina, *Cradle for Leadership*, p. 3

[13] Memorandum, 1931, No. 3, Memorandum of Army Training (India), BL, IOR/L/MIL/17/5/2199.

[14] Memorandum, 1932, No. 5, Memorandum of Army Training (India), BL, IOR/L/MIL/17/5/2199.

played a pivotal role in the affairs of the NDA as its first principal. Gibson's account attests to a gradual institutional growth curve for the NDA. It also confirms that the NDA's early academic precepts grew out of the pre-existing training schemes that had been devised in the ISPCCs at Nowgong, and also at a similar institution at Almora in northern India. The earliest experiments in institutionalizing cadet training at the NDA were also constituted along inter-service lines, as Gibson noticed both officers and other ranks of the three services worked together to train younger prospective officers for the three services.[15] Gibson found the training imparted at these ISPCCs to be favourable since the results of cadets after a six-month period were found to be mostly identical when measured by different selection boards.[16]

As an educationist working in India in the early twentieth century, Gibson brought a wealth of experience into this nascent 'confederate' of military academies that came up in quick succession in India. Starting his career in 1937 as a housemaster at the Doon School, he soon gravitated into the military administrative landscape, which took him in 1942 to the Kitchener College as a special instructor. He eventually moved to the NDA as its first principal in 1949. Gibson's long tenure in heading and directing various academic institutions across India allowed him to inculcate a robust scholastic character to these emerging academies, not least the NDA. The NDA's later struggles, as will be discussed in the last section of this chapter, in managing the demands of an essentially military training programme with issues of imparting a more generalized education was part of the legacy that it inherited mainly from these earlier educational-cum-training academies.

The ISPCC's success rested on its ability to weld together elements of late nineteenth-century military-academic requirements with the demands of the twentieth century. Despite its unexplained insistence

[15] J.T.M. Gibson, *As I Saw It: Records of a Crowded Life in India, 1937–1969* (New Delhi: Mukul Prakashan, 1976), p. 281.

[16] Gibson, *As I Saw It*, p. 284. Around 80 per cent test results matched, in Gibson's words, when results were compared between the ISPCC staff and the formal Services Selection Board.

on admitting students of a 'fighting class', the ISPCC offered instruction in military subjects such as map work, tactics, and military administration and organization, in addition to the regular subjects, thereby offering a broad-based education to its students who would not be misfits in the civilian space of higher education, if they were unable to get into the military.[17] Besides, the ISPCC was a watershed in training policies, as its curriculum was offered to both prospective officers for Sandhurst (and then later the IMA and NDA), but also to the 'younger and better educated type of Indian officer or NCO,' with the aim of turning him out as a leader who can train and lead a platoon in peace and war, and command a company in an emergency'.[18] The significance of this academic protocol signified the priority that came to be accorded to educating and training individuals of all occupational hues, including the NCO cadre.

It is easy to dismiss the ISPCC experiments as fly-on-the-wall episodes in the larger story of the development of institutions in India, and more specifically the NDA, but the narrative of Indian military academies should essentially be built by examining the recurring patterns of institutionalization at a smaller scale that were occurring since the late nineteenth century. The dominant narrative around the NDA pays scant attention to its 'pre-1949' origins, much of which relates to the smaller and tentative experimental measures that shaped its 'signature' organizational contours after 1947. Thus, the NDA came to inhabit a space that was rapidly changing with time, albeit in its favour. There was greater acceptability towards integrated service training globally and a changed belief system on military educational practices had already begun to alter the institutional map as it stood at the turn of the twentieth century, especially in India. Most military institutions that emerged in India have had a transformational influence on the larger training architecture in which they vied for space and legitimacy like in the case of the IMA. The NDA, too, in a way, modified and recalibrated the terms on which institutional innovation was to be discussed.

[17] The Kitchener College Nowgong Syllabus, 1931, BL, IOR/L/MIL/17/5/2304.
[18] The Kitchener College Nowgong Syllabus, 1931, BL, IOR/L/MIL/17/5/2304.

FROM THE COUNCILS TO THE COMMITTEES: OBSERVATIONS OF AN INDIAN OFFICER

The National War Academy (NWA) Committee, which was entrusted with the task of examining the question of a National War Memorial and the form it was to take after its brief stationing as an officer-training school in central India, was headed by Auchinleck. Gen. Auchinleck, in turn, was assisted by members of the Viceroy's Council belonging to finance, education, lands, as well as Commonwealth relations, among other key departments.

However, before this committee drafted its proposals on the precise institutional contours of the NDA, it was the observations and reports of an Indian Army officer—not fully accounted for in the published accounts—that made the task of the committee considerably easier and established a resonance between his and the committee's opinions on Indian military institutional reform. The NDA's formation, therefore, is important to understand the underlying institutional synergies that were beginning to draw the military closer to advising the government on critical matters of Indianization. This developing relationship would further blossom in the reorganization and establishment of the NDC in 1960.

Brig. K.M. Cariappa, who was to later become the first Indian commander-in-chief of the Indian Army in 1949,[19] played an important part in setting up the early institutional framework for the NDA. However, much of Cariappa's observations have not been taken into account in the earlier published works on the NDA. This section, therefore, will bring to light Cariappa's observations on foreign military academies, which set much of the context for the NDA's planning. It also helps provide the precise evidence on the basis of which it is possible to explain the exact pathways along which the NDA absorbed ideas from the United States Military Academy, a feature that is frequently cited in the historiography but never fully explained or unpacked.[20]

---

[19] Cariappa, a brigadier in 1947, was made a general officer by 1949. This accelerated promotion feature was characteristic of the years after 1947, where a shortage of senior Indian officers compelled the government to rapidly promote the existing middle-ranking cadre to fill critical staff and command appointments.

[20] It is unclear whether Cariappa visited these institutions as part of a delegation that was being led by another British officer Brig. Bateman and which

Cariappa's observations on the US and Canadian military institutions and correspondence with their military authorities on crucial educational and administrative aspects of cadet instruction were useful 'terms of reference' for the NWA Committee. Thus, Cariappa's interventions and suggestions, much like the Skeen Committee's that offered to redress the problems of Indianization of officers by means of an 'institutional solution', helped pave the way for the NDA to be imagined as a facility dedicated to providing a uniform standardized method of education to cadets, so as to enable them to move onto higher military institutions for training.[21]

Cariappa's correspondence with authorities at the United States Military Academy and Canada provide fascinating insights into the early stages of planning for an inter-service academy in India. Cariappa was considerably impressed with the 'magnificent atmosphere of efficiency, completeness, comfort, and high standard of equipment' at West Point, where a cadet spent '3–4 years of his early life in the Army'.[22] This could not, in his view, but produce really efficient officers, imbued with a sense of pride and dignity of the highest order.[23] Cariappa's fulsome praise for West Point drew from a larger assessment of the West Point facilities—from student halls of residence to its 'tuck shop'. He also carefully examined the multiple modes of entry to gain training at West Point, a feature that was of key interest to him. Cariappa noted the prevalence of 'Honour Schools' across USA—essentially a variant of the feeder training network that existed in India—playing an important role in supplying well-trained candidates to West Point, in addition to the other 'nominated' routes to cadetships from the US states and other overseas dependent territories. In a sense, then, the assessment

---

visited principle military institutions in USA, the UK, and Canada. See India's National War Academy, *Times of India* Report, 17 September 1946, India's National War Academy-1, Training India's Future Defenders IOR/L/I/202.

[21] Letter from Gen. Thos T. Handy, GSC, Deputy Chief of Staff, to Brig. K.M. Cariappa, Reorganization Committee (India), 22 October 1945, Part I, Group I, Cariappa Papers, NAI, New Delhi, India.

[22] Group XXII, Part XI, Observations on West Point by Brig. Cariappa, September 1945, Cariappa Papers, NAI, New Delhi, India.

[23] Group XXII, Part XI, Observations on West Point by Brig. Cariappa, September 1945, Cariappa Papers, NAI, New Delhi, India.

of West Point spoke to the enduring significance of the multi-tiered architecture of military training and set the broad institutional context that the NDA was required to inhabit: as a space designed for inter-service training, drawing its candidates from a surrounding network of several feeder institutions.

Cariappa's 'observations' carried weight, for it paved the way for the unofficial adoption of West Point as the suitable model for the NDA, edging out the Canadian institution, even though the latter had better civil–military channels for rehabilitating its graduates. Kingston, the Canadian academy, in contrast to West Point, offered a more regular educational component to graduates who chose not to opt for regular or permanent commissions. The Canadian military academy recommended such graduates 'for special entry into the faculty of Applied Science in certain Canadian universities' or, in the case of law graduates, for the Bar.[24] While this element of ensuring continued learning for non-commissioned graduates may have found favour with the Indian authorities, certain associated aspects of American military training infrastructure sealed the deal in favour of West Point as the model for the NDA.

The American model struck a chord with the Indian authorities due to the segmented nature of military institutionalization in USA and the importance it gave to all aspects of military training, including administrative and logistical issues. The coexistence of a parallel administrative training infrastructure alongside West Point and other officer-training schools in USA signified key 'post war arrangements for training establishments', adhering to the principle that 'every military problem' involved an 'administrative aspect which must be as closely studied as the tactical or strategic side of the problem'.[25] This feature found special favour with Cariappa, as it spoke to official Indian concerns about the administrative challenges that were being faced in the effort to Indianize the military, evident in the case of the IMA, which threw up a host of functional challenges in its operation. The American system

---

[24] Group XXII, Part XI, Observations on West Point by Brig. Cariappa, September 1945, Cariappa Papers, NAI, Delhi.

[25] Letter from E. Austain, Principal Administrative Officer (India), General headquarters (GHQ), New Delhi to Brig. K.M. Cariappa, HQ, Jumna Area, Delhi, 11 December 1945, Cariappa Papers, NAI, New Delhi.

of a comprehensive education and training programme presented a worthy solution to counter the systemic hiccups that were liable to surface during further Indianization of the officer cadre. This evolution of an integrated military training infrastructure was not unique to USA. The role of 'military apprenticeships' had begun to attract official attention in the UK as well when, in 1947, a series of training academies in the technical sciences opened up across England, aimed at producing well-educated and skilful technicians but also had the stated aim of 'developing boys' who could rise to 'ranks of importance in the Army's great technical corps'.[26] Thus, in appreciating the military industrial collegiate facilities in Britain and USA, some critical suggestions emerged with respect to the proposed 'Indian West Point'. At a deeper level, these elements of a 'technical–civil nexus' in military training resonated with the interconnected nature and underlying aims of Indianization policies in India, that is, meeting the demand for more Indian officers through an architecture that carried the impulses for the qualitative transformation of the Indianized force in consonance with the changing ethos of military system.[27] The aforementioned proposals and reports were accepted 'in principle' by the government and were passed onto the hands of the NWA Committee, which was a select group of service and non-service members, academicians, and others who typified the inter-service character the academy was to take in the years to come through the diversity of their own academic, official, or non-official service backgrounds.[28]

[26] See, for instance, 'Making Technicians for the Army', 13 September 1958, Press Report from the 'Harrogate Advertiser', consulted in the Brig. Noel Joseph Chamberlain Papers, Liddell Hart Centre for Military Archives, King's College London, UK.

[27] Letter from General Staff Branch, GHQ to PSO & Secretary, Military Dept, India Office, Whitehall, 21 June 1946, Higher Administrative Training, BL, IOR/L/WS/1/819. These features were also beginning to get incorporated into the higher echelons of military institutions. Some of the proposals outlined in the letter favoured the inclusion of 'higher administrative matters of industry and supply' in the Staff College syllabus while recommending a group of Indian officers to train in the UK and USA annually to gain a firmer grasp over these issues.

[28] Defence Services Military Academic Committee, BL, IOR/L/WS/1/803. The committee, under the chairmanship of Auchinleck, comprised

Understanding the 'terms of reference' for the upcoming academy as given to the committee is crucial to unlocking the institutional history of the NDA. Aside from the regular mandate of drawing out a larger territorial and operational map of the institution, the committee was also tasked with probing if more feeder institutions were required to be set up, a theme that would continue to be discussed well after 1947. This need to establish clear lines of entry into the new academy brought back many similar strategies that were employed during the establishment of the IMA more than a decade earlier in 1932. However, in the case of the NDA, this was tempered with a more 'academic' flavour mainly through the actions of the committee, which set about visiting other service academies in USA, the UK, and Canada again, to gain a fuller understanding of their ways of functioning and administration.[29]

The question whether the emergence of the NDA impacted the development of other feeder schools is an important one. However, there is little evidence to pursue such a line of enquiry, mainly because the feeder school network that was set up in the early twentieth century continued to function and furnish graduates for the NDA, and no new institutional networks were forged. However, J.T.M. Gibson recorded in his memoir, albeit sketchily, that 'residential schools were established as feeders' to the NDA.[30] Auchinleck, addressing the National Defence

---

the following: the chief of the GS; the flag officer commanding, RIN; the air officer commanding, Royal Indian Air Force (RIAF); secretary to the GoI, War Department; the educational advisor to the GoI; Sir Mirza Mohammed Ismail, prime minister of Jaipur state; Rao Bahadur Rao Raja Narpat Singh, Jodhpur; Dr Amarnath Jha, vice chancellor of Allahabad University; Khan Bahadur Mian Afzal Hussain, former vice chancellor of Punjab University; W.X. Mascarenhas, principal of College of Engineering, Poona; and A.E. Foot, headmaster of Doon School, Dehradun.

[29] Telegram from GoI, War Dept, to Secretary of State, India, sent 26 August 1945, Defence Services Military Academic Committee, BL, IOR/L/WS/1/803. In addition to West Point, the committee, in a span of two months, visited the naval academy at Annapolis, USA, as well as planned to visit officer academies across the UK. This was not as extensive a tour as was undertaken by Cariappa, and was meant as a survey visit along the principle elements that had been laid down by the Indian officer.

[30] Gibson, *As I Saw It*, p. 285.

Council in October 1945, also 'hoped' that the NDA would function in conjunction with feeder schools to set credible standards in delivering quality education to cadets, but he, too, did not point towards the possibility of setting up new colleges.[31]

Any such signs of a reorganization of the feeder network appeared only later—almost two decades after the NDA had started to function—in the form of an inquiry committee that was appointed to make recommendations to augment state-wide recruitment levels into the defence services.[32] The newly reorganized state of Maharashtra, in which the NDA was located, instituted this committee. It was chaired by a senior Indian Army general to study the feeder institutions in the state in order to examine the reasons behind the shortfall in the recruitment numbers.[33] The committee testified the continued importance of the feeder training network in the hierarchy of Indian military institutions. In assessing the functioning of the Ahmednagar

[31] Report of an address by Auchinleck to the National Defence Council on the future of India's armed forces, issued by the Public Relations Directorate, GHQ, India, GB 133 AUC/1103, Auchinleck Papers; John Rylands Library (Special Collections), University of Manchester Library.

[32] Report of the Committee on the Pre-Cadet Training and Feeding-cum-Training Centres in Maharashtra, 10 April 1974, Lt Gen. S.P.P. Thorat Papers, NMML Archives, New Delhi, India. The committee was appointed by the State in response to the 'shortfalls' in the recruitment into the defence services from Maharashtra, and to make recommendations to overcome it. It comprised the following as members: Lt Gen. S.P.P. Thorat (Retired), chairman; Lt Col V.B. Sathe (Retired), member; and Col L.W. Araj (Retired), member-secretary.

[33] Report of the Committee on the Pre-Cadet Training and Feeding-cum-Training Centres in Maharashtra, 10 April 1974, Lt Gen. S.P.P. Thorat Papers, NMML Archives, New Delhi, India. During the 1962 Sino-Indian border conflict, additional feeder centres were established in heavily recruiting districts in Pune, Satara, Ratnagiri, Mahad, Nagpur, Amravati, and Aurangabad in May 1963. However, they were closed down in October 1963. The committee appointed by the state in 1973–4 to review military recruitment from the state, recommended that the 'pre-cadet training centre' at Ahmednagar be reorganized into a service preparatory institute and shifted to Pune. This also meant that the institution would now be responsible in delivering a regular, matriculate education, in contrast to the fragmentary and apprenticeship-based training.

pre-cadet training centre and its relocation closer to the 'main academy', the report provides evidence of the interlinked nature of military institutionalization in India. The surest way to increase entry into the military was to ramp up its feeder networks. Thus, a significant share of official attention went in shoring up the educational offerings and training at these feeder schools in the later years of the 1970s. Krishna Menon, as defence minister in independent India, was also involved in the establishment and expansion of the 'Sainik Schools'[34] that were intended to function as 'feeders' to the military.[35]

While the primary nature of the NWA Committee's membership remained similar to that of the IMA, in that it was government-led and comprised government functionaries, what distinguished the former from the latter was the size and scope of the project at hand. The NDA was seen as a large undertaking that would establish it as the foremost defence training academy in India. Independence appeared imminent, if not apparent in the mid-1940s, and this lent a degree of urgency to the project. Of course, one of the major obstacles in the establishment of the NDA immediately after the War was finance. Post-War ravages and a restricted economy had made it well-nigh impossible to commission a new academy, and this played a key role in ensuring that the new academy had its initial start from within the confines of the IMA at Dehradun, with a final date reserved for its eventual transfer to its original location.[36]

The NDA proposals forwarded by the NWA Committee in 1947 were revived as a 'national project' after a short delay by a newly formed Indian government under Jawaharlal Nehru. The question of the NDA received renewed attention in the post-Independence scenario, as it followed on from a fiercely pitched nationalist movement's demands for a 'nationalized' Indian Army. This happened in the wake of larger defence reorganization, wherein the unified Indian command that had hitherto existed was now trifurcated into service-specific domains of

[34] Translatable to 'serviceman's school'.

[35] Janaki Ram, *V.K. Krishna Menon: A Personal Memoir* (Delhi: Oxford University Press, 1997), p. 117.

[36] 'Important Matters Which Need Progression By Staff Branches at Army HQ', File 7901-87 from 1 June 1948 to 1949, POS 287, Roy Bucher Collection, NAM London, UK.

the army, navy and, air force, each headed by an officer of the rank of a full general or equivalent from within those services, now jointly under the Ministry of Defence's control. This outward change of offices and chain of command altered, indubitably, the parameters within which a new inter-service academy was to operate, and set the framework of debates that took place on the role and responsibilities of the NDA vis-à-vis the three autonomous armed services.

INSTITUTIONAL REFORM AFTER 1947

The changed morphology of higher defence management that had led to a de-facto separation of services and control was not an unimportant side story to the establishment of the NDA. The NWA Committee, instituted in 1945 to examine the NDA project, had 'strongly laid down the winding up of the various service-specific training facilities in India as a necessary pre-condition for setting up the NDA' in order to focus on teaching and learning integrated service training solely at the NDA.[37]

However, with the trifurcation of the services, each of the service-specific domains inherited their own set of officer-training facilities, which continued well after the NDA was in place. This by itself did not mean a repudiation of the idea of inter-service training, but significantly 'chopped and changed' the original blueprint of the NDA.[38] While the NDA retained its status as the first step in the training of 'raw entrants', other channels for commissions remained wide open and indeed thrived well after Independence.[39] This is reminiscent of the initial years of the IMA, which also maintained alternative routes to commissioning arrangements, thereby succeeding in creating multiple channels of gaining officership.

Semi-autonomous service arms at this time meant that voices and opinions from the perspective of the navy and air force too would

---

[37] Raina, *Cradle for Leadership*, p. 11.

[38] Raina, *Cradle for Leadership*, p. 11.

[39] As a graduate, one could directly join the IMA (or the navy/air force equivalent) for service-specific training upon clearing an examination, bypassing the NDA route. Separate channels for engineers and doctors were also devised subsequently.

carry as much weight as the army; this was all too apparent when the government, after having accepted the proposals of the NWA Committee in September 1947, referred them back to the service chiefs to solicit their views. This resulted in a critical modification, causing the academy to be formed initially as an 'experimental' inter-service wing to the IMA. This, in the words of the NDA's Commandant Maj. Gen. E. Habibullah, was attributable to 'vested interests' that had got entrenched in the services, each of whom forwarded their own list of priorities for the upcoming academy.[40]

The vision behind an inter-service training institution such as the NDA was to bring together the three services in joint combat exercises through training young recruits and inculcating tenets of combined operations early on, so that future commissioned officers who would go on to command crucial positions would bring to bear exactly the kind of expertise they were fed on. What was perhaps overlooked was the fact that service integration would bring along service-specific anxieties and concerns onto the table as well, thus causing the negotiations on military reform to contend with their views on what constituted the best measures for reform and training.

The ambiguity regarding the future course of the academy resulted in many a change in its nomenclature, which underpinned the deeper fault lines relating to the form, functions, and training responsibilities of the academy. From being referred to as the Junior Inter-Service Wing, to Experimental Inter-Service Wing, to Armed Forces Academy, to its present-day title, the National Defence Academy, institutional reform in India after 1947 presented the articulation of different streams of thought on training. These different streams were part of an evolving ecosystem within which these autonomous sites of military training appeared. After a further round of inter-service negotiations, the three service chiefs now suggested that training at the NDA could be 'pruned and adjusted'.[41] While the experimental inter-service course could take place uninterrupted in Dehradun, this would, in turn, lay the path clear for the preparation of the cadet's 'real training

[40] E. Habibullah, in collaboration with Col B.K. Narayan, *The Sinews of Indian Defence* (New Delhi: Lancers Publishers, 1981), pp. 100–1.

[41] Raina, *Cradle for Leadership*, p. 22

in his Service academy'. The Royal Indian Navy (RIN) establishment, in particular, was desirous of attracting young recruits and insisted that the course length be kept to three years only, whereas cadets interested in joining the army could take an extra fourth year.[42]

The NDA, which to many stakeholders appeared as too 'army-driven' in approach, was now sought to be toned down, if not a downgraded, in its overall status as a primary site for training cadets. The NDA was now not to remain the 'sole supplier of commissioned officers to the three services',[43] but became one of the many avenues open for candidates to pursue military training in order to gain an officers' commission. Indeed, service-specific training won on its own right, since cadets, after passing out from the NDA, proceeded for further training in the service academies before they finally earned their commissions. Therefore, the relative downgrade in the status of the NDA, coupled with the efforts to locate it away from the political and national nerve centre of New Delhi or even the IMA to a western Indian state, could have had important political implications.

The emergence of the NDA symbolized the transition to a more integrated tradition of training and instruction; it was also a cause and a result of this difficult process of 'inter-service cooperation', which, until the NDA's establishment, had been approached mainly through an 'experimental' basis. Its establishment also reflected the ways of compromise and bargain through which it carved an independent space for itself in the Indian military institutional landscape. This contested terrain of institution-building in India was made even more apparent in the years of its construction and establishment, which flagged up issues of inter-state governance and administration.

---

[42] MB1/D44/6, copy of a paper enclosing a copy of the minutes of Defence Committee meeting No 2 of 1948, concerning various matters to do with the services in India, 18 February 1948, Mountbatten Papers Database, Special Collections, University of Southampton, UK.

[43] Among a few 'conspiracy theories' regarding this development was the fact that the ministry wanted an inter-service institution, primarily to clip the wings of the army establishment to temper its service related superiority. See, for instance, Habibullah, *The Sinews of Indian Defence*, pp. 97–9.

PLANNING A MILITARY INSTRUCTIONAL SPACE: ADMINISTRATIVE AND ACADEMIC CHALLENGES

Active planning at the site of the academy at Khadakvasla, a Pune sub-urb,[44] began in June 1948 under the control of the NDA Construction Committee, chaired by the defence secretary and W.X. Mascarenhas, a one-time associate of the legendary engineer-scholar, M.Visvesaraya.[45] Aside from the operational and logistical difficulties in constructing the NDA, it was the process of its planning and negotiations on its institutional character that highlighted the ideological, political, academic, and social fault lines of the Indianization process as well as institution-building in post-Independence India.

As an interim measure, it was suggested by the Chiefs of Staff Committee in India to set up a 'Junior Experimental Wing' of the IMA at Dehradun.[46] Thus, while planning for the 'Indian National War Academy' was in progress, the formation of an 'Inter-Services Wing' of the IMA was approved, following which the NDA began recruiting cadets for training.[47] This inter-services wing constituted the junior wing of the academy, while the military wing—the IMA—continued to train cadets for the army. The objective behind this measure was to enable the cadets to 'appreciate the inter-services aspect of the armed forces for three years at the Junior Wing while providing adequate academic instruction'.[48] Also, the officers' training school at Mhow (near Indore in the erstwhile Central Provinces) was directed to train cadets for regular commissions in 1946. These arrangements were supposed to last only for a year, pending the establishment of the NDA.[49]

The iconography of the construction processes and the wide journalistic coverage of the NDA's establishment lent it a particularly unique place in the India's post-Independence history. Being regarded

---

[44] This was the state of Bombay, which later became the state of Maharashtra in Western India in 1960 after the linguistic and political reorganization of the Indian polity.

[45] Raina, *Cradle for Leadership*, p. 24

[46] Lal, *The National Defence Academy*, p.6. This junior wing was eventually shifted to Pune where the new NDA was established in the 1950s.

[47] Report in *The Tribune*, 4 April 1948.

[48] Report in *The Hindustan Times*, 3 November 1945.

[49] Report in *The Hindustan Times*, 4 November 1945.

as the first inter-service academy and the fact that it was being built in the inaugural years of the new republic afforded the NDA a great deal of public attention.[50] The conscious effort to memorialize a sense of history arising out of the construction of this national enterprise was indicative of the ways in which ambitious colonial projects, such as the planning of urban zones like New Delhi in the early twentieth century, represented the need to reflect and radiate the prestige of the colonial state outwards.[51] The groundswell of governmental and logistical support to the NDA dovetailed with the wider institution-building wave of the post-Independence years, where, aside from educational projects, a wide variety of state-owned enterprises—financial, agricultural, scientific, and industrial—were set up. Needless to say, a project of the size of the NDA courted a fair amount of attention from all those who saw themselves as a part of it.

After Independence, though, the onus was on internalizing this spirit into the body politic of the 'sovereign republic', and this manifested in the physical drawing of the NDA campus as a detached cantonment overlooking the city in its neighbourly precincts, signifying the emergence of a military training institution with the power to project the military prowess of the State in an urbanized zone. It also reflected a degree of eagerness with which the hegemonic State wanted to commence—what Yasmin Khan has termed—the 'nation-statist' initiatives after Independence.[52]

Habibullah, the officer who was one of the earliest commandants of the NDA, called the setting up of the NDA as a 'Marx Brothers' Show'.[53]

---

[50] Report in *The Hindustan Times*, 3 October 1949. In order to exercise control over the project effectively, a supervisory board and a construction committee were set up by the government under the chairmanship of Sardar Baldev Singh, the defence minister.

[51] Narayani Gupta, *Delhi between Two Empires, 1803–1931: Society, Government and Urban Growth* (Delhi: Oxford University Press, 1981), pp. 178–80.

[52] Yasmin Khan, 'Remembering and Forgetting: South Asia and the Second World War', in *The Heritage of War*, Key Issues in Cultural Heritage Series, ed. Martin Gegner and Bart Ziino, pp. 177–93 (Abingdon and New York: Routledge, 2012), p. 191.

[53] Maj. Gen. E. Habibullah, 'The Great Migration', in *The National Defence Academy of India, Memorial Volume: 1978*, ed. T. Raina, pp. 33–8, (Pune: NDA, 1978), p. 36.

The similarities between the hugely successful twentieth-century Broadway comedy team and what was happening miles away in Pune were all too apparent to Habibullah in the intense activity and 'planned disorder' of the task to construct and operationalize the NDA. The new academy moved to its new location at Khadakvasla only in 1955, following a massive relocation operation marked by considerable logistical hardship at a substantial financial cost.[54]

The permanent site for the construction of the NDA came to be chosen after a hectic round of negotiations between the states and the centre, as well as after the struggles to balance service-specific demands of the navy and air force, who insisted on the new academy's proximity to the sea and an airfield. The debate, arguably, was sparked off by the NDA committee's questionnaire, which first placed the question on choosing a suitable location for the institution.[55] Out of the many replies which the committee received, it was mainly Pune, Karachi (now in Pakistan), Bangalore (now Bengaluru), Bombay (now Mumbai), and Dehradun that made it to the unofficial shortlist. However, after Independence, Pune emerged as the likely choice. Interestingly, it was also considered as an ideal place for a new Indian Staff College to be established in India, since the one in Quetta was to be split in 1947.

In the process of choosing a site for the NDA, Pune was hardly an outlier. There already existed within the future confines of the upcoming academy a combined training centre, wherein training after 1943 was being organized under the newly established Directorate of Combined Operations.[56] Therefore, geographically and institutionally, the academy did not quite inhabit a barren space, and in fact may have been favoured to be set up near Pune, primarily because of some rudimentary form of combined operations training that existed there, which could have aided the development of a more professionally organized military academy. However, the pace at which the working

[54] India's National War Academy, BL, IOR/L/I/202. According to the calculations outlined in the report, which were tentative, the initial cost of the project was estimated to be around Rs 15 crores, including the site, buildings, equipment, and the like.

[55] Raina, *Cradle for Leadership*, p. 19.

[56] Alan Jeffreys, 'Training the Indian Army, 1939–1945', in *The Indian Army, 1939–47: Experience and Development*, ed. Alan Jeffreys and Patrick Rose, pp. 69–86 (Farnham, Surrey, and Burlington, VT: Ashgate, 2012), p. 85.

committee of the NWA committee worked to vote for Poona (now Pune) was ground to a halt, when the desired stretch of land spanning up to 10 square miles was refused in a free allotment by the Bombay state.[57]

The refusal to grant additional land came close on the heels of the state government's disappointment when it apparently learnt that the new academy's training agenda had been abridged. From being a full-fledged commissioning academy, the state government later learnt—much to its dismay—that the final-year training of the cadets will take place in the service academies, upon which the officers' commission will be granted.[58] It was unusual for a state government to bristle at such a development given the wide gulf that existed between the states' and the centre's domains on military issues, much less on intricate details of officers' commissions. The NDA land transfer issue was eventually resolved, yet the episode was a critical reminder of the centrality of the states or provinces in the subcontinent's military institutional development.

States and provinces had played a critical role in the endowment, formation, and characterization of the military institutions they were associating themselves with. These ties of state-based collaboration in institution-building continued even after 1947. The NDA, therefore, needs to be seen as a twentieth-century milestone in a long journey of provincial collaboration in the establishment and sustenance of military networks. As pointed out in earlier chapters, even in the late nineteenth and early twentieth centuries, the states or princely states collaborated in significant ways in the establishment and functioning of military spaces like the feeder schools. This collaboration took many forms—administrative, financial, and educational. Therefore, the NDA inhabited a new, but not unfamiliar terrain of state-based collaboration in military institution-building practices.

The NDA's institutional and physical iconography derived in part from other existing military institutions at this point such as the IMA. Built in 1932, primarily in the image of Sandhurst, the IMA story took a backseat in the years of the NDA's birth. However, many of

---

[57] Cited in Raina, *Cradle for Leadership*, p.21

[58] T. Raina, 'Introducing the NDA', in *The National Defence Academy of India, Memorial Volume: 1978*, ed. T. Raina (Pune: NDA, 1978), p. 18.

the earliest architectural battles that were fought on the fields of Khadakvasla (the site of the NDA) carried a distinct imprint of what came to be famously known as the 'Sandhurst Syndrome'.[59] This phrase was coined by Mascarenhas, the chief engineer for the NDA project, and it brings to light how different organizational conceptions and models were associated with the construction plans of the NDA. At the organizational level, the construction of the NDA brought to light intergenerational differences over views on military training spaces.

Officers trained at the IMA or Sandhurst in Britain voiced their opinions, which occasionally sat at odds with the younger crop of officers who were fast emerging and who looked up to newer, other non-British institutions for inspiration. One of Krishna Menon's biographers termed these differences as resulting from the hangover of the 'Imperial Staff College dominated past' of the officers, which presented considerable obstacles for the Defence Ministry to pursue reforms.[60]

Mascarenhas recounts how on two occasions he was asked to modify the plans of the upcoming academy (mainly the designs for the parade ground and the mess) to suit the patterns after which the IMA was built and to implicitly model it after Sandhurst.[61] The Construction Committee's struggles with plans for the creation of a single Mess symbolized the changes (and also differences) in organizational and architectural sensibilities with an earlier generation of officers who were bred and socialized in the British mores of 'Messing' conventions.

The reorganization of the physical space inside the NDA gave rise to a substantial discussion on the precise ways in which its layout could speak to the mid-twentieth century's modernistic sensibilities of design and institutional management. The Indianization of the proposed mess at the NDA, for instance, was an issue that attracted considerable official attention and finds a mention in another biography of the NDA.[62]

---

[59] W.X. Mascarenhas, 'A National Monument: Planning and Execution', in *The National Defence Academy of India, Memorial Volume: 1978*, ed. T. Raina, pp. 23–6 (Pune: NDA, 1978), p. 23.

[60] T.J.S. George, *Krishna Menon: A Biography* (London: Jonathan Cape 1964), p. 251.

[61] Mascarenhas, 'A National Monument', p. 25

[62] Lal, *The National Defence Academy*.

Much of the emphasis, gleaned from public reportage and institutional accounts, was on hiring Indian staff that was familiar with cooking different cuisines and able to imbibe western styles of management.[63] However, the discussions surrounding the NDA's Mess systems, apart from its immediate fixation with logistical arrangements, had deeper institutional and historical roots.

As a site for convivial and communal dining as well as for inter-personal communications, the mess represented the social equivalent of the military operational field theatre for the officers. Even in other non-Indian contexts, as Robin Luckham has pointed out, the mess forms part of the 'prescribed' element of the 'military way of life'.[64] It was, therefore, a site conceptualized for an unofficial, off-the-cuff interaction among members that was otherwise impossible within the confines of a military workplace. Ironically, though unsurprisingly, for it was often situated in the rarefied and hierarchical ambience of the cantonment, the mess was also a space which was extensively controlled by military authorities to regulate social–official behaviour among officers. These controlling strategies took the form of establishing intricate sartorial, dining, and socializing rules that dictated movement and conduct in the mess to a significant degree, thereby resulting in the conceptualization of a site that successfully replicated the hierarchical chains of command that were operational at the workplace.

As Stephen Cohen has also noted, the space of the mess had been instituted by the British long before any Indians were commissioned, and their rules and conventions governed more than just 'dining etiquette … but also prescribed a system of social behaviour and control'.[65] The mechanism of regulating the mess acquired an even more important role in the context of the Indian Army, whose administration and functioning was never devoid of any political interest. Thus,

---

[63] Editorial, 'Loyalty to Country Essential: How Proposed Military Academy Can Succeed', *Hindustan Times*, 22 December 1945.

[64] Robin Luckham, 'Officers and Gentlemen of the Nigerian Army', *Transition* no. 39 (October 1971): 38–55, p. 53.

[65] Stephen P. Cohen, *The Indian Army: Its Contribution to the Development of a Nation* (Berkeley: University of California Press, 1971), pp. 164–5. The author remarked how each unit had its own rituals, laws, and customs, which contributed to the effectiveness of the Mess as a 'focal point for loyalty and as an instrument of group control'.

social interactions among a wide constellation of officers had always to be looked for signs of unrest or disharmony or even subversion.[66] The space of the mess and its regulatory constraints continued to subject officers well after Indianization had begun. The officers came to be socialized professionally through this institution, which, in many ways, 'controlled their personal and political beliefs'.[67]

For some, the mess projected an alien image of an institution planted artificially on Indian soil because there happened to be no such formal institution in pre-British indigenous military forces. However, during the NDA planning, some others supported the idea of the mess because it presented a glimpse of modernity which had little or no institutional linkages with other pre-British military organizations in the subcontinent, most of which were organized on irregular lines and had rarely experienced the cohesion which the colonial army came to be known for and much of that cohesion, it was opined, was a product of the socialization that took place in the mess.[68]

Fundamentally, the questions over the removal or retention of the mess at the NDA hinged on the aspect of interpersonal and institutional

---

[66] Gen. J.N. Chaudhuri, chief of the army staff in India (1962–6), recollected his interactions with Nehru in 1963 over the 'desirability of officers talking politics in the mess' after the 1962 Sino-Indian conflict. Chaudhuri, in his words, assuaged the fears of the political leadership by downplaying the importance of such discussions among officers. He added that an 'occasional criticism of government policy' did not imply 'a lack of loyalty to the government or the country.' See, Gen. J.N. Chaudhuri, 'Nehru and the Indian Armed Forces', Jawaharlal Nehru Memorial Lecture, 5 May 1973. Available at https://www.cambridgetrust.org/assets/documents/Lecture_5.pdf; 27 August 2020.

[67] On a visit to the Soviet Union's military installations in 1957, Gen. Thimayya, army chief (1957–61), had interesting observations on the tenor of the conversations among Russian officers in the social setting of the Soviet Mess. 'In visiting the messes', Thimayya had noticed that the officers behaved in a manner as they would in any other officers' mess in any army: 'They were cheerful, rowdy and frank in their conversations and I heard frequent disparaging references to civilian ministry officials and financial control.' See File No. 6: Gen. Thimayya's Talk to Officers at Defence Services Staff College (DSSC), 21 November 1958, Thimayya Papers, NMML Archives, New Delhi, India.

[68] Lt Col D.K. Palit, 'Are Officers' Messes Suited to Indian Conditions?', *Journal of the United Service Institution of India* vol. LXXVI (January 1946): 10.

relations that prospective officers were envisioned to imbibe at the new academy. The fate of the mess, then, effectively depended on how far the new academy would go in transforming the ideological lens with which officers would view their commissions. If the academy was able to foster a nationalist element in officership, then the mess could perhaps play a key role in sustaining and even perpetuating the nationalist ethic of military service. The spatial reorganization of the NDA, therefore, necessitated in the eyes of some, to demand that the issues of 'loyalty of soldiers', the removal of caste and religious barriers among officers, and the 'Indianisation of the spaces within which they interacted with each other' be taken up in earnest at the highest official level.[69] Calls for the new military academy to introduce drastic organizational changes advocated that the 'clash of loyalties' in terms of caste, religion, and so on, could only be resolved by making loyalty to the country the obligation of military service.[70] There were, in addition to the discussion on the institution of the mess, requests and calls for designing a 'National Flag', an anthem and a set of formal 'colours for the Academy' which would impart a nationalist as well as a unified character to it.[71]

Thus, the ideological scope of Indianization went far beyond its immediate mathematical determinism of replacing British officers to face a host of institutional challenges associated with the task of running an officers' academy. The NDA, therefore, transformed its scope from being mainly responsible for training more Indian cadets into a space that was now to be entrusted to mirror the sensibilities and priorities of an independent country.

A host of administrative and cadet-centric challenges marked the early years of the NDA. These challenges related to the quality of the cadet intake in the academy, which in turn gave rise to numerous suggestions for improving the academic standards of the cadets, bringing back to life the early struggles of the IMA and feeder institutions in

---

[69] Report in *The Hindustan Times*, 22 December 1945.
[70] Report in *The Hindustan Times*, 22 December 1945.
[71] Report in *The Hindustan Times*, 22 December 1945. The report also pointed out that instructors at the proposed 'West Point' should all be Indian and that the 'inclusion of even one British officer would disturb the atmosphere which is to be built at the academy'.

attracting and training a diverse set of prospective officers. However, another set of challenges profoundly affected the NDA, which was unique to the period in which the academy had emerged. It reflected the anxieties of a changing defence force, which, in addition to the demands of being Indianized, was also beginning to get increasingly concerned with the wider educational significance of the defence force's training. Military institutional reform and its Indianization, in the years after 1947, was increasingly veering towards developing academies that were capable of acting as not just formal officers' training schools but also as partners in the equally important civilian higher educational network.

The issue of affiliation of military academies to civilian universities would come to play a central role in the development of other major military institutions. Nonetheless, with the NDA, it marked the beginning of a change in approach towards the education that was being provided for officers and cadets. The idea behind having the NDA affiliated to a university was to give the 'collegiate' aspect of education at the academy a more formal and regular character.[72] However, the fact of securing recognition for its courses was initially rejected by the Defence Committee of the cabinet. The finance minister had opposed the idea of gaining recognition as he felt this could lower the status of the NDA to the level of a degree college or such. He asserted that this would have diverted the attention of the cadets to pursue their 'real aim' of training to become good officers.[73]

One of the key themes here is to explore and highlight the ways in which the NDA balanced the demands of running a responsible educational institution in twentieth century with the more obvious need to ensure its status as an inter-service training academy for the armed

[72] India's National War Academy, BL, IOR/L/I/202. It was proposed to place adequate emphasis on the academic aspect of the education, so that after the initial officer requirements of the services were satisfied, a certain percentage of the output might be allowed to enter civil life. The idea was that apart from the technical training, the youths when they leave the institution, will have acquired academic instruction to the level of bachelor of science (BSc), which, it was hoped, the existing universities would recognize.

[73] MB1/D44/6, copy of a paper enclosing a copy of the minutes of Defence Committee meeting No 2 of 18 February 1948, Mountbatten Papers Database, Special Collections, University of Southampton, UK.

forces. This was starkly apparent in an inter-university conference at the NDA, where the commandant, in his address to the vice chancellors, termed his institution as a 'University of Arms' that had much to learn about 'student discipline', 'examination reform', 'limiting student numbers', and other administrative and functional challenges in running civilian universities.[74] The issues highlighted by the commandant formed a veritable perimeter of administrative issues, the solution to which would be the focus of the NDA's attention.

Problems in setting the level of academic instruction started right away after the academy's inauguration in 1949. This was compounded by the fact that the first batch of cadets did not enter the NDA upon passing an examination but were selected out of a large pool of sixteen-to seventeen-year-old gentlemen who had recently matriculated.[75] The 'somewhat rushed' start to the academy, Gibson (the first principal of the academy) said, did not afford much time in trying to understand the academic and intellectual levels of the cadets.[76] The authority to conduct the examination was vested with the Federal Public Service Commission (later rechristened as the Union Public Service Commission) in New Delhi, but no clear consensus had emerged in setting a pattern for the entrance examination, resulting in holding the inaugural examination at abeyance.

The indecision in designing a common entrance examination scheme, which also plagued the IMA in its early years, was compounded by the government's decision to reform the recruitment policy for the academies, which brought a differently educated group of students to the NDA. This exerted considerable amount of pressure on the examination authorities who had to design papers while keeping in mind the average educational levels of the prospective cadets. Gibson regretted while noting in his memoirs that the uneven academic and educational

---

[74] Proceedings of the Vice Chancellor's Conference convened by the Ministry of Education at National Defence Academy, Khadakvasla on 15–16 June 1960, Ministry of Education, GoI (Publication No. 545, GoI Press, 1961), Shelf mark: Asia, Pacific & Africa V 15059, BL, London, UK.

[75] J.T. Gibson, 'Broad General Education at the JSW', in *The National Defence Academy of India, Memorial Volume: 1978*, ed. T. Raina, pp. 27–31 (Pune: NDA, 1978).

[76] Gibson, 'Broad General Education at the JSW', p. 27.

standards of the earliest batches at the NDA compelled its authorities to accept and teach a less-advanced syllabus to a differentially educated cohort of cadets.[77]

A brief survey conducted by the academy to gauge the level of the first batch of cadets yielded interesting results. More than half of the cadets who were informally tested in general matriculation-level subjects did not succeed in scoring more than 33 per cent in each of the subjects they were tested for.[78] The results were enough for the NDA Syllabus and Establishment Committee to design fresh syllabi and also collaborate with the Public Service Commission to institute a standardized testing mechanism.

Successive batches entered the NDA after passing an all-India test and then appearing before the Services Selection Board, with the result that there was uniformity among the educational levels in the cadets. However, this did not offer an immediate solution to the problem of underperforming cadets.[79] By 1957, that is, two years after the NDA began to function as a regular inter-service academy from its new location, the complains regarding the NDA's high rate of failure and withdrawal of cadets reached a crescendo. Several complaints, with diverging points of concerns, were directed against the NDA, ranging from terming the NDA's products as being sub-standard to calling the assessment strategies of the academy as too lenient, thereby

---

[77] Gibson, 'Broad General Education at the JSW', p. 27. The problem may also have been linked with the issue of the language that was the medium of instruction. Gibson later conceded that it was the lack of knowledge of English which may have let students down, since many students had acquired their matriculation in regional languages.

[78] Gibson, 'Broad General Education at the JSW', p. 28. Of the 187 cadets (of the first course/batch or the incoming class) examined, the statistics were: mathematics—12 scored above 66 per cent and 100 below 33 per cent (an unspecified number of cadets had not studied mathematics beyond the age of 14); general science—6 scored above 66 per cent and 73 below 66 per cent; English—12 scored above 66 per cent and 93 scored below it; geography—5 scored above 66 per cent and 130 below it; and history and current affairs—11 scored above 66 per cent and 69 below it.

[79] See Brig. C.B. Khanduri, *Thimayya: An Amazing Life* (New Delhi: Knowledge World, 2006), pp. 154–5.

highlighting the chaotic early years of its functioning and developing a coherent protocol of cadet assessment.[80]

It was the high incidence of failure that finally caught the government's attention. The Ministry of Defence, then headed by Krishna Menon (who was to play a key role in determining the fate of another military academy—the NDC in Delhi [discussed in the Chapter 4]), called into question the assessment methods of the academy and the financial loss that was being incurred on to the government by the withdrawal of cadets, each of whom were supported by government subsidies since tuition at the NDA was being paid for by the central government.[81] The sentiment about big flagship projects and the need to ensure their continued operational success had not undergone any significant transformation since the time of the IMA, which had to be always portrayed as a successful, viable training space in the face of the latter's struggle to cope with under-performing cadets.

The issue of withdrawals seemed to be resolved when the NDA blinked and took back a few cadets,[82] but the practical problems in training the cadets to a uniform standard remained. Cadet failure at the NDA had also come to be viewed against the context of the Indian military's policy to adopt newer, more progressive methods of recruitment. In fact, the controversy surrounding the new methods of recruitment started the moment the NDA, as well as other officer-training facilities at Mhow and Bangalore, had started to put them into use—as early as 1945. Mere entrance to the academies as a cadet was not a guarantee to earn a commission now. It had come to be replaced with a continuous system of evaluation of cadets, and all the under-performing cadets who were not considered fit for granting commissions were asked to leave.[83] The idea of selecting cadets by means of an entrance examination was not new and was also used in the case

[80] T.N.Vyas, 'Teething Troubles', in *The National Defence Academy of India, Memorial Volume: 1978*, ed.T. Raina, pp. 39–41 (Pune: NDA, 1978), p. 39.

[81] Vyas, 'Teething Troubles', p. 39.

[82] Vyas, 'Teething Troubles', p. 40. Out of a total of twenty-three failed cadets in 1957, only a 'few' were asked to leave.The exact number, however, is unspecified.

[83] Report in *The Hindustan Times*, 27 December 1946.

of the IMA as well; what was novel about the selection processes after 1947, however, was the enhanced focus on the interview process of the candidates, which determined, in large part, whether the candidate was fit to pursue a career in the military as an officer, eschewing the preference for lineage and class in favour of a more progressive, skills-based selection process.[84]

This renewed focus earned its fair share of supporters and detractors. The interview process, conducted by specially constituted Services Selection Boards, carefully recalibrated recruitment parameters and criteria for judging the candidates afresh for their suitability for a career in the armed forces. A wide measure of support for this new entrance regulation, interestingly, came from within the services that portrayed these regimens as part of a scientific officer selection protocol for the armed forces. This was critical in acquiring what was described in a not too unfamiliar trope as a professional officer corps, which would perform their duties unmindful of their social, cultural, and political backgrounds and surrounding milieu.[85]

The military authorities, at times, went out of their way to convince the validity of their ideas, inviting the press and other senior military functionaries to witness the functioning of the Services Selection Board, whose selection methodologies derived from the best German and US protocols of cadet assessments.[86] This 'foreign context' pitch by the military authorities in bolstering the case for interviews, if not entirely successful in allaying the fears of those who took the examination, certainly had a ring of factual accuracy to it, as a few key higher foreign military training institutions had begun to test its efficacy as

[84] Report in *The Hindustan Times*, 25 January 1947. The report clearly favoured the new system of selection because it made selection practices 'merit based' and 'democratic'. The article pointed out that due to earlier systems of selection, the 'well-connected or the more presentable' had a big advantage over recruitment processes.

[85] Lt Col Rajendra Singh, 'Is Scientific Selection Successful?', *JUSII* vol. LXXVI (October 1946): 335.

[86] Report in the *Hindustan Times*, 25 January 1947. The head of the Selection Board located in Meerut, in fact, invited members of the press and Army Nationalization Committee to oversee the functioning of the selection boards to cast light on the 'transparency' with which the tests were being conducted.

an assessment tool. Similar changes in the recruitment processes were also instituted in Britain where a newly restructured Staff College, whose own institutional reorganization had a key impact on the Staff College in Quetta (and also later in India), had instituted a qualifying examination—a new addition since the Second World War—coupling it with the written examination as a guide to measure the officers' potential.[87] The NDA, therefore, did not just represent the arrival of a national institution for training along inter-service lines but was also shaped by the prevailing currents about determining the value and importance of delivering a military-based education to matriculates.

A critical structural and 'intellectual' stocktaking of the NDA was undertaken in 1958, the same time the NDA was deliberating upon the fate of its under-performing cadets. Interestingly, at this time, the academy also passed over into the hands of a naval commandant—the first non-army officer to ever take command of the inter-service academy. Vice Admiral B.A. Samson, the naval commanding officer (CO) of the NDA, was directed by the chiefs of Staff Committee to study the current academic course structures at the NDA and asked to make recommendations to upgrade the course modules. Two important issues surfaced in this directive. The first was to upgrade the status of the academic course at the NDA to that of a 'degree course', and second, to get the course recognized by a university in India.[88]

The need to upgrade the course at the NDA may have been pushed forward as a result of Gen. Thimayya's (Indian Army chief, 1957–61) visit to the United States Military Academy at West Point in 1958, where he was 'particularly impressed by the great emphasis placed on academic training' and the necessity of 'obtaining an undergraduate or a Bachelor's "B.Sc." degree, before an officer was commissioned.'[89] This, in Thimayya's opinion, was a real necessity for augmenting the role of science in modern warfare while enabling an officer to obtain 'civil employment at any stage in his life, being in possession of a recognised

[87] Report in *The Tribune*, 18 April 1948.

[88] Vice Admiral B.A. Samson, 'Aiming at Higher Standards', in *The National Defence Academy of India, Memorial Volume: 1978*, ed. T. Raina, pp. 47–9 (Pune: NDA, 1978), p. 48.

[89] File No. 6, Gen. Thimayya's Talk to Officers at DSSC, 21 November 1958, Thimayya Papers, NMML Archives, New Delhi, India.

university degree.'[90] In consonance with his views, Samson remarked on the merits of a 'broad and thorough academic and professional base' as being essential to intelligent action and intelligent planning at this stage of 'defence complexity'.[91]

With an eye on India's evolving foreign policy on non-alignment at the time and out of the immediate strategic context of India's location in relation to its neighbours, the qualitative change in the appreciation of the role of the defence forces necessitated the formation of a new breed of officers. This new officer corps, which, apart from consisting of professional officers, was also expected to take up appointments within India and abroad to manage security scenarios, where they would invariably end up interacting with different classes of professionals—'scientists and government officials'—all of whom were 'academically, apparently, highly qualified'.[92] This meant that a more interdisciplinary module of education would now have to be devised to suit the demands of a changing occupational mandate of the armed forces.[93]

The change in the portfolio of responsibilities that the Indian Armed Forces had to bear lay in India's international commitments to global security, which, in addition to conventional warfare, entailed peace-keeping and legal arbitration over repatriation of refugees in Korea in the 1950s, among other campaigns. This new roster of responsibilities necessitated a force that was capable of handling professional complications that could arise in the conduct of such business, since, in resolving a 'number of national and international tricky problems', the

[90] File No. 6, Gen. Thimayya's Talk to Officers at DSSC, 21 November 1958, Thimayya Papers, NMML Archives, New Delhi, India.

[91] Samson, 'Aiming at Higher Standards', p. 48.

[92] Samson, 'Aiming at Higher Standards'.

[93] The discussions surrounding the political education of the cadets came to occupy a powerful grip on the minds of the senior military leadership. In a visit to the Soviet Union in 1958, Gen. Thimayya was struck by the extensive educational programmes that were being run to support Russian forces, in addition to shoring up their logistical support base, much of which had been obliterated after 1945. See File No. 6, Gen. Thimayya's Talk to Officers at DSSC, 21 November 1958, Thimayya Papers, NMML Archives, New Delhi, India.

exercise may have 'little or nothing to do with being a soldier, sailor or airman'.[94] This feature of deputing military officers in non-combatant diplomatic assignments would prove instrumental in setting the context for the establishment of the NDC in 1960.

The set of recommendations that was eventually forwarded by the NDA's commandant was aimed at restructuring the course syllabi from a traditional, basic sciences-based and humanities-based general education—including service-specific training as it existed after the Second World War—to a more novel methodology. Samson, in collaboration with other members on the restructuring committee (the full proceedings of which have not been made public), then went on to recommend a diversification of the course through including what he termed as 'vital humanities'.[95] This included teaching emerging disciplines like public administration and international relations

The NDA's affiliation to a civilian university is an important episode in the story of its establishment and reorganization of its academic curriculum. However, formal measures to explore affiliation arrangements did not commence until the mid-1960s, with the appointment of a defence ministry–led Syllabus Revision Committee in 1968.[96] The committee comprised H.N. Kunzru, D.S. Kothari, J.P. Naik, and Dr S. Bhagvantham, among other university chancellors who recommended that degree arrangements were necessary for post-service rehabilitation of officers.[97]

These deliberations highlighted the vital pathways along which the education being imparted to cadets was sought to be brought under the overall academic arrangements of a civilian university. This would be a continuing feature in the case of future academies that were set up, but in the case of the NDA at least, it seems to have been settled smoothly. Future negotiations regarding affiliations would involve hectic rounds of hammering out issues of autonomy and institutional control, but the collegiate system of education that had been introduced at the NDA, owing to Gibson's efforts, did not pose any substantial problems, save for the fact that the affiliating institution sought by

[94] Samson, 'Aiming at Higher Standards', p. 48.
[95] Samson, 'Aiming at Higher Standards', p. 48.
[96] Raina, *Cradle for Leadership*, p. 77.
[97] Raina, *Cradle for Leadership*, p. 77.

the government—the New Delhi-based Jawaharlal Nehru University (JNU)—was a postgraduate research university that only ran a handful of undergraduate courses. Jawaharlal Nehru University worked in conjunction with the NDA's newly created Academic Committee with the 'purpose of directing and guiding all academic matters'[98] to facilitate the affiliation arrangements.

The NDA ran its academic-cum-military education courses on what were then considered to be modern lines of a collegiate education and paralleled the developments at JNU. The affiliation—in the words of the then-NDA commandant Air Marshal M.B. Naik (air force), under whose tenure it took place—was preceded by a rigorous examination of the NDA's academic policies and 'the scope and extent of education' that was being imparted.[99] Naik also reiterated that affiliation arrangements were only sought to strengthen the academic import of the NDA education and in no way did the 'content of service training get diluted' with the introduction of the new academic programme.[100] Naik was perhaps addressing these concerns which were emanating from within the military circles, bringing back to life the initial military institutional struggles of the early twentieth century, which will be discussed in the next chapter. The tensions inherent in the twin roles earmarked for the NDA did not sit well with Habibullah, whose opinions on various aspects of the NDA were quite vocal and who called for an objective clarity on the precise cadets that would populate the NDA; graduates in arts and science, he added, did not mean they were better educated.[101]

The affiliation arrangements for the NDA throws up vital questions and problem areas for the reconfiguration of military education and instruction, and also the changing profile of the 'consumers' of that education. Contemporaneous observers were not slow in realizing the important role that education had to play in the life of the officers. Commentators including Naik, the NDA's then-military head,

[98] Air Marshal M.B. Naik, 'University Affiliation', in *The National Defence Academy of India, Memorial Volume: 1978*, ed. T. Raina, pp. 50–2 (Pune: NDA, 1978), p. 51.

[99] Naik, 'University Affiliation', p. 51.

[100] Naik, 'University Affiliation', p. 51.

[101] Habibullah, *The Sinews of Indian Defence*, pp. 102–3.

conceded that syllabus requirements would have to change in the future to keep track of developments in international political economy and geopolitics, both of which had an impact on India's security.[102] Thus, the NDA's early evolution from an experimental wing to a full inter-service academy in the years after Independence offers an alternative reading of the history of the relationship between India and its armed forces and the management of Indian officers. Although rooted in the obvious paradigm of military training and tactics, the institution, by itself, stood as a mirror to the evolving political realities of the period. Whether it was the centre–state relations in influencing the establish-ment of the academy or carving out newer educational protocols for the cadets, the NDA went beyond its immediate military identity into becoming a more potent symbol of nationhood and security, all the while managing the links between the civilian and military arms of post-Independence governance in India.

[102] Naik, 'University Affiliation', pp. 50–2. Naik also hinted at introducing further structural reforms in the NDA, ones that pertained to the reforms in Indian school education system, advocating a further two-year programme of education prior to joining undergraduate courses in universities.

4 The National Defence College

Higher Training and Its Management after 1947*

No other military training or instructional institution embodies the tensions, challenges, and exhilaration of the post-Independence decades in India quite like the NDC, situated in New Delhi and inaugurated in 1960. Established almost over a decade after Independence, the college sits at the crossroads of modern Indian history. It is an integral story in the management of the three services and their senior officers in order to forge a 'strategic culture' in India. Additionally, the institution of the NDC also provides a distinct civilian context to the narrative of military policy and reform. This was essentially the highest military institution that would 'bring together selected senior officers from various organisations of the Government of India in addition to the armed forces for the purpose of giving them a structured exposure to diverse issues related to national security of a modern state'.[1]

The creation the NDC and its functioning in the immediate years was the culmination of a long process involving extended deliberations.

---

* An earlier and different version of this chapter analysing the NDC and contemporary institution-building efforts geared towards the inception of a National Defence University in India appeared in the Economic and Political Weekly. Please see: Vipul Dutta, 'Educating Future Generals: An Indian Defence University and Educational Reform', *Economic and Political Weekly* vol. 53, no. 32 (2018): 47–54.

[1] Maj. Gen. G.D. Bakshi and Maj. Gen. A. Mukherjee, *Lamp of Wisdom: History of the National Defence College, New Delhi* (New Delhi: NDC), p. 6.

By the turn of the 1960s, while India possessed all the required training architecture for the primary and middle-level ranking officers, the NDC represented something that had been absent for the better part of the post-Independence decades in India—an inter-service institution that could bring together senior officers from different services. Several of these senior officers for whom the NDC was established in 1960 were graduates of the earlier academies (discussed previously), which were set up in India as part of the military Indianization and institution-building starting in the latter half of the nineteenth century. The NDC was the highest institutional training space devised for this Indianized generation of military officers in India and continues to remain so.

The idea behind the NDC drew from international precedents. Similar institutions existed elsewhere in the world. Its establishment in India is notable because it occurred at a critical juncture. It was created for senior officers of the Indian military, representing a generational upgrade, given the fact that senior ranks were only beginning to take emerge in the late 1950s, owing to the 1947 partition of the subcontinent into two new nation-states of India and Pakistan, which had caused a significant shortage of manpower at the higher military levels in both the new nations. The NDC was also envisaged as an institution devoted to the study of national security and strategy. Thus, institutionally, the NDC marked a paradigm shift in training, not dissimilar from the Indian Staff College,[2] which, in the early twentieth century, functioned as an instructional space that delivered specialist knowledge to officers.

Not the usual Indian equivalent of a British or American 'sister institution', the NDC went on to carve a distinct institutional identity for itself in the succeeding decades. This should not mean that the college disavowed any international linkages. Indeed, the immediate model of operations that the college adopted was the IDC in London (now known as the Royal College of Defence Studies), where a few vacancies were reserved for Indian officers. However, the precise ways

---

[2] In order to assess the institutional challenges faced by the Staff College and its evolution within the subcontinent as an intellectual military space, please see: Vipul Dutta, 'The "Indian" Staff College: Politics and Practices of Military Institution-Building in Twentieth Century India', *Journal of Strategic Studies* vol. 42, no. 5 (2019): 600–25, doi: https://doi.org/10.1080/01402390.2019.1570148.

in which the IDC influenced the emergence of the NDC has not been sufficiently analysed. This chapter, therefore, will highlight the inter-institutional linkages between the two institutions which have hitherto attracted cursory attention.

The NDC was meant to train growing officer corps who were in the midst of an evolving operational context in the years after Independence. A significant section of the Indian Army's senior officer corps was engaged not just insecurity tasks and warfare, but was also part of international missions that made the Indian Armed Forces more intellectually cosmopolitan in its operational capabilities. The NDC, I argue, was a result of this intellectual cosmopolitanism pervading the Indian defence establishment after 1947.

This chapter will examine the years leading up to the formation of the NDC. Effectively, this will involve a study of the post-Independence years that fostered the demand for such an institution. The analysis of the formation of the NDC is connected to the development of a senior officer cadre. Therefore, this chapter appraises this institution through a sustained study of the higher officer ranks and their occupational assignments in order to critically reflect on the military institutionalization practices of the mid-twentieth century—an important theme that this chapter analyses and contextualizes in the larger wave of institution-building that swept across the subcontinent since the late nineteenth century. In this respect, this chapter connects the NDC with the longer arc of military institution-building in India—a theme not fully analysed in the scarce literature on the NDC.[3] Following the pattern employed in the previous chapters, I will examine the history of the emergence of the NDC, by studying the mechanisms through which the military liaised with the government in establishing an institution that went beyond its utility to just the armed forces.

COMPARISONS WITH BRITAIN: POLITICS AND THE ISSUE OF VACANCIES

Literature surrounding the NDC is meagre. Apart from an institutional biography,[4] there appear to be no other published works on the

---

[3] This chapter will broaden the discursive context surrounding the emergence of the NDC in the backdrop of post-Independence security-related events.

[4] Bakshi and Mukherjee, *Lamp of Wisdom.*

institution's history. This is not surprising, given the fact that the case of other academies has been largely similar. Official correspondence and newspaper reports, as well as memoirs of former alumni of the NDC, are helpful in charting the years leading up to the establishment of this institution, but they do not offer a fuller picture of the higher military institution-building practices that this book in general, and this chapter in particular is interested in.

The biographical account of the NDC traces the origin of the idea behind the institution in the post-Independence context and the political establishment that took over the reins of governance after 1947. This group included India's first prime minister, Jawaharlal Nehru, as well as Vallabhbhai Patel (India's first home minister) and scholar-diplomat K.M. Panikkar.[5] That the same galaxy of leaders and diplomats should be involved with the NDC as well as with other foreign policy and domestic security arrangements of the period is hardly surprising. Both Patel and Panikkar were associated with the accession of princely states and reorganization of India's internal boundaries. Panikkar was part of the States Reorganisation Commission of 1953, a body set up by the government to review and recast state boundaries on linguistic lines, a veritable domestic security challenge in the aftermath of Partition when not a few states were wary of joining the union, and whose integration occasionally involved active participation from senior military officers. Added to this was the 1948 Kashmir conflict and other large-scale military campaigns. Thus, the opening decades of the post-Independence phase of Indian history are host to a succession of international conflicts and phases of domestic reorganization, exercising a great influence on not just the relations between India and Pakistan but also India's relations with the West.

This international nature of security threats was also highlighted in the prime minister's speech during the inauguration of the NDC in April 1960. Terming the NDC as a 'positive necessity', Nehru called for a greater integration of governmental and military institutions in the appraisal of security issues facing the country.[6] Alluding to his

---

[5] Bakshi and Mukherjee, *Lamp of Wisdom*, p. 2.

[6] Speech at Inauguration of the National Defence College, 27 April 1960, in *Selected Works of Jawaharlal Nehru* [*SWJN*], Volume 60, Second Series, ed. Madhavan K. Palat, pp. 627–31 (New Delhi: Jawaharlal Nehru Memorial Fund, 2015).

non-alignment policies, which many termed as idealistic, the prime minister was aware and sensitive to the needs of developing a broad framework for the management of crises and security-related issues from a realist perspective, and regarded the NDC as one of the tools to do so. Significantly, the speech highlighted the central tenet that defence 'was not merely battle' but a 'term of such wide connotation' that it was imperative for 'higher grade defence officers' to develop a broad perspective on defence matters.[7] Aside from the acknowledgment of the changed principles of warfare and their impact on strategic planning, the speech laid bare the rough outlines of the new institution that was being planned out. The NDC, therefore, encompassed the widely felt strategic need to accommodate and analyse strategic threats in an institutional and academic way.

The lack of any substantive historical accounts of the NDC fails to offer an accurate context for the development of this institution. This chapter will shed light on the larger public discourse around which this idea was put across. It will also offer glimpses of what the senior generation of officers thought about this new institution, not all of whom embraced the new wave of institutional growth for the military. The previous chapter on the NDA highlighted the several turf battles that took place in relation to the new inter-service academy that was coming up and exhibited the generational as well as organizational gap between the services on the issue of officer training. The post-Independence decades, too, carried over similar points of differences that seem to have been ironed out in the narrative surrounding the development of not just higher military institutions such as the NDC, but also the ways through which the training needs of senior Indian officers was appreciated in this period.

Nehru and his cohort of ministers and secretaries did not work out the details of the new college in isolation. The prime minister was also in touch with other senior Indian officers like Gen. Thimayya, in whose international travels to foreign officers' academies, especially to the Soviet Union, the prime minister took keen interest.[8] There were

---

[7] Speech at Inauguration of the National Defence College, 27 April 1960, in *SWJN*, Volume 60, Second Series, ed. Madhavan K. Palat, p. 629.

[8] 'Army: Equipment, Training and Education', Note to Defence Secretary, New Delhi, 28 September 1957, *SWJN*, Volume 39, Second Series, ed. Mushirul Hasan, pp. 437–8.

active channels of communication between the prime minister and also other military officers, notable among them, the ex-commander-in-chief and later field marshal K.M. Cariappa: a key player in the establishment of the NDA in 1949, who was asked about his opinion on the new plan. An active public figure well into the 1970s and 1980s, Cariappa was part of the first batch of KCOs that was screened and selected for training in India, and managed to become the symbol of the Indian political demand of the early twentieth century, asking for more Indian officers for the Indian Army. The officer, therefore, was no stranger to the contemporaneous debates on how best to staff the new Indian Army and what it really meant to be an Indian officer.[9]

In Cariappa's correspondence with Nehru, the former did not quite match the excitement with which the idea of NDC was met in the government. In a letter to the prime minister in 1960, Cariappa termed the setting up of the new college as an 'avoidable luxury'.[10] Being an alumnus of the IDC in London, Cariappa did not share in the wider enthusiasm of setting up a college of high calibre to study 'our potential enemies—Pakistan and China'.[11] Terming such an institution as incompatible with India's oft-stated foreign policy aims of non-alignment, the retired general opined, rather imprecisely, that the establishment of the college could possibly compel India into getting involved with military pacts with other countries, thereby violating India's aims. Whether this was a response to solicited advice or simply proffering his personal point of view, Cariappa's views were not finally taken on board, at least for the moment.

Cariappa added further by writing about other existing institutions that could be used to deliver advanced studies on potential enemies in his letter. He directed the prime minister's attention to the Staff College and the Intelligence Bureau, and, intriguingly, the chiefs of Staff Committee, where a few selected officers could do a short course, approximating to a technical apprenticeship. Cariappa chose to offer an

---

[9] For a glimpse of Cariappa's views on the nationalization of the Indian Army, see, for instance, C.B. Khanduri, *Field Marshal KM Cariappa: His Life and Times* (Atlanta, New Delhi: Atlanta Publishing, 2013).

[10] Letter from Gen. K.M. Cariappa to Nehru, 8 July 1960, Cariappa Papers, Part II (B), Group XXI, S.No. 37, NAI, New Delhi, India.

[11] Letter from Gen. K.M. Cariappa to Nehru, 8 July 1960, Cariappa Papers, Part II (B), Group XXI, S.No. 37, NAI, New Delhi, India.

unusual opinion that favoured the use of existing military infrastructure in delivering specialist knowledge to senior ranking officers. Despite acknowledging the fact that the new institution was to be modelled on the lines of the IDC—Cariappa's alma mater—the general perhaps, at the time, did not appreciate the institution that was being planned at this time, overlooking the institutional significance and need for a higher training space for senior officers in India.

Relegating plans for higher officer training onto smaller, secondary military institutions went against Cariappa's own training and career trajectory. Besides, the type of knowledge the NDC was supposed to generate and inculcate was at odds with the militaristic and service-specific ambience of the other institutions, which were neither designed nor equipped to provide training to senior officers of not just the armed forces but also senior civil servants to forge intergovernmental linkages on national security.

Studying at the IDC in 1947, shortly before being recalled to India to oversee the partition of the armed forces, Cariappa regarded his half innings at IDC as instrumental in helping him effectively discharge his duties after Independence.[12] However, why Cariappa chose to offer this advice despite his stint in a similar institution is worth probing. The cost of setting up the new college (approximately Rs 350,000) was prohibitive to him, while the Staff College, according to him, could be equipped with 'the full paraphernalia of a National Defence College', thereby saving money which was 'urgently required for other nation-building projects'.[13] However, the die had been cast in favour of the NDC. The favourable reception to the idea of the NDC could have been partly to do with the fact that the college was not only an inter-service institution but also looked upon the participation of civil servants as integral to its constitution. Whether the same institution, albeit totally militaristic in its nature, would have found a similar degree of reception, is a question worth asking.

The IDC in London had more to do with the establishment of the NDC than being a mere model of inspiration. The decision to

---

[12] Brig. T.I.G. Gray (ed.), *The Imperial Defence College and the Royal College of Defence Studies, 1927–1977.* (London: HMSO, 1977), p. 37.

[13] Letter from Gen. K.M. Cariappa to Nehru, 8 July 1960, Cariappa Papers, Part II (B), Group XXI, S.No. 37, Cariappa Papers, NAI, New Delhi, India.

constitute the NDC came in part due to the limited vacancies that were beginning to be made available in London. However, this was not the only driving factor or the 'primary impetus', as the biography points out.[14] The move towards setting up the NDC was also because the Indian establishment, including Nehru, shared the growing ambivalence with regard to sending a small batch of officers overseas to gain knowledge that could have been imparted in India.[15] Besides, the financial commitment in sending out officers for higher training to London on a range of courses was beginning to be seen as too prohibitive and did not match the perceived benefits.[16] The issue of sending Indian civilian officials to IDC was also frowned upon and opposed by Nehru.[17] These objections and counter-claims formed a large part of the discourse associated with the development of the NDC and had an important role in determining the future course of the institution.

Thus, placing the development of the NDC within the context of a restrictive pool of opportunities for Indians abroad simplifies the narrative of institutional growth in India. First, it limits the narrative to a cause-and-effect argument; and second, it obscures the complicated and recalibrated context in which the issue of higher military training was discussed in India after the Second World War. More than the issue of the IDC closing the 'window of opportunities' for the Indian Army, it might be worthwhile to examine the changed landscape in which London found itself vis-à-vis the colonies and the larger Commonwealth. In the aftermath of the Second World War, the IDC opened in 1946 in London, but not before recalibrating its position within the British security framework as well as its relations with

---

[14] Bakshi and Mukherjee, *Lamp of Wisdom*, p. 5

[15] 'Army: Equipment, Training and Education', Note to Defence Secretary, New Delhi, 28 September 1957, *SWJN*, Volume 39, Second Series, ed. Mushirul Hasan, pp. 437–8.

[16] 'Training in the Imperial Defence College', Note to Defence Secretary, New Delhi, 17 October 1957, in *SWJN*, Volume 39, Second Series, ed. Mushirul Hasan, p. 439.

[17] 'Training of civilians in the Imperial Defence College', Note to M.K. Vellodi, Cabinet Secretary, 24 November 1957, in *SWJN*, Volume 40, Second Series, ed. M. Mukherjee, p. 312.

the Commonwealth and other security apparatuses that were being formed in post-War Europe.

Central to the reorganization and reopening of the IDC was the latter's relationship with India. Decolonization and the transfer of power to former colonies had changed the face of the post-War Commonwealth, resulting in a transformation of the terms with which newly independent countries would want to engage with Britain as far as defence matters were concerned. This directly affected the case of officers of the Indian Army who had been sent to the IDC before 1947. The changed constitutional status of India and its soon-to-be independent Indian Armed Forces now posed a challenge as to how Indian officers would come to be accommodated in the new college in London. This was not limited solely to India as this post-War scenario affected other nationalities too. The first post-War course of the college had no overseas students or civil servants, save for a few American military students who were included for the first time, but without publicity, 'at the request of the United States Chiefs of Staff'.[18]

However, the case of the Indian Army officers attracted official attention in London because of the imminent partition of the subcontinent, and while every issue attached to the division of the forces—in addition to the division of the subcontinent—was embroiled in a controversy, the task of sending out officers to train would not have remained uncontroversial for long. The issue of the Indian Army officers crept up in 1945 in a letter that Gen. Auchinleck, the commander-in-chief of the Indian Armed Forces in India (1941, 1943–7), wrote in response to a note from London's War Office that highlighted the grave concerns about delivering the specialist-cum-confidential knowledge to officers attending IDC who did not belong to the British Army.[19] Coupled with this was the overall delicate balance of power structure in Europe that favoured a more guarded approach towards sharing strategic knowledge in the immediate post–Second World War security

---

[18] Gray, *The Imperial Defence College and the Royal College of Defence Studies*, p. 14.

[19] Letter from Viscount Montgomery of Alamein, Chief of the Imperial General Staff, to Auchinleck, 30 January 1947, GB 133 AUC/1213, FM Auchinleck Papers, John Rylands Library (Special Collections), University of Manchester Library, UK.

context.[20] Officers and personnel from an army that was soon to be independent from British rule were not seen as party to a recalibrated security framework in Britain. These fears, however, did not find a place in the official call that went out asking the dominions to select and send officers for the course that was scheduled to begin in early 1947.

Gen. Auchinleck, while acknowledging the changed security scenario, mounted his criticism on the school commandants in Britain who favoured such a policy, in contrast to the policy advocated by the chiefs of staff (COSs) that recommended a general dominion-wide representation in the college as had been happening before.[21] While the biography of the NDC gives no such precise indication of a policy shift, the official correspondence between the War Offices in London and New Delhi bears testimony to the tensions and anxieties that radiated across defence circles in India and Britain due to the intractable political problem arising out of the failure of any constitutional settlement between major political parties in India, thereby relegating matters relating to defence and security issues in a considerably uneasy quarter.

Auchinleck expressed his disappointment that the issue of Indian officers going to the IDC was being discussed without taking his views into account, and termed the timing of this proposed move to refuse Indians from attending IDC as 'unfortunate', coming as it did during the ongoing tripartite negotiations between India, Britain, and Nepal on retaining the services of the Gurkhas in the military.[22] The general

---

[20] Minutes of a Meeting held at Horse Guards Parade on 4 April 1945 to discuss the organization of the post-War Staff Colleges, BL, IOR/L/WS/1/789. The director of military training was ready to welcome foreigners at Arms Schools, but remarked that at Staff Colleges and higher training institutions, foreign officers were a nuisance from a security aspect, and seldom derived much value through the language difficulty. He hoped that any tendency to go off to USA or Moscow would be overcome by the attendance at Arms Schools.

[21] Letter from H.E. FM Auchinleck, Commander-in-Chief, India, to War Office, UK, 3 December 1946, BL, IOR/L/WS/1/806.

[22] Record of Interview between Lord Mountbatten and FM Auchinleck, 5 April 1947, in *Constitutional Relations between Britain and India: The Transfer of Power 1942–7* (*TOP*), Volume X, ed. N. Mansergh and E.W.R. Lumby, pp. 133–4 (London: HM Stationery Office, 1970–83).

argued for parity for India as long as the latter remained part of the Commonwealth, and added further that should the IDC refuse taking in officers from India, he would 'put a ban on sending British officers of the Indian Army also' to London.[23]

Auchinleck's reference to British and Indian officers of the Indian Army foregrounds yet again the political and racial fault lines that existed in this organization. From Auchinleck's account, it seems the uneasiness with regard to Indian Army officers, which institutions such as the IDC experienced, was to do with the fact of passing on critical and sensitive information to a contingent of officers who, in the future, simply put, might not put it to use to further Britain's interests, if, for instance, India refused to join the British Commonwealth.[24] The issue seemed to have gained some traction in Whitehall, for in a chiefs of Staff Committee meeting in December 1946, the committee decided that for 'political reasons', it was not prudent to recommend at this 'eleventh hour that Indians should be excluded from the course'.[25] It was decided by the committee that any 'really super-secret information is not divulged to the students' and that since it was 'impossible to treat Indian students and UK/Dominion students differently', the ban on disclosing sensitive information to Indian students would extend to others as well.[26]

The episode also highlighted the importance with which the British military had come to regard to its relations with India and Pakistan after 1947, seeking opportunities to tie the newly independent States onto a security-cum-defence pact. Britain—mindful of the fact that its security interests were also now aligned with those of western Europe—was desirous of presenting Commonwealth as a fount

---

[23] Letter from H.E. FM Auchinleck, Commander-in-Chief, India to War Office, UK, 3 December 1946, BL, IOR/L/WS/1/806.

[24] Letter from Auchinleck to Lt Gen. Sir Geoffrey Scoones, Principal Staff Officer to the Secretary of State for India, FM Auchinleck Papers, GB 133 AUC/1215, John Rylands Library (Special Collections), University of Manchester Library, UK.

[25] PS/USS Note: Attendance of Indian Officers (Army and ICS) at the IDC, 11 December 1946, BL, IOR L/WS/1/806.

[26] PS/USS Note: Attendance of Indian Officers (Army and ICS) at the IDC, 11 December 1946, BL, IOR L/WS/1/806.

of its power that could present a 'united front' to the world.[27] The Commonwealth defence negotiations were an effort by Britain to rally its former colonies around the cause of containment of this Soviet-led socialist aggression. It was with this view in mind that Britain started to focus its attention on developing an official consensus in India and Pakistan towards the idea of forging a Commonwealth defence arrangement.

Britain envisaged immense possibilities in pursuing Commonwealth defence negotiations after Independence in order to secure a foothold over its imperial possessions in Southeast Asia and to prevent India from getting dominated by the Soviet Union's interests in the region.[28] The containment of Soviet influence across South Asia also prompted USA to bring newly independent countries within its security ambit. These security arrangements took the form of the South East Asia Treaty Organization (SEATO) and Central Asia Treaty Organization (CENTO) among others, but gaining entry into these did not attract much interest from the Indian political leadership.[29] The talk of a Commonwealth treaty was also portrayed as a measure to forward a 'joint imperial service contribution' in the assistance of the newly established council of the United Nations.[30]

The talks relating to Commonwealth defence were mired in controversy and a fair amount of political-diplomatic chaos. Britain offered the terms of assistance arising out of the prejudiced security of both India and Pakistan in 1947 due to the underdeveloped nature of their military infrastructure. Yet, Britain had also conceived of India's

[27] Anita Inder Singh, 'Keeping India in the Commonwealth: British Political and Military Aims, 1947–49', *Journal of Contemporary History* vol. 20, no. 3 (1985): 469–81, p. 471.

[28] 'Appreciation on the strategic value of India to the British Commonwealth of Nations', Chiefs of Staff Committee Notes, GB 133/AUC/1188, FM Auchinleck Papers, John Rylands Library (Special Collections) University of Manchester Library, UK. Also see, Singh, 'Keeping India in the Commonwealth', p. 473.

[29] 'The Prime Minister on a Military Approach to Security, 15 January 1960', *Select Documents on India's Foreign Policy, 1947–1972*, Volume I, ed. A. Appadorai, pp. 53–4 (Delhi: Oxford University Press, 1982).

[30] Note on the '1946 Course' at the IDC, London, GDFR 2/8, Capt. GA French Papers, Churchill Archives Centre, University of Cambridge, UK.

role in a 'loose organization of commonwealth defence' that could potentially make use of Indian military resources in any war in which the 'Commonwealth might get involved'.[31] The British COSs, with an eye on potential defence pacts, were anxious to offer long-term defence arrangements to the two new dominions. Yet, the negotiations were impeded by a crucial factor: Any long-term defence negotiation would have required the stationing of British troops in India—an issue that was controversial and could not attract any political unanimity in India.[32]

In a statement given at a session of the JDC (the body constituted to undertake the division of the Indian Armed Forces) a week before independence was granted in August 1947, Lord Ismay, the COS to Viceroy Mountbatten, admitted to the political complexity in which the defence negotiations were meant to be carried out.[33] In addition to this, the negotiations, Ismay added, were sought to be carried out through a 'system of liaison staff under the respective High Commissions of India and Pakistan'.[34] Of course, the hurried, violent, and convulsive atmosphere of Partition, coupled with the administrative challenge of dividing military resources, ultimately put paid to the British COSs' efforts to pursue a Commonwealth defence treaty due to the absence of any 'conditions' that could have guaranteed their military interests in

[31] Singh, 'Keeping India in the Commonwealth', p. 473.

[32] Note entitled 'British Officers in India', 3/7/68/5, Ismay Papers, Liddell Hart Centre for Military Archives, King's College London, UK. The report laid out the divisions in Indian opinion on the subject of retaining British officers after 1947. While Nehru and his 'senior soldiers' wanted to retain some officers and technicians, his other Congress colleagues, led by Vallabhbhai Patel, and others junior military officers 'wanted to see the whole British element eliminated'. Eventually, though, a significant number of British officers stayed back, many of them in advisory capacities or on secondment, but a significant number also served in command positions, heading the air force and naval wings.

[33] Statement made by Lord Ismay at the Joint Defence Council Meeting on 6 August 1947, ISMAY 3/7/12/4, Ismay Papers, Liddell Hart Centre for Military Archives, King's College London, UK.

[34] Statement made by Lord Ismay at the Joint Defence Council Meeting on 6 August, 1947, ISMAY. 3/7/12/4, Ismay Papers, Liddell Hart Centre for Military Archives, King's College London, UK.

the subcontinent.[35] Besides, both India and Pakistan, engrossed in the Kashmir conflict in 1948, showed relative indifference to the idea of a Commonwealth defence agreement.[36]

However, the chaotic and overwhelming administrative context of the 1947 partition could not obscure the possibilities that were pursued between India and Britain to continue to look for areas on defence cooperation, within or without the Commonwealth.[37] While there was no formal Commonwealth military commitment, India continued to rely on Britain for 'defense matters' on purchase of military equipment and supplies.[38] India's membership to the Commonwealth advisory Committee on Defence Science was also sought to be renewed in 1947, along with the subject of 'disclosing classified information to India',[39] reflecting the nature and possibilities of bilateral cooperation between the two nations on defence issues.

These possibilities for cooperation existed even between India and Pakistan when they signed the Inter-Dominion Agreement in 1948 in the hope of reversing the tide of migration from East Bengal.[40] Possibilities were also explored when other efforts were made to find common ground during the No-War Pact correspondence between Indian and Pakistani prime ministers in the framework of an evolving bilateral relationship in 1950.[41] This space for cooperation was further highlighted in 1959, when the idea—albeit short-lived—of a 'joint defence' was proposed by Pakistan in the wake of Chinese

[35] Singh, 'Keeping India in the Commonwealth', p. 473.

[36] P.S. Gupta, 'India in Commonwealth Defence, 1947–1956', in *Power, Politics and the People: Studies in British Imperialism and Indian Nationalism*, pp. 308–22 (New Delhi: Permanent Black, 2001), p. 310.

[37] Singh, 'Keeping India in the Commonwealth', p. 477.

[38] C.H. Heimsath and S. Mansingh, *A Diplomatic History of Modern India* (Delhi: Allied Publishers, 1971), p. 49.

[39] Rear-Admiral Viscount Mountbatten of Burma to the Ear of Listowel, Mountbatten Papers, Letter from Mountbatten to the Secretary of State, 27 June 1947, *TOP*, Volume XI, pp. 677–9.

[40] Joya Chatterji, *The Spoils of Partition: Bengal and India, 1947–1967* (Cambridge and New York: Cambridge University Press, 2007), p. 129.

[41] Pallavi Raghavan, 'The Making of the India–Pakistan Dynamic: Nehru, Liaquat, and the No War Pact correspondence of 1950', *Modern Asian Studies* vol. 50, no. 5 (2016): 1645–78. doi 10.1017/S0026749X15000554.

incursions into Tibet, but was not followed up.[42] These cooperating impulses were also evident during post-War negotiations regarding the officering of the Indian Army by British officers, many of whom wished to continue their service in India, but due to the compulsions of the domestic political conflicts in the subcontinent, only a few could be retained.[43] Moreover, studying the Commonwealth defence arrangements primarily through the Indo-British bilateral framework offers only a partial account of the ways in which personnel training was developed, as many decolonized countries formed bilateral partnerships with Commonwealth countries other than the UK.[44]

Thus, the establishment of higher military training institutions after 1947 in India, such as the NDC, were not solely a reaction to the closing down of opportunities for Indian officers abroad. The Commonwealth defence pact could not be signed due to historical and contextual reasons. In the same decade during which Britain attempted to initiate the discussion on a Commonwealth treaty, it did so with a host of other dominions in West Africa and Southeast Asia.[45] Also, for both India and Pakistan, the treaty, which set out to offer assistance in the event of victimization of the new dominions by external aggression, could not have worked out in the context of the 1948 Kashmir conflict, where Indian and Pakistani armies were at loggerheads, thereby putting the British political leadership—including their senior officers who stayed back to guide the new Pakistani and Indian militaries—in

[42] Letter from UK High Commissioner in India to the Commonwealth Relations Office, 14 May 1959, File DO 35/8997, Combined India and Pakistan Defence Policy, TNA, Kew, UK.

[43] Post War Officering of the Indian Army, BL, IOR/L/WS/1/924 (A).

[44] M.S. Rajan, *India and the Commonwealth: Some Studies* (Delhi: Konark, 1990), p. 161. Rajan estimates that a number of Asian-African and Caribbean countries were said to have had established 'fresh links' with other Commonwealth countries like Canada and Australia for the 'supply of military stores and training personnel'.

[45] Letter from R.F.C. Butcher, Research Department to G. Wigg, 19 May 1961, WIGG/3/6, George Edward Cecil, Baron Wigg Papers, Special Collections, LSE Library, UK. Apart from Ghana which did not have a treaty by 1961, Nigeria, Cyprus, Sierra Leone, and Malaya had either signed pacts with Britain or were preparing to negotiate for one.

a diplomatic quandary.[46] A telegram sent by the British high commissioner in Delhi to the Commonwealth Relations Office in London in 1949 captures the sense of unease and tension that pervaded the ranks of senior British military staff as well as the COSs in Delhi, who were relaying their fears of an imminent military conflagration between the two new dominions onto their British diplomatic establishment in New Delhi, treating the latter as a confidante to speak about such matters.[47]

Moreover, the practice of sending Indian officers for a stint at British institutions resumed after a brief gap in 1947.[48] S.D.Verma, the first commandant of the Indian Staff College, was selected to attend the IDC in 1950.[49] This was also accompanied by sending officers to USA.[50] Moreover, around 260 British officers at the regional level worked in India, testifying to the shared bonds of decision-making in the difficult years of Partition and Independence.[51] These shared spaces

[46] Singh, 'Keeping India in the Commonwealth', p. 474. Singh suggests that neither the events of Partition nor the Kashmir hostilities lessened the desire of the British to keep India in the Commonwealth. Yet, in the context of a defence pact—were it to have materialized—these events would have acquired a significant degree of importance and complicated Britain's involvement.

[47] Inward Telegram to the Commonwealth Relations Office from the UK High Commissioner in India, 30 August 1949, File DO 35/2275, UK Relations with India and Pakistan, TNA, Kew, UK. The high commissioner reported in the telegram that he had advised Admiral Parry, the navy chief (formerly RIN), who had come to discuss the Kashmir situation with the diplomat, to 'take as long as possible' in the preparation of the plans that the Indian cabinet wanted to see, and should use the 'background of their own experience' to insist on the proper workings of the COS organization.

[48] General Talk to Indian Officers of the Indian Army by Maj. Gen. K.M. Cariappa, September 1947, Part I, GROUP XXII, S.No. 9, Cariappa Papers, NAI, New Delhi, India. In a lecture given in September 1947, Cariappa asserted that officers would continue to be sent to attend courses in the UK and USA.

[49] Lt Gen. S.D. Verma, *To Serve with Honour: My Memories* (Kasauli: S.D. Verma), 1988, p. 74.

[50] Exchange of Officers between USA and India, WS 14070, BL, IOR/L/WS/1/827.

[51] Report of a Press Conference of Gen. Bucher, Commander-in-Chief, Indian Army, in *The Tribune*, 30 October 1948.

for cooperation on security matters were also explored again by India and Pakistan, when both States were prodded to consider setting up a joint defence arrangement in 1965. Although chimerical in its vision to establish a joint security force, the proposal reflected the eagerness with which each possibility was actively considered by all the sides concerned.[52]

The fact that the NDC borrowed certain institutional features from the British institutions shows that channels of inter-institutional knowledge transfer remained open throughout the post–Second World War years and after.[53] These channels were established through other foreign missions too (in collaboration with London), and in the fledgling years of post-War Indian foreign policy establishment, a cluster of middle-ranking Indian officers were given the opportunity to survey and study a wide range of military training, feeder, and other technical apprenticeship schools in Europe to offer suggestions on enhancing the efficacy of the military institutional network back in India.[54]

Thus, any examination of the conditions that necessitated the development of the NDC would have to shift the gaze to the pattern and nature of military institutionalization within India in a broader context.

[52] Letter from Lt Gen. Tuker to FM Ayub Khan, 18 November 1965, Document 4/7, 71/21/4, Lt Gen. Tuker Papers, IWM, London, UK.

[53] Several Indian vacancies were opened in a wide range of British Staff Colleges as well as Small Arms Schools after 1945. This was done knowing fully well the developing political situation in India, and while concerns about sharing sensitive knowledge remained, there was no official call made to forbid Indians from coming to train at higher military institutions such as the IDC. See, for instance, Minutes of a Meeting held at Horse Guards Parade on 4 April 1945 to discuss the organization of the post-War Staff Colleges, BL, IOR/L/WS/1/789.

[54] Officers like Col S.M. Shrinagesh, stationed at the Indian Military Mission in Berlin, Germany, and later chief of the army staff (1955–7), visited a large number of industries in addition to certain military instructional schools in Europe. See Letter from Chief, Indian Military Mission, Berlin, to War Staff India Office, 3 July 1946, BL, IOR/L/WS/1/807. Similarly, Maj. Batra, another Indian officer training at the Staff College in Britain, was offered the opportunity to make a liaison visit the US Staff College in Kansas. See Draft Telegram from the secretary of state for India to the GoI, War Dept, 9 February 1946, BL, IOR/L/WS/1/807.

Just as the late nineteenth-century institutional network laid the basis for the emergence of a higher training institution in the form of the IMA, which, in turn, provided the context for inter-service academies to appear on the horizon after 1945, it was the developing context of higher military institution-building practices and Indianization which can better explain the establishment of the NDC.

It is also critical to view the IDC's stance in the late 1940s because it sat at the forefront of the regional and international developments relating to security and defence, not least by virtue of the nature of its constitution. The NDC, too, borrowed certain organizational elements from the former. Institutions like the IDC were seen afresh in the establishment after the War in 1945.[55] The IDC's charter differed from the pre-War IDC 'in that it was no longer required to examine and report on the occasional concrete problem referred to it by the Chiefs of Staff'.[56] The onus now seemed to be on a holistic approach and, in the words of the IDC biographer, 'increasingly few of the lectures had a direct military connotation and more and more were concerned with the political, economic and scientific and sociological aspects of the world scene and their implications for defence'.[57]

This approach to international issues had an immediate resonance with the IDC mainly because of the speed with which they came to be taught and studied there. So, for instance, the military part of the syllabus was updated in the latter part of the 1950s and 1960s with

---

[55] Note on the Imperial Defence College, 1946 Course, GDFR 2/8, Capt. GA French Papers, Churchill Archives Centre, University of Cambridge, UK. The note details the formation of the IDC in 1927 and the role played by the inter-War years. It added that:

> During the interval between the two World Wars, much thought was devoted to improving the machinery for the higher direction of war. Churchill, who foresaw the future need for combined staffs, propounded the idea of a college where senior and carefully chosen officers of the fighting and civil services, drawn from all parts of the Empire should study jointly the problems and factors of the higher direction of British Commonwealth defence.

[56] Gray, *The Imperial Defence College and the Royal College of Defence Studies*, p. 14

[57] Gray, *The Imperial Defence College and the Royal College of Defence Studies*, p. 14.

the introduction of lectures on the North Atlantic Treaty Organization (NATO) and Disarmament. This amalgamated the IDC's twin roles of a higher defence institution and a place for discussing current policy issues with a specialist staff that did not necessarily comprise only academic practitioners, but military officers too.[58] This twin role also typified the journey and trajectory of the NDC and was central to its continued functioning in the years to come, suborning operational and political hurdles that came in order to integrate decision-making structures at the higher intergovernmental level.

The years after the Second World War were crucial for the IDC in London because a number of non-military subjects were introduced into the syllabus, 'indicative of the increasing swing away from the pre-War need for officers and officials to concentrate on the problems of the deployment of forces worldwide, towards the growing necessity to have as comprehensive a knowledge of the contemporary world as possible.'[59] This included delivering modules on the dominions wherein lectures on India, for instance, in the initial years, were delivered almost exclusively by high commissioners, the first being Mr Krishna Menon himself, later to be India's defence minister.

The evolving methods of instruction at IDC arising out of a changed international context for defence forces saw the dominions emerge as important players. They came to be regarded as critical areas of study in their own right, and generals who had served in the former colonies came to occupy an important place in the ways in which IDC stood to make sense of the post-War decades. The first post-War course had K.M. Cariappa as its student. In addition to the British generalship associated with the Southeast Asian command who lectured at IDC, P.M.S. Blackett, who later moved on as scientific advisor to the Indian prime minister, was also present 'representing the scientific profession'.[60]

[58] Gray, *The Imperial Defence College and the Royal College of Defence Studies*, p. 14.

[59] Gray, *The Imperial Defence College and the Royal College of Defence Studies*, p. 14.

[60] Gray, *The Imperial Defence College and the Royal College of Defence Studies*, p.16. The post-War years were crucial in carving out a distinctive identity for the IDC. No longer required to function as a purely military institution, it updated its syllabi in keeping with the changing position of the security

The similarities between the NDC and the amended charter of the IDC are notable.[61] Conceived as a higher training institution with interdisciplinary learning aims, the post-War amendment into the IDC charter defined the aim of the college as 'to help to fit selected members of the Armed Forces and Civil Service of the United Kingdom and the Commonwealth for high responsibilities in the field of defence.'[62] Subsequent amendments directed further changes to the college and the decade of the 1960s—which itself saw the emergence of multiple such colleges in other parts of the world—increased the international character of the IDC as it helped foster an international exchange of military officers.[63] Thus, the years leading up to the formation of the NDC are characteristic of a rich intellectual and organizational exchange of ideas defying a reductive approach in defining the development of higher military training architecture in India.

It was against this intellectual and organizational backdrop that India's defence minister, Krishna Menon, expressed his keenness to have an Indian defence college that could train senior Indian officers in adequate numbers. It was decided to institute a Parliamentary estimates committee attached to the Ministry of Defence in July 1958 and to review 'the whole policy of deputing military and civilian officers to the Imperial Defence College, London'.[64] The committee was aware of the training methodology imparted at London suggested that the

---

framework vis-à-vis Britain. All wartime service chiefs lectured at the IDC in the years following the Second World War, complemented by lectures on other non-military subjects relating to constitutional history, theology, and so on.

[61] Gray, *The Imperial Defence College and the Royal College of Defence Studies*, p. 8. Issues regarding syllabi and the curriculum were borrowed from the IDC as well the National Defence College of Canada and National War College in Washington, D.C., USA.

[62] Gray, *The Imperial Defence College and the Royal College of Defence Studies*, p. 23.

[63] Gray, *The Imperial Defence College and the Royal College of Defence Studies*, p. 23. Pakistan sent its first representative in 1950 as did the United States Department of State. In the 1960s, Nigeria, Jamaica, and Zambia sent their officers in 1961, 1964, and 1966, respectively. Hong Kong, Trinidad and Tobago, and Sierra Leone followed soon after in 1967–8.

[64] Bakshi and Mukherjee, *Lamp of Wisdom*, p. 5.

'feasibility of establishing a college in India on the pattern of the Imperial Defence College should, therefore, be considered'.[65] This proposal was approved by the Defence Committee of the cabinet in 1959 and the presidential sanction for setting up the college was issued shortly thereafter.[66]

This push for setting up of the college is often seen as a direct result of the limited number of vacancies at the London institution. However, the larger history of the movement to get the NDC is more than just about vacancies, as this chapter has argued throughout.

INDIAN OFFICERS AND THE 'SENIOR STAFF' AFTER 1947

The emergence of the NDC is incomplete without an examination of the larger context of the growing number of senior Indian officers that had begun to emerge at this time. In other words, it is important to illuminate the state of the military after Independence—its officers, to be precise—and identify the contours of this rapidly changing force. Such an exercise is important in order to highlight that the establishment of the NDC was necessitated by an expanding officer corps, for which it was imperative to provide higher training to mitigate future strategic challenges, and create a task force for higher armed formations and other joint military–diplomatic assignments.

A significant section of the Indian officers who began to earn commissions after 1919 saw their first combat engagement during the Second World War. A considerable number of them also went on to earn senior ranks in the post-Independence army. At least ten of them were appointed to the office of the chief of the army staff in successive years, with several retiring as senior general officers. In addition to the KCIOs, numbering about fifty and trained at Sandhurst from 1919 to 1934, there was also a large contingent of several hundred officers who had been trained at the newly instituted IMA from 1932.[67] By 1947,

65 Bakshi and Mukherjee, *Lamp of Wisdom*, p. 5.

66 Bakshi and Mukherjee, *Lamp of Wisdom*, p. 5.

67 Cited in, Steven I. Wilkinson, *Army and Nation: The Military and Indian Democracy since Independence* (Cambridge, MA, and London: Harvard University Press, 2015), p. 87.

Indian graduates of Sandhurst as well as the IMA had attained the ranks of lieutenant colonels and colonels, and the most senior among them were 'ready to move into the top command positions'.[68]

However, despite accelerating promotions for this middle-ranking officer cohort, there was still a substantial deficiency in the numbers of senior-ranking Indian officers who had had considerable combat and 'higher' staff experience. For instance, at the time of Independence and after the transfer of officers to each of the new dominions, 'only one of eight Major Generals, and none of the Lieutenant Generals had been Indian'.[69] Besides, only 5 per cent of the brigade and subarea commanders, and fewer than 10 per cent of the regimental and battalion commanders, had been Indian at Independence.[70] Indianization of the senior officer ranks carried imminent dangers as far as maintaining professional standards was concerned. More importantly, the issue at stake was not just in acquiring experienced officers but their greater participation in the higher levels of decision-making. As Nehru put it to Mountbatten, 'It was not merely a question of promotion but of association at high levels.'[71]

This post-Independence inheritance of officers was critical in the development of the NDC and represented the clear need to manage and synchronize the military's training needs at this time. 'Jointness in military operations'[72] had been the motif of the Second World War operations. The importance of 'jointsmanship' in training the military had been realized at the officer/cadet entry levels, but not at the senior or higher officer level. The NDC thus filled this gap that had existed

---

[68] Wilkinson, *Army and Nation*, p. 87.

[69] Wilkinson, *Army and Nation*, p. 86.

[70] Wilkinson, *Army and Nation*, p. 86.

[71] Pandit Nehru to Rear-Admiral Viscount Mountbatten of Burma, 11 July 1947, *TOP*, Volume XII, pp. 105–6. Nehru was interested in having more Indians associated with the Armed Forces Nationalisation Committee, which eventually included Thimayya on its board. The committee was instituted in January 1947 to look at the service-specific numbers of Indian officers in the armed forces and develop a scheme to augment those numbers. For details on the plans and formulations of the committee, please see Recommendations of the Armed Forces Nationalisation Committee, 1947, Gen. Thimayya Papers, NMML Archives, New Delhi, India.

[72] Bakshi and Mukherjee, *Lamp of Wisdom*, p. xix.

ever since 1947 on the issue of the training of senior officers in matters of national security. The NDC's arrival, therefore, needs to be contextualized in this broad reappraisal of the role of the Indian military that was given momentum after Independence during the domestic and international conflicts the Indian military was deployed in. Chief among them were the Kashmir conflict of 1947–8, the Hyderabad operation of 1948, as well as foreign missions such as the Neutral Nations Repatriation Commission (NNRC) of the early 1950s in Korea in which India played an active role as an international arbiter. The widely subscribed view of the NDC fostering a new culture of training for senior military as well as civilian officers masks a forgotten history of how the institution itself has been shaped by the experiences, conflicts, and management of events that took place almost a decade before the NDC's inauguration, paving the way for the formation of an intellectual context for the NDC to develop.

The intellectual context is important to make sense of the institutional innovation because it highlights the years in which the military and government underwent structural and organizational changes. It also portrays the NDC as a by-product of the decades of the 1940s and 1950s, which played a crucial role in the way the institution of the Indian Armed Forces and its mandate came to be envisaged. Therefore, in order to understand why the NDC shaped up the way it did, it is important to first understand what its constituency, that is, the senior military officers, was engaged in at this time.

Kashmir and Hyderabad, 1948

The accession of the princely states into the new Indian union after Independence provided one of the most formidable challenges to the government led by Prime Minister Nehru. Battling the ravages of Partition and communal riots, the integration of states was a crucial task to secure the newly constituted borders of the union. It was also considered a security issue, since quite a few of the princely states had not decided to merge with either of the two new nation-states. In the case of Hyderabad, where negotiations for accession were hitting a roadblock, and Kashmir, which faced an attack by Pakistan-backed tribal insurgents in 1947–8, the Indian authorities were compelled to take action through their armed forces to secure the accession of these two states and ward off foreign interference.

Part of the domestic and international foreign policy context in the management of these conflicts was laid down by Nehru's own ideas on the use of force. This percolated down to the military circles and the foreign policy establishment which he led during the years he was prime minister. Raghavan's incisive work on Nehru's foreign policy gives a ringside view of how crises were approached by the latter and his advisors.[73] The 'inter-departmental structures for decision-making',[74] however few present at the time of Independence, were under immense stress. This was compounded by the low numbers of experienced Indian senior GS at this time, aided in part by the insufficient numbers of Indian officers making it to the top ranks. Nonetheless, some crucial civil–military links were forged during the management of these conflicts. In the case of Hyderabad and Kashmir, the military acted in close cooperation with the civilian government and the strategy of resisting the invaders followed the policy laid down by the ministries in charge. This integrated strategy of planning laid the intellectual and academic groundwork for the establishment of the NDC in critical ways.

The actions of the military during these crises were not divorced from how the governmental establishment approached the issues at the time. It was the admixture of liberal and realist outlooks, Raghavan argues, 'that predisposed Nehru to favour coercive rather than controlling strategies', and a predilection 'for coupling military moves to pressurize the adversary with diplomatic ones to explore opportunities for a settlement'.[75] Such an approach laid the groundwork for a synthesis between military policy and the government in mitigating conflict scenarios.

In the case of accession of the Hyderabad state into the Indian union, military action followed a long and parlous round of negotiations between India and the princely state,[76] and force—when used

---

[73] Srinath Raghavan, *War and Peace in Modern India* (Delhi: Palgrave Macmillan, 2010).

[74] Raghavan, *War and Peace in Modern India*, p. 23.

[75] Raghavan, *War and Peace in Modern India*, p. 19.

[76] For a detailed account of the political negotiations, please see V.P. Menon, 'Hyderabad II', in *The Story of the Integration of the Indian States*, pp. 337–68 (Calcutta: Orient Longmans, 1956).

eventually—was measured and directed in close cooperation with Nehru and his top advisors.[77] Gen. J.N. Chaudhuri, who spearheaded the operation, provides an account of his role in the operation, but also gives a wider view of the civil–military liaison in this incident.[78] Chaudhuri's career bears testimony to the changing profile of the Indian Army in the years that he served. A graduate of Sandhurst and later the IDC, London, he also fought in the Second World War, and eventually retired as the chief of the army staff. Chaudhuri, like many Indian officers, had been rapidly promoted to take charge of the planning and staff positions that had become vacant after 1947. However, nothing could have prepared the officer for the challenges that lay ahead.

Chaudhuri's first posting, after Independence was in the planning division of the Army headquarters (AHQ) in Delhi and it took him little time to realize the challenges that Indianization posed to efficient working of the army in times of an emergency. Chaudhuri (then a brigadier) was posted to a staff position in the AHQ (his first so far) in 1947, but recounts the challenges in getting on with his newly assigned task of organizing a national territorial army through a barely functioning office and with an assistant holding the rank of a lieutenant colonel who had no experience in planning.[79]

Shortly thereafter, Chaudhuri was promoted to the rank of major general, and assigned command of an armoured division that had been selected to conduct operations against the Hyderabad State Forces. Chaudhuri's rapid promotion signalled that there was a shortage of senior officer cadre in the Indian Army at this time, and thus, it seemed

---

[77] Sarvepalli Gopal, *Jawaharlal Nehru: A Biography, Volume II—1947–1956* (New Delhi: Oxford University Press, 2012), pp. 38–42.

[78] B.K. Narayan, *General J.N. Chaudhuri: An Autobiography* (New Delhi: Vikas, 1978).

[79] Narayan, *General J.N. Chaudhuri*, p. 141. The plans for raising a national territorial army failed eventually, but Chaudhuri's account raised important questions on the issue of running and thinking anew about institutions. In his view, the plan failed primarily because they 'had little Indian experience to draw on' and the proposals were modelled on the British TA. The causes, however, went deeper. Central to the failure of the proposals was the absence of any mechanisms to procure weapons and equipment for this force, a trend that gathered pace only after the conflict with China in 1962.

necessary to promote certain officers rapidly who bore substantial experience at this time. The officer's account lends fulsome praise to the civilian establishment of the time, and a sizeable amount of that is spent on his close and amiable relationship with the then-home minister, Sardar Vallabhbhai Patel, during the course of the Hyderabad operation. Although the overall charge of the army at this time was in the hands of the commander-in-chief, Gen. Roy Bucher, Chaudhuri, as commander and later the military governor of Hyderabad, was in regular contact with both the military as well as the civilian heads of government.

Nehru's reliance on diplomacy to mitigate conflict meant that military manoeuvres had to be carried out subtly so as not to wreck the delicate negotiations that were being carried out with the nawab of Hyderabad. However, the fact that Chaudhuri had already been appointed commander of a force that was to be used in the operation meant that steps needed to be taken to operationalize and deploy the division, a time-consuming process, without which only a false sense of readiness could have been relayed to the Indian government were it to suddenly order military action. This, according to the general, is what eventually happened when the order to mount an armed attack came through from New Delhi. While the orders for mobilization came, the government continually pressed the deployment of the troops down south. The GS, on the other hand, resisted deployment near Hyderabad for reasons of re-equipping and training the Division. While this tussle over deployment between the largely British officered GS and the Indian government was resolved in favour of deployment (signalling the government's dominance), it nonetheless puts Chaudhuri in a tight spot, which impeded his mobility for a long time.[80]

S.D. Verma, the officer who played a key role in setting up the Staff College, also briefly officiated as the commander of the Armoured Division that was to carry out Operation Polo, the codename for the Hyderabad operation. Verma contends that as military commander, he had to regularly inform his units about the policy action that was being contemplated in order to reinforce that the operation was not being conducted in 'some foreign land'.[81] The aim of the operation, Verma

---

[80] Narayan, *General J.N. Chaudhuri*, p. 150.

[81] Lt Gen. S.D. Verma, *To Serve with Honour: My Memoirs* (Kasauli: S.D. Verma, 1988), p. 66.

added, was to 'relieve the civilian population' and that no 'misbehaviour' against the residents would be allowed.[82] However, later operations suggested otherwise, as the military did engage in heavy-handed campaigns to dislodge communists and detained thousands of people.[83] Moreover, the military's attempts to aid in the deportation and/or repatriation of non-Indian Muslims during the operation frequently brought the military into the evolving debates between informal understandings of belonging and the more formal legal interpretations of citizenship.[84] Verma's efforts to reinforce the changed principles of a military campaign onto his troops, and the subsequent events in the campaign prove that the nature of armed operations in a domestic context had begun to change. The Hyderabad operations reflected the significant non-military contexts in which the armed forces were required to function and mitigate challenges, bringing the latter into the domain of popular politics interspersed with questions of belonging and political ideology.

The military action in Hyderabad was the final measure that the government took after multiple rounds of negotiations failed to resolve the dispute. Chaudhuri's challenge in trying to convince the civilian structures of the government of the need to have a machinery to prevent law and order problems—anticipated also by Verma—points to the early linkages between government agencies that needed to be developed in times of conflicts. The difficulty may have had more to do with limited organization resources and less with the alleged apathy or indifference of the government. Since Independence, the acute shortage of troops and officers had serious implications for the internal security during Partition, and this shortage affected the military's capability in assisting the civilian authorities in effectively countering the communal violence and other operations, to establish a credible security framework.

Gradually, an integrated task force began to be formed that comprised officials from the civilian, medical, police, and engineering

---

[82] Verma, *To Serve with Honour*, p. 66.

[83] Taylor C. Sherman, 'The Integration of the Princely State of Hyderabad and the Making of the Postcolonial State in India, 1948–1956', *Indian Economic and Social History Review* vol. 44, no. 4 (2007): 489–516.

[84] Taylor C. Sherman, 'Migration, Citizenship and Belonging in Hyderabad (Deccan), 1948–1956', *Modern Asian Studies* vol. 45, no. 1 (2011): 81–107.

branches of the government that would work in tandem with the military force and bolster internal security.[85] Chaudhuri, who had also been acting as the chief of general staff by this time, attests to the joint meetings that took place, in which representatives from the home and state ministries sat alongside chief secretaries and inspector generals of police to understand the workings of each other's respective domains, reflecting the interdependent nature of conflict management that the NDC later imbibed as one of its core intellectual and training objectives.

The 1948 conflict in Kashmir presented similar challenges. A Muslim-majority princely state ruled by a Hindu king and contiguous to the boundaries of Pakistan and India—with immense geographical and strategic features—presented itself as a conflict for the two newly independent countries. The king's prevarication over joining either India or Pakistan, after signing an interim 'Standstill Agreement', compounded the political crises, leading to an intrusion of armed tribal gangs from the northwest to invade the state and present a fait accompli to the Indian authorities.[86] The civil–military management of the 1948 'war' extended well beyond its immediate scope, and provided an additional layer of context to understand how the emerging corpus of senior Indian GS and officer ranks proceeded to manage the conflict.

The geographical location of the Kashmir valley presented a challenge for the Indian forces to effectively mount an operation against the raiders, and the precarious land routes of the state with the rest of the country meant that a large number of troops had to be airlifted into Kashmir.[87] Notwithstanding the limited infrastructure for the airlift and the ongoing conflict in Hyderabad state, the management required an intensive collaboration of the military with the government. Unlike the Hyderabad case, Nehru felt that unilateral concessions in Kashmir would not result in a resolution, and unless 'India drove home the costs of continued military action', the attackers could not be compelled to desist.[88] Thus, a more aggressive military stance had to be developed

[85] V.P. Menon, *The Story of the Integration of the Indian States*, (Calcutta: Orient Longmans, 1956), pp. 377–9.

[86] Menon, *The Story of the Integration of the Indian States*, p. 395

[87] Humphrey Evans, *Thimayya of India: A Soldier's Life* (Dehradun: Natraj Publishers, 1988), p. 266.

[88] Raghavan, *War and Peace in Modern India*, p. 123.

in addition to the negotiations, and this involved training and arming an outfit of 'irregulars' in Kashmir to combat the guerrilla tactics of the raiders.[89]

During April–May 1948, Gen. Thimayya proved to be a key military figure in the Kashmir war and succeeded Maj. Gen. Kalwant Singh in the Jammu and Kashmir Force, which was split into two commands, with Thimayya taking charge of the Srinagar division.[90] Thimayya, a KCO from Sandhurst and Quetta (and later commandant of the NDA), came to regard his Kashmir experience in exceptional terms. The officer regarded the battle as a 'combination of jungle and mountain warfare', and disregarded the heavily publicized role of artillery because of the geographical location of the raiders, who had come to occupy an elevated terrain as opposed to the grounded Indian forces.[91] Apart from the one-off airlift of the troops, he also discounted the use of air power since the enemy were largely dug-in, and much of the tactics was 'solid infantry work'.[92]

The operations in Kashmir went a long way in reinforcing the need to educate and train the earliest cohort at the NDC in the art of jointsmanship in warfare. Moreover, Thimayya's experience in Kashmir, interestingly, gave rise to another institutional innovation immediately after the hostilities were paused in the valley. The difficulties experienced in mountain warfare compelled Thimayya and his staff to propose the establishment of a training facility in high-altitude warfare for soldiers,[93] and bore important and unnoticed lessons that the military learnt after the conflict.[94] Thus, the NDC's emergence, which the institutional or official biography sees in the context of the Kashmir operations, had at least one immediate and

---

[89] 'Letter to Baldev Singh (Defence Minister) on Kashmir, 22 April 1948', in *SWJN*, Volume 6, Second Series, ed. S. Gopal, pp. 177–9.

[90] Menon, *The Story of the Integration of the Indian States*, p. 411.

[91] Evans, *Thimayya of India*, p. 270

[92] Evans, *Thimayya of India*, p. 271.

[93] Brig. C.B. Khanduri, *Thimayya: An Amazing Life* (New Delhi: Knowledge World, 2006) p. 139.

[94] Khanduri, *Thimayya*, p. 139. A smaller facility called the Division Ski School was eventually started with the aid of the pre-existing Ski Club of India. This facility eventually laid the foundation for the much larger institution, The High Altitude Warfare School in Gulmarg, Kashmir, India.

additional institutional development in fortifying the military's training regimen.

These early but important signs of cooperation between the military and civilian government during the Kashmir and Hyderabad operations signalled the 'institutional gap' that existed in training senior officers in the principles of higher direction of war, who until the NDC's emergence, learnt these principles 'on the job'. The NDC, thus, emerged at a point in time when the need for such an institution was being acutely felt, even though it was not consistently expressed. The small group of Indian officers at the time of Independence, who had been rapidly promoted to senior ranks, had experience of combat and tactics, but their familiarity with higher management of conflict was inadequate.

Korea, 1953

An example of the more strident foreign policy context, and the role played by senior Indian officers with regard to their roles and responsibilities after 1947, is provided by the events relating to the NNRC in Korea. The NNRC was formed in 1953 in the aftermath of the Korean Armistice Agreement that was signed after the Korean War. The NNRC's mandate was to repatriate and/or settle all those prisoners of war (POWs) who had refused to repatriate to either the North or South Korean states as they stood after 1953. The international interest in the crisis, combined with political overtones of the Cold War (the North Koreans were backed by the Chinese and the Soviets and the South Koreans were supported by the US-led faction), meant that only a neutral country could have been approached for arbitration. India's avowed non-aligned foreign policy posture allowed it to assume charge of the repatriation commission in order to work with the opposing camps to peacefully settle or repatriate refugees and prisoners of the Korean War.[95]

Although Thimayya was assigned as the chairperson of the NNRC, he did not arrive in Korea alone. Initial planning on India's proposed role suggests that Nehru was considering appointing a military officer as the Indian representative along with a political

[95] Heimsath and Mansingh, *A Diplomatic History of Modern India*, p. 72.

advisor.[96] Subsequently, India provided a 'custodian force', roughly the size of a brigade comprising three battalions and an ancillary staff,[97] under the charge of another officer, Lt Gen. S.P.P. Thorat, who would later retire as senior commander and member of the National Defence Council. The force, called the Custodian Force India (CFI), arrived in Korea complete with its retinue of engineer and infantry units along with a sizeable field ambulance and medical team.[98]

The sheer international implications of repatriating refugees back to states who stood on opposing sides of the Cold War camps meant that India had to tread a fine line on adjudicating over various issues relating to the conflict. The conflict had critical legal, political, and international ramifications, and came to be governed by a set of injunctions drafted by the United Nations, in accordance with articles pertaining to the Geneva Convention. Therefore, India's participation in the arbitration processes and attendance at political conferences on Korea were keenly watched not just by the Americans and the United Nations, but also the Chinese, each of whom had different views on the manner in which India was to adjudicate over repatriation.[99] The 'terms of reference', as they came to be called, provided the mandate to the NNRC to essentially explain to the prisoners their rights relating to their repatriation or settlement in a country of their choice. The terms of reference also laid out the procedure of the member states as to how these explanations to the refugees would be carried out.[100]

---

[96] Outward Telegram from the Commonwealth Relations Office to UK High Commissioner in India (Acting), 1 July 1953, File FO 371/105507, TNA, Kew, UK.

[97] K.C. Praval, *Indian Army after Independence* (New Delhi: Lancer International, 1987), p. 152.

[98] Khanduri, *Thimayya*, p. 163. Khanduri states that the entire CFI establishment comprised initially of a brigade. This brigade consisted of three field ambulance units, five infantry units, and a unit each of the postal, engineering, and field workshops. This entire contingent was also assisted by joint Red Cross Teams.

[99] See File FO 371/105533, Efforts to arrange a post-armistice political conference on Korea, TNA, Kew, UK.

[100] The complications arising out of the processes of educating the refugees about the intricacies of repatriation have been discussed in greater details by K.C. Praval in his account. See Praval, *Indian Army After Independence*, pp. 155–61.

It took little time for the situation to develop complications. The selective interpretations made by the member states with regard to the NNRC terms inhibited the efficient functioning of the body, giving way to acrimonious discussions between the Korean-Chinese and the United Nations's commands over the release of prisoners.[101] The gaps created in understanding the processes were swiftly filled in by Cold War rivalries and created a 'mountain of recrimination, vituperation, charges and counter-charges', causing a 'repeat of the days of the long war that caused some 300,000 casualties'.[102] Some of the conflicts were about the actual terms of engagement for the prisoners, outlining the procedure for explanation teams to approach the refugees without precipitating violence or clashes which were a frequent feature during the proceedings.[103]

All these prevailing conflicts and tensions over the precise inter-pretations of the document presented a unique non-military context in which the Indian Armed Forces were deployed. Mirroring the experience of the Kashmir and Hyderabad conflict, in which hitherto unpractised forms of warfare were learnt, the NNRC experience was a formidable diplomatic assignment for the Indian forces which rep-resented a steep learning curve. Thimayya found himself surrounded by a diverse cast of civilian government and security officials: civil servants (B.N. Chakravarty, served as the alternate NNRC chairman); Indian diplomats (P.N. Haksar); and an officer from the Indian Police Service who served at the NNRC. The Indian Armed Forces's stint in Korea—complete with its newly emerging corps of senior-level and middle-level officers—represented a group of officers who passively learnt a great deal about the management of international conflicts that involved a substantive monitoring of certain associated legal, political, and humanitarian aspects related to warfare.

---

[101] Lt Gen. S.P.P. Thorat, *From Reveille to Retreat* (New Delhi: Allied Publishers, 1986), pp. 156–7.

[102] Khanduri, *Thimayya*, p. 171.

[103] Khanduri, *Thimayya*, pp. 169–71. Paragraph 3 of the terms of refer-ence suggested that no amount of force could be used against the prisoners for their repatriation process. However, over the question of prisoners who refused explanation consistently for fear of retribution or anything else, it was 'perforce agreed that minimum force should be used'.

The NNRC experience was a microcosm of the changed operational and institutional ecology which the Indian Armed Forces and its officers inhabited. It did not necessarily involve combat but involved 'peace-making' and 'peace-keeping'. The subsequent international peace-keeping operational deployments of the Indian Army in Africa and Middle East would become increasingly apparent in later years.The NNRC, though, represented the first such non-combatant experience for the Indian Armed Forces, and it was central to the development of the NDC, which later enshrined these international intergovernmental policy making encounters in its academic components. Thus, the Korean experience helped underscore the need for the establishment of higher training institutions such as the NDC.

LATER ACADEMIC AND ADMINISTRATIVE ISSUES

The initial years of the NDC, after it was established in 1960, highlight the struggles that the new institution made in the post-Independence phase of military reorganization and Indianization. From the discussions on its role and mandate to something plainly administrative issues like its construction and land transfer, each episode in the life of the NDC uncovers an important part of its history and the linkages it developed with the government as it negotiated each turn in its fortunes. Krishna Menon, India's defence minister, who attended the NDC's inauguration along with the prime minister, warned that 'the National Defence College should not become a carbon copy of these institutions [IDC and the Defence College of Canada], but evolve as per the needs of the Indian situation and context'.[104]

The 1962 conflict with China placed the college in a broader context of military policy vis-à-vis governmental policies on military reorganization. It also highlighted the urgency with which the government approached questions of national security. Institutionally, this was also evident in the formation of a National Defence Council in 1962. The council comprised senior retired and serving officers of the armed forces who were entrusted with the task to advise the government on all aspects of the security situation arising out of the 1962 conflict.[105]

---

[104] Bakshi and Mukherjee, *Lamp of Wisdom*, p. 11.

[105] Subject File No. 9, Lt Gen. S.P.P.Thorat Papers, NMML, Delhi, India, Report in the *Times of India*, 4 November 1962.The council included five

The formation of the council was accompanied by instituting parallel consultative structures within the defence ministry to mitigate the threat posed by the Chinese in the northeastern frontier. This resulted in approaching senior retired officers, such as Gen. Thimayya and Lt Gen. S.P.P. Thorat among others, to serve in the ministry in advisory capacities.[106]

The fact that the NDC was established in the 1960s made it unrealistic to expect immediate dividends from an institution whose true worth can only be measured in successive decades. Since the 1960s, the college has produced senior-ranking military officers and civil servants who have come to occupy high offices in national and international fora. However, a critical appraisal of the 1960s—the decade of its establishment—is crucial for understanding the public and domestic context in which decisions concerning the NDC came to be taken. It comes across as a site where an ever-widening circle of middle-ranking and senior-ranking officers with varied operational and managerial skills were sought to be brought together to link the industrial, economic, and administrative decision-making structures of the country.

Issues of command and control were central to the constitution of the college. During the years of its initial functioning as well as well into the 1970s and 1980s, the college grappled with the precise character it was supposed to have. The debate between being a higher military institution or a research centre (or both) seemed to be the lynchpin for the institution's successive growth story. Each new decade in the NDC's history brought forth similar issues of academic and organizational control, but the kernel for each new dilemma was rooted in the unresolved or rather the unresolvable dichotomy that was inherent in higher military institutions of the Indian military.

---

union ministers besides Jawaharlal Nehru, five state chief ministers, the Kashmir premier, three COSs, four retired officers of the defence forces, five officials, and seven non-officials. The four retired officers were Gen. Rajendra Sinhji, Gen. K.S. Thimayya, Vice Admiral R.D. Katari, and Lt Gen. S.P.P. Thorat. The council's functions were essentially 'to take stock of the situation and arrange for national defence, and advise the govt on matters relating to national defence'.

[106] Report in *The Statesman*, 23 November 1962, also present in Lt Gen. S.P.P. Thorat Papers, NMML Archives, Delhi, India.

The official account dwells at length on the multiple schools of thought that viewed the college differently. A section among these numerous governmental circles thought of instituting a civilian principal and faculty—akin to the NDA—to direct the wide-ranging diversity of subjects that were being taught at the NDC. This was in contrast to the military view which stressed the necessity of having a directing staff to guide students, most of whom would be military officers, which would ensure that the 'military aspect was not lost in theoretical abstractions and generalizations.'[107] This eventually gave rise to the mixed approach where a selection of civilian directing staff drawn from the civil and foreign services coexisted with the military directing staff.

This tussle between the college's role and identity on whether to be a research institution or a purely defence training institution continued further when the discussions on adding a civil degree to the NDC qualification, which would augment the 'value of the NDC in the literary circles', took place.[108] The proposal for awarding an master of philosophy (MPhil) degree at the end of the course was taken up since the early 1970s with different universities like the University of Allahabad and the Delhi-based Jawaharlal Nehru University, but the matter did not progress further. It was during Gen. Manekshaw's tenure as chief of the army staff (1969–73), who also served as the commandant of the Staff College earlier, that the issue of affiliation for military academies was taken up more actively.

Manekshaw's insistence on equating 'examinations the service man passes' with 'university equivalents' was thought to have had an 'incidental side benefit', which was that 'the retired serviceman could boast of a civil degree, the chief requirement for job seekers…'.[109] The initial proposal, as one of his biographies suggests, was to

> [e]quate graduation at the National Defence Academy with a Bachelor's degree; graduation at the Defence Services Staff College with a Master's degree; and successful completion of the National Defence College

[107] Bakshi and Mukherjee, *Lamp of Wisdom*, p.15.
[108] Bakshi and Mukherjee, *Lamp of Wisdom*, p.144.
[109] Lt Gen. Depinder Singh, *Field Marshal Sam Manekshaw, M.C.: Soldiering with Dignity* (Dehradun: Natraj Publishers, 2002), p. 79.

with a Ph.D. Likewise, lower examinations could also be equated with corresponding school certificates.[110]

Although the proposal did not see light of day while the general served in his office, it acquired an institutional after-life, in which the other academies like the Staff College and the NDA continuously worked to get civilian affiliation. Manekshaw's tenure also envisioned the prospect of granting study leave to officers so they could 'seek admission to colleges and universities to obtain higher education, to benefit both the service and the individual'.[111]

The NDC's quest to be regarded as a research space meant that it had to align its academic structures in accordance with existing university regulations. However, its profound military character and the charter stood in the way. Hence, securing autonomy for the NDC as a research institution was perceived to be the solution. The eventual commencement of the MPhil programme from 2006 (as mentioned in the biography) happened after awarding autonomous status to the institution under the affiliating arrangements of the University of Madras.[112] This gave the NDC the flexibility to design its own courses, control the curriculum, and devise its own evaluation protocols. The Board of Studies and the Academic Council comprised the senior military directing staff and other faculty members nominated by the commandant of the NDC, a lieutenant general or equivalent in the air force or navy, in addition to a representative by the university.[113] This autonomous arrangement for the NDC within university regulations provides insights into the constant sense of dilemma that is inherent in military institutions wishing to incorporate principles of a civilian or non-military higher research facility, but which also wanted to retain their essential mandate to provide a professional military education to their officer ranks.

This complex partnership with civilian universities, however, raises more questions than it answers about the ways in which Indian military institutions have allied with civilian universities in the past.

---

[110] Singh, *Field Marshal Sam Manekshaw, M.C.*, pp. 79–80.
[111] Singh, *Field Marshal Sam Manekshaw, M.C.*, p. 80.
[112] Bakshi and Mukherjee, *Lamp of Wisdom*, p. 148.
[113] Bakshi and Mukherjee, *Lamp of Wisdom*, pp. 146–7.

The more recent discussions on the imminent establishment of the Indian National Defence University, which intends to subsume existing military training institutions under its command, will provide an interesting view into this complex phenomenon. Civilian recognition for military academic coursework also highlights the need that is felt by military institutions to fit into the larger academic framework that can recognize and give due academic credit to the study undertaken at these institutions.

The NDC reflected a changed institutional landscape for the Indian military and its officers. Marking a generational shift in the ranks of Indian officers, the earliest of whom came after the First World War with a higher commissioned rank, the NDC was a milestone in the Indianization narrative. Starting from the initial struggle to reorganize the late nineteenth-century military feeder network to the early twentieth-century constitutional tussles for an Indian Sandhurst and the post-Independence establishment of the NDA, the establishment of the NDC was, and remains, the highest stage for officer training in India, and could well be regarded as the denouement of the Indianization narrative of the Indian military seen through the prism of its diverse set of officers' training institutions.

Conclusion

This book has highlighted an important but forgotten aspect of the Indian military that has escaped the attention of historians. By focussing on the emergence and evaluation of the officers' academies and training institutions of the Indian military, I have tried to argue for a more differentiated yet comprehensive view of the Indian military. This view offers an alternative perspective on the Indianization and institution-building processes of the military, by examining its 'building blocks'—the sites where the constituency of the military, that is, officers and cadets, were trained, socialized, and, after 1947, aligned and infused with the distinct ethos of nationhood.

Studying the Indian military academies and feeder institutions provides a new and additional layer of understanding about the armed forces that have played a long and important role in the defence of the subcontinent. If anything, the importance of the Indian military in the defence and security domain during the years after Independence, has only increased and given rise to a significant body of scholarly literature dealing with the various operational, tactical, and strategic contexts in which the Indian military has been deployed.

Even as the Indian Armed Forces have had a significant presence in the wider military historiography, focussing on the tactical and operational aspects of its deployment, the view that this historiography has offered to us is only partial. This is because the historiography overlooks a wide range of institutions that have lent a distinctive influence on the ways in which the military transitioned through the latter half of the twentieth century. The first military academies and feeder schools in the subcontinent appeared towards the end of the nineteenth century, and since then, they have been a regular and integral feature of the institutionalization and Indianization of the military as it progressed through the years of the first half of the twentieth century. However, in most historical accounts of this defence organization, the academies have been relegated to a corner. Never fully apparent, but visible from the sidelines, the academies are an inseparable element of the history of the Indianization, professionalization, and development of the Indian military.

Institutional innovation in the Indian military has gone hand in hand with other momentous events that it has witnessed. The earliest wave of armed conflict for the Raj in the mid-nineteenth century resulted in the setting up of feeder colleges and schools along India's northwestern region, and later, with the advent of the First and Second World Wars, policy discussions for more central and formal academies began in earnest. It is, thus, surprising, that despite such a historic time-frame, ranging from the late nineteenth century until the post-Independence decades, during which the Indian military took part in some important armed conflicts, not much has been reflected on the 'structures' through which the organization officered itself.

While references to the IMA or the Indian Sandhurst do occur in Indian history writing, a more nuanced view of the architecture of the Indian military can be conceived only by documenting the larger historical processes of institution-building that had been taking place long before the IMA was inaugurated in 1932. The story of the missing academies of the Indian military, the metaphor with which this volume's first chapter began, should be traced back to the late nineteenth century. It is a period when policy measures for Indianization were advocated not just by Indian officials, but crucially, also by members of the Viceroy's Executive Council and officers from the Indian Army, thereby questioning the conventional analyses which often attribute all military reform solely to the actions of the nationalist Indian leaders and blames the slow pace of Indianization mainly on colonial indifference.

The interconnected nature of military Indianization and institution-building can be brought into focus by integrating colonial and post-Independence periods. Such an approach illuminates the successive waves of reform, review, and expansion that swept across the military's training spaces, and significantly affected the manner in which Indian officers were commissioned. By bringing together periods of the colonial and post-colonial government, a broad canvas of military institutionalization becomes apparent, which enables us to understand the contingent, often contradictory, and chaotic policy-led measures that gave rise to these academies and determined their training and educational practices. This time period contextualizes the advent of these military institutions within the larger framework of the domestic and international political climate, and illuminates the changes in the official visions that guided the formation of these institutions.

Military Indianization, as a political issue of the early twentieth century, cannot be wholly understood without studying the actual institutional mechanisms or the 'hardware' through which Indianization was to take place. Protracted arguments and debates in the legislative assembly in the twentieth century mask the precise administrative and institutional challenges that were met in the wake of replacing British officers with Indian ones. These challenges carried over from the late nineteenth century when the feeder training institutions of the military first encountered problems relating to the training of a diverse and disparate group of prospective military officers. The nature of these problems magnified in the subsequent century, when higher officers' academies came to be developed, partly to satisfy nationalist demands for more rapid Indianization, but also to shore up the Raj's security framework.

In addressing the educational needs of those who wanted to join the military, a considerable broadening of the scope of Indianization took place, and it significantly impacted the character and pace of the process of replacing British officers with Indians. Policies and measures implemented to reorganize the existing educational programmes, and the sites at which these programmes were delivered, were aimed at reviewing the educational arrangements of precisely those who were meant to replace the British officers in larger numbers. Thus, Indianization policies were intimately linked with patterns of military institution-building in India, and this link was first evident in the early regional network of military feeder academies of the late nineteenth century.

By the early twentieth century, this link tying up Indianization along with the administrative challenges of military institution-building was becoming clearer. The link between Indianization and the sites where Indianization was actually carried out also meant that the quantitative increase in Indianization, that is, the demand for acquiring more Indian officers, would have to be carried out alongside a qualitative assessment of those who would go on to Indianize the military. This qualitative assessment was related to the examination and re-evaluation of the existing military educational practices at institutions that were engaged in preparing countless Indian 'gentlemen' into principles of officership. Thus, policies of institutional upgradation, overhauling the feeder networks, and exploring ways to connect professional military educational modules with civilian spaces of higher learning, came to be pursued almost at the same time as the beginning of the discourse of Indianization. This intertwined nature of military institution-building was in full display with the emergence of officers' academies of the twentieth century, but its roots lay in the preceding century. Therefore, twentieth-century Indianization was a two-faced policy discourse that aimed to refashion and reformulate the process of the replacement of British officers.

The IMA's emergence in 1932 marked a break from former military institutional developments in India, as it was the first commission-awarding facility to appear in the subcontinent. The IMA's immediate constitutional and legislative provenance, however, lay in the RTC held in London in 1931, a meeting which has since been studied largely for its political consequences but hardly at all for the significant military implications that followed. The conference paved the way for the committee to review the fractious issues of commissions and regiment-based Indianization, as well as the recruitment policies towards different communities like the Anglo-Indians, in order to arrive at an institutional solution that had the potential to transform the nature of Indianization that had been pursued until 1931. The conference and consultative committees formed to plan the IMA's establishment laid bare the political fault lines, not just within the Indian political opinion but also between academicians, military officers, and the princes, with respect to military institution-building. It highlighted the multidimensional and differently motivated agendas that worked in tandem with these consultative committees instituted to review military institutional reform.

Contrary to most assumptions about this development, the academy was not implanted onto the Indian landscape. It took elaborate negotiations to decide on the precise form and constitution of the 'Indian

Sandhurst', which punctured the claims of any sort of Indian political unity on military issues at this time. Besides, the institutional experiences in administering the IMA and its training and cadet induction policies, derived much from the manner in which the pre-existing military network of the Raj functioned. It has been easily overlooked that the IMA was born out of the interactions and experiences of administering and examining a vast network of regional, feeder network of colleges and institutions that were set up in the late nineteenth and early twentieth centuries, and this same network was again reorganized in the wake of the IMA's emergence, testifying to the interconnected nature of military Indianization and institution-building in the subcontinent.

Transformations in the inter-service aspect of the Indian military set the terms for the next phase of institution-building that commenced after the Second World War. This phase was marked by the inauguration of inter-service military institutions in India after 1947: the NDA in 1949, and later, the NDC in 1960. However, it is important to highlight that this turn in the process of setting up newer academies was not an exclusive by-product of the post-Independence scenario.

Much of the planning for these higher military institutions took place in the years after the Second World War, when changing principles of warfare combined with the need to reorganize and enhance the value of a military education to officers, resulted in the creation of these inter-service institutions. These higher military spaces symbolized India's self-reliance on maintaining a hold over the production, delivery, and sharing of strategic-military knowledge by producing a set of skilled and holistically trained military officers. But it is important to point out the shared and diffusionist international contexts in which ideas for such academies emerged in India.

The NDA, inaugurated in 1949 and built largely on the lines of the United States Military Academy at West Point, came to be regarded as the 'Indian West Point', much like the 'Indian Sandhurst' years ago. However, the NDA's future institutional trajectory belied this easy christening. Started as a primary entry-level institution for cadets to train in a three-year undergraduate inter-service collegiate education, it replaced the IMA as the flagship programme for training for prospective officers. Consequently, the IMA then became a solely service-specific training arm for the Indian Army that recruited its own cadets but also trained the graduates of the NDA for commissions.

The NDA's own history mirrored the changed principles of defence organization in India. The division of the Indian Army into three separate units—army, navy, and air force—after 1947, each under a full general or equivalent officer, meant that the inclusion of newer stakeholders into the now national enterprise of setting up a new academy would be a far more layered, if not complicated affair than before. This trifurcation of the armed services raised as many concerns as the numerous objectives they were meant to fulfil. A devolved and divided military force (in addition to the Indian paramilitary contingents: not the focus of this book) guaranteed the promise of a civilian government's supremacy in the Indian polity. However, it also kept the military from speaking and acting in a unified voice on matters that concerned them because it fractured authority and created semi-autonomous voices of official military opinion on several matters, none of which could completely override or suppress the other. The multiplicity of official opinion on military institutional reform, therefore, further complicated the post-Independence character of military institution-building.

The character and compositional ideas about the NDA marked a break from those that shaped the IMA a decade earlier, reflecting the subtle sociological changes that were beginning to inform post-Independence ideas about Indianization. Cast as the Sandhurst generation, the outward and ostensibly American sensibilities of the NDA sat at odds with the supposedly old English air of the officers and officialdom that had given birth to the IMA. Modelled primarily on the lines of an American academy, the NDA was seen in various quarters to be a more modern military university enclave.

The differences in the modes through which the higher military institutional network was conceptualized in India after 1947 needs to be studied through the prism of changing visions underlying the development and management of the training and educational needs of a growing cadre of Indian officers. Service-specific conditions and inter-service turf wars make for an interesting case study of the earliest years of the NDA. Notions of the ideal cadet and the location of the academy and its educational and founding principles, all gave rise to a multiple debates between the newly organized military and the central and state governments in India, reflecting the impact of the historical centre–state–military triangulation on military institution-building practices in the subcontinent.

The post-Independence context, marked by State-centred institution-building patterns, helped give a nationalist aura to the newer academies, such as the NDA and NDC, as they managed to capture a part of the imagination of a wide cross-section of the public, professional, and political spheres. This also partially explains why the academies of the post-1947 years attracted a more lively editorial coverage and journalistic reportage as compared to the earlier set of institutions. The growth in the popular coverage of military academies after 1947, examining the various aspects relating to training and education testified to the widening circle of interest for military issues in the subcontinent. Yet, the ideas behind these institutions charted a longer historical journey and often challenged the statist conceptions which marked their early years of functioning.

The establishment of the NDC in 1960 marked the highest stage of institutional development for officer training in India. Contrary to the official accounts of the institution, the NDC was also a part of a larger wave of institutional reform and Indianization that gathered greater speed after 1947, but whose roots lie in the same late nineteenth-century efforts to afford a greater degree of representation to the Indian Army.

The NDC's conception reflected the changed principles of crisis management and security imperatives in India. Its remit did not remain restricted to the armed forces but expanded considerably to include the civil and diplomatic services, which elevated the national discourse around security and policy issues to the status of a shared enterprise. The NDC started out with the aim of training the nascent group of middle-ranking and senior-ranking officers of the military in higher staff, command, and related appointments. The NDC's emergence, therefore, capped an organizational churning within the military after 1947. This organizational churning within the military now demanded the latter to seek insights into conflict management and resolution from a variety of non-military contexts in order to synchronize the appreciation and mitigation of strategic threats and challenges to the country.

The events ranging from the Kashmir and Hyderabad conflicts, to the diplomatic engagements of the NNRC, set up after the

1950 Korean War, exposed the Indian Armed Forces to multiple organizational and occupational demands, thereby also delivering a significant degree of operational experience for the forces. Thus, the NDC not only developed the inter-service operational acumen of the armed forces but also came across as a site that could potentially make available a pedagogic and academic corpus of knowledge of the previous decades' experiences in managing conflict. The NDA and the NDC, thus, represented, with varying degrees of interest and institutional mandate, the need to deliver specialized military knowledge in an environment of service cooperation between the different armed wings in association with the civilian structures of government.

Bonds between the military and the State share a deep institutional covalence in the twentieth century. These bonds were first made visible in the formation of the earliest network of feeder training colleges, whose struggles and challenges in training the Raj's prospective military officers, coincided with the initial demands to make the Indian Army more open to Indian officers. Gradually, as the constitutional status of India began to move closer towards self-rule and nationhood appeared imminent, these bonds resurfaced again in the wake of the reorganization of the higher military training architecture. By the mid-twentieth century, the feeder training colleges were determining the institutional trajectories of the later officers' academies, and also the latter's interactions with a diverse cast of Indian 'gentlemen' who came forward to become 'officers'.

This cast of Indian men came from different sociocultural backgrounds, which these academies trained and commissioned in increasing numbers, to rapidly place them in lieu of British officers in India. But while this replacement took place, a parallel wave of reform aimed at providing a robust educational programme to these officers also gathered steam and aligned itself closely with the process of Indianization and institution-building processes. The reorganization of officer training occurred in the context of the changing occupational mandate of the Indian military, and this process determined the institutional contours of each new military academy that came up in the subcontinent in the period under discussion in this book. Hence, Indianization processes functioned in close collaboration with certain military institutional practices; to study the former without looking at the latter is to study the military's transition through the twentieth century only partially.

Studying military academies historically is crucial to understand the manner in which governments and military authorities engaged with each other to address the simultaneous demands of acquiring more Indian officers and exploring ways to offer a relevant course of instruction that could safeguard Indianization by commissioning well-trained officers ready for a career in the military service; a service whose terms of operations were constantly changing.

This volume, therefore, links matters of training policy with the more familiar politically driven demands that took up the case of the Indian officers from the early twentieth century. A robust civil–military institutional nexus in matters of counter-insurgency, disaster relief operations, and issues of nuclear and strategic management has always been under the academic radar. The military officers' training and feeder academies, however, have hardly been scrutinized in the same spirit. This book has aimed to address this gap.

The waves of military institutionalization that swept across the subcontinent from the turn of the twentieth century recast our understanding of the ways in which the state and the military have changed since then. Military academies reflect the changing priorities in the military policies that were espoused through different channels and governmental sensibilities, and often led to mixed results for those involved in the process—students, cadets, instructors, and officers. A sense of shared political, economic, and ideological context in the formation of these spaces for training provides a more layered account of the Indian military, which has been largely viewed through a mono-institutional standpoint or in terms of its operational and compositional integrity during campaigns and conflicts.

This volume has attempted to highlight a neglected element in the journey of the Indian military as it transitioned from colonial rule to serving under an independent nation. It has laid bare the complications and contradictions, as well as ties of cooperation that were developed over the course of a century, in mitigating the institutional and administrative challenges faced during Indianization. Indian military institutions today are often projected by the military and the state to portray a steadfast image of pride and self-sufficiency in safeguarding the country's security. Most of these academies are by-words for the military itself. Joining the NDA or IMA, or graduating from the NDC, remains a rite of passage for many of the cadets and officers, and often the only way to 'generalship'. Yet, the history of this network remains obscured. Indeed, where attempts have been made to correct this anomaly, an unfortunate amnesia sets in when it comes to expanding their contemporary history and probing the ideas behind their establishment, which first germinated long before Independence came in 1947.

Military institution-building and reform continues to be a relevant discourse globally. The broader international context surrounding the formation and functioning of military academies today throw up questions of inclusion, administration, and training in a similar vein as this book has highlighted, further substantiating the fact that an institutional history of the military's embedded institutions is critical to appreciate contemporary military institution-building patterns. Current organizational challenges in raising a 'national military academy' near Kabul, Afghanistan—a British legacy in the wake of the withdrawal of foreign troops from Afghanistan—and the establishment of Joint Services Staff College in Qatar in the Middle East with British assistance speaks to nineteenth- and twentieth-century developments, where the Indian subcontinent was witness to a substantive growth of military institutions and whose reform and subsequent expansion arose out of a layered international context of ideas relating to military institutionalization.

Contemporary concerns about issues of recruitment and the question of who to recruit, together with struggles to achieve gender parity in the forces, are central to militaries in many countries today, including India. However, it is important to appreciate the nature of these problems through a historical perspective. A more perceptive view of today's challenges in managing military academies and officership can be offered by a critical examination of what other academies of another age did to rectify their problems relating to recruitment and education, while trying to devise uniform training standards for a disparate group of educated candidates interested in pursuing a military career.

Present-day challenges of opening the officer cadre of all the fighting services to Indian women, ongoing legal and juridical struggles being mounted by those committed towards securing permanent commissions for women in select branches of military services, and the impending reorganization of the military feeder network to shore up recruitment by offering a level playing field to female students are better understood in the light of the historical developments through which the Indian military has been frequently sought to be made more representative of existing sociological demographics. Attempts to pave the way for women to take an active role in the armed forces in all the commissioned and non-commissioned ranks is another manifestation of a further round of Indianization that awaits the Indian military today. The manner in which military institutions will be reorganized to facilitate their entry at all levels of military training will be scrutinized with a keen interest, whenever it happens.

This book does not proffer policy advice on running military academies but the policy implications arising out of what is mainly a historical exegesis are obvious. Current discussions on the formation of Indian National Defence University will mark a new age of military institutional reform and it has indeed already initiated familiar lines of enquiries into matters of affiliation and the patterns of inter-institutional knowledge transfer that will take place at this proposed institution. A more retrospective gaze, therefore, can help make sense of the contemporary state of the Indian military institutions and the manner in which they have adapted to fit in with the political, economic, and sociological demands made on the military. Studying past forms of collaboration and the complex interweaving of military policy with institution-building will hold the key to this next round of institutional innovation being planned for the future. The military academies of India are a map of the officers, cadets, and the country in which they emerged and are important witnesses to the history of India itself.

Appendix

APPENDIX A.1 Chronology of Major Military Institutional Developments in the Indian Subcontinent, c.1900s-1960*

1871–88	Establishment of the Chief's colleges mainly to train and educate the princes and aristocrats in Rajkot, Ajmer, Indore, and Lahore. Their limited pool of students paved the way for newer structures to develop in order to include the sons of Indian military personnel in the twentieth century.
1901	The ICC is founded to impart officer training to the princes.
1905	The Staff College opens in Deolali (southwestern India); relocated to Quetta in 1907. Catered only to British officers of the Indian Army at this time.
1921	Establishment of the Prince of Wales Royal Indian Military College to act as a feeder institution to Sandhurst.
1925	Lawrence School Lovedale (south India) designated as the 'Lawrence Memorial Royal Military School, Lovedale' upon receiving a royal ascent, signifying the change in its institutional mandate and aims of education.
1925–6	Appointment and submission of the Indian Sandhurst Committee, also known as the Skeen Committee, to study the feasibility of setting up an Indian Officers' Training academy in the subcontinent.
1925–30	Creation and expansion of the King George's schools in the northwest: Jhelum, Ajmer, and Jalandhar. Expanded to accommodate children and wards of Indian military personnel.
1929	Kitchener College is established in Nowgong (central India). Later to be focussed upon as an 'experimental' site for testing inter-service training protocols that would form the basis for the evolution of the NDA.

1925–33	Expansion of the Lawrence School network to include Anglo-Indians in its portals. Begins forging early institutional links with the military architecture of the subcontinent.
1931	Indian Military College Committee, also known as the Chetwode Committee, is appointed. Its report recommends the formation of Indian Military Academy (IMA), popularly regarded as the 'Indian Sandhurst'.
1932	Inauguration of the IMA at Dehradun (present-day Uttarakhand).
1947	Partition announced for the subcontinent. The Indian Staff College is planned to be relocated from Quetta.
1948	Establishment of the Indian Staff College, later known as the DSSC in Wellington (in present-day Tamil Nadu).
1949	Inauguration of the NDA; relocated in 1955 to Khadakvasla near Pune in Bombay state (now Maharashtra).
1960	Establishment of the NDC in New Delhi.

Note: * The placement of Lawrence Schools in this table, even though they were founded earlier and were not formally military feeder schools like the other institutions discussed in this book, is to be seen in the context of the early years of the twentieth century when they were expanded and liaised with the military to a considerable extent.

Source: Compiled by author.

Bibliography

ARCHIVAL SOURCES

Nehru Memorial Museum and Library, New Delhi, India

K.S. Thimayya Papers
S.P.P. Thorat Papers
Dr B.S. Moonje Papers
Cabinet Office Papers, Vols I–V

History Division, Ministry of Defence, GoI, New Delhi, India

Papers of the Indian Sandhurst Committee Report, 1925
Report on the Decisions on the Indian Sandhurst Committee, 1928
War Diary of the Staff College 601/1413/WD
Report on the Army School of Education 601/1416/WD Part A

National Archives of India, New Delhi, India

K.M. Cariappa Papers

India Office Records, British Library, London, UK

IOR L/WS: Records of the War Staff Secretariat
IOR L/MIL: Records of the Military Department
IOR L/PJ: Records of the Public and Judicial Department
IOR L/PS: Political and Secret Department Records
IOR V/9: Legislative Council and Legislative Assembly Proceedings
IOR/L/I: Information Department Records

Liddell Hart Centre for Military Archives, King's College London, UK

Maj. Gen. Arthur Reginald Chater Papers
Brig. Noel Joseph Chamberlain Papers
Gen. Hastings Lionel Ismay Papers
Gen. Sir Ronald Adam Papers

National Army Museum, London, UK

Gen. Sir Roy Bucher Papers

Special Collections and Archives, London School of Economics and Political Science (LSE), UK

George Edward Cecil (Baron Wigg) Papers

Special Collections, University of Southampton Library, Southampton, UK

Mountbatten Papers Database (MB1/D Series)

John Rylands Special Collections, University of Manchester Library, UK

FM Auchinleck Papers

Churchill Archives Centre, Churchill College, University of Cambridge, UK

FM Slim Papers
Capt. Godfrey French Papers
Viscount Esher Papers

The National Archives, Kew, UK

DO 35: Records of the Dominion Office and Commonwealth Relations Office
DO 196: Records of the Commonwealth Relations Office and Commonwealth Office
FO 371: Records of the Foreign Office

The Imperial War Museum, London, UK

Lt Gen. Sir Francis Tuker Papers

Published Primary Sources

Appadorai, A. *Select Documents on India's Foreign Policy, 1947–1972, Volume I.* Delhi: Oxford University Press, 1982.

Hasan, Mushirul (ed.). *Selected Works of Jawaharlal Nehru,* Volume 39, Second Series. New Delhi: Jawaharlal Nehru Memorial Fund, 2007.

Mansergh, N. and E.W.R. Lumby (eds). *Constitutional Relations between Britain and India: The Transfer of Power 1942–7.* London: HM Stationery Office, 1970–83.

Mukherjee, M. (ed.). *Selected Works of Jawaharlal Nehru,* Volume 40, Second Series. New Delhi: Jawaharlal Nehru Memorial Fund, 2009.

Palat, Madhavan (ed.). *Selected Works of Jawaharlal Nehru,* Volume 60, Second Series. New Delhi: Jawaharlal Nehru Memorial Fund, 2015.

Philips, C.H., H.L. Singh, and B.N. Pandey (eds). *The Evolution of India and Pakistan: 1858 to 1947, Select Documents.* London: Oxford University Press, 1962.

Prasad, B. (ed.). *Official History of the Indian Armed Forces in the Second World War, 1939–1945: India and the War.* New Delhi: Combined Inter-Services Historical Section, 1966.

Rao, B. Shiva (ed.). *The Framing of India's Constitution: Select Documents,* 5 Vols. New Delhi: The Indian Institute of Public Administration, 1966.

Sastri, K.A. Nilkanta (ed.). *A Great Liberal: Speeches and Writings of Sir P.S. Sivaswamy* Aiyar. Bombay: Allied Publishers, 1965.

Superintendent Government Printing, India. *The Army in India and Its Evolution: Including an Account of the Establishment of the Royal Air Force in India.* Calcutta: 1924.

Institutional Journals

Journals of the Royal United Service Institution of India
Journal of the United Service Institution of India

Memoirs, First Person Accounts, and Biographies

Evans, Humphrey. *Thimayya of India: A Soldier's Life.* Dehradun: Natraj Publishers, 1988.

Gantzer, Hugh and Colleen Gantzer. *Never Give In: A History of the One Hundred and Twenty Five Years of the Lawrence School, Lovedale.* Madras: Orient Longman, 1984.

George, T.J.S. *Krishna Menon: A Biography.* London: Jonathan Cape, 1964.

Gibson, Jack. *As I Saw It: Records of a Crowded Life in India, 1937–1969.* New Delhi: Mukul Prakashan, 1976.

Gopal, Sarvepalli, *Jawaharlal Nehru: A Biography,* Vols I–III, New Delhi: Oxford University Press, 2012.

Khanduri, C.B. *Thimayya: An Amazing Life.* New Delhi: Knowledge World, 2006.

———. *Field Marshal KM Cariappa: His Life and Times.* New Delhi: Atlanta Publishing, 2013.

Maurice, Sir Frederick (ed.). *The Life of General Lord Rawlinson of Trent: From His Journals and Letters.* London: Cassell, 1928.

Menezes, S.L., Lt Gen. *Fidelity and Honour: The Indian Army from the Seventeenth to the Twenty-First Century.* Delhi: Oxford University Press, 1999.

Muthanna, I.M. *General Cariappa: The First Indian Commander-in-Chief.* Mysore: Usha Press, 1964.

Narayan, B.K. *General J.N. Chaudhuri: An Autobiography.* New Delhi: Vikas, 1978.

Ram, Janaki. *V.K. Krishna Menon: A Personal Memoir.* Delhi: Oxford University Press, 1997.

Rudolph, Susanne H., Lloyd I. Rudolph, and Mohan Singh Kanota (eds). *Reversing the Gaze: Amar Singh's Diary—A Colonial Subject's Narrative of Imperial India.* Boulder: Westview Press, 2002.

Singh, Depinder, Lt Gen. *Field Marshal Sam Manekshaw, M.C.: Soldiering with Dignity.* Dehradun: Natraj Publishers, 2002.

Singh, Harbakhsh, Lt Gen. *In the Line of Duty: A Soldier Remembers.* New Delhi: Lancer Publishers, 2000.

Thorat, S.P.P., Lt Gen. *From Reveille to Retreat.* New Delhi: Allied Publishers, 1986.

Verma, S.D., Lt Gen. *To Serve with Honour: My Memoirs.* Kasauli: Lt Gen. S.D. Verma, 1988.

Wright, Charles. *Service before Self: A Tribute to the Indian Military Academy before and after Partition.* Eggleston: Raby, 2002.

NON-ARCHIVAL SOURCES

Alavi, Seema. *The Sepoys and the Company: Tradition and Transition in Northern India, 1770–1830.* Oxford: Oxford University Press, 1995.

Bajpai, Kanti, Saira Basit, and V. Krishnappa (eds). *India's Grand Strategy: History, Theory, Cases.* New Delhi: Routledge, 2014.

Bakshi, G.D., Maj. Gen. and Maj. Gen. A. Mukherjee. *Lamp of Wisdom: History of the National Defence College, New Delhi.* New Delhi: NDC, 2010.

Barkawi, T. 'Culture and Combat in the Colonies: The Indian Army in the Second World War'. *Journal of Contemporary History* vol. 41, no. 2 (2006): 325–55.

Barr, Niall. *Pendulum of War: The Three Battles of El Alamein.* London: Jonathan Cape, 2004.

Barua, Pradeep. *Gentlemen of the Raj: The Indian Army Officer Corps, 1817–1949.* Westport, CT: Praeger, 2003.

Basu, Shrabani. *For King and Another Country: Indian Soldiers on the Western Front, 1914–18.* New Delhi: Bloomsbury India, 2015.

Bayly, C.A. and T.N. Harper. *Forgotten Armies: Britain's Asian Empire and the War with Japan.* London: Penguin, 2005.

———. *Forgotten Wars: The End of Britain's Asian Empire.* London: Allen Lane, 2007.

Black, Jeremy. *Rethinking Military History.* London and New York: Routledge, 2004.

Bond, Brian. *British Military Policy between the Two World Wars.* Oxford: Oxford University Press, 1980.

Caforio, Giuseppe (ed.). *Handbook of the Sociology of the Military.* New York: Springer, 2006.

Callahan, Raymond. *Churchill and His Generals.* Lawrence: University of Kansas Press, 2007.

Chatterji, Joya. *Bengal Divided: Hindu Communalism and Partition 1932–1947.* Cambridge: Cambridge University Press, 1994.

———. 'The Fashioning of a Frontier: The Radcliffe Line and Bengal's Border Landscape, 1947–1952'. *Modern Asian Studies* vol. 33, no. 1 (1999): 185–242.

———. '"Dispersal" and the Failure of Rehabilitation: Refugee Camp-Dwellers and Squatters in West Bengal'. *Modern Asian Studies* vol. 41, no. 5 (2007): 995–1032.

———. *The Spoils of Partition: Bengal and India, 1947–1967.* Cambridge and New York: Cambridge University Press, 2007.

———. 'South Asian Histories of Citizenship, 1946–1970'. *The Historical Journal* vol. 55, no. 4 (2012): 1049–71.

Chatterji, Joya and D. Washbrook (eds). *The Handbook of the South Asian Diaspora.* Abingdon, Oxon and New York: Routledge, 2013.

Chaudhuri, J.N., Gen. 'Nehru and the Indian Armed Forces'. Jawaharlal Nehru Memorial Lecture, 5 May 1973. Available at https://www.cambridgetrust.org/assets/documents/Lecture_5.pdf; accessed on 27 August 2020.

Cohen, Stephen P. 'The Untouchable Soldier: Caste, Politics and the Indian Army'. *The Journal of Asian Studies* vol. 28, no. 3 (1969): 453–68.

———. *The Indian Army: Its Contribution to the Development of a Nation.* Berkeley: University of California Press, 1971.

———. *The Pakistan Army.* Karachi: Oxford Pakistan Paperbacks, 1998.

Colley, Linda. 'The Indian Armed Forces and Politics since 1947: Putting Difference in Context'. Jawaharlal Nehru Memorial Lecture, 24 April 2003. Available at https://www.cambridgetrust.org/assets/documents/Lecture_25.pdf; accessed on 20 August 2020.

Copland, Ian. *The Princes of India in the Endgame of Empire, 1917–1947.* Cambridge: Cambridge University Press, 1997.

Corrigan, Gordon. *Sepoys in the Trenches: The Indian Corps on the Western Front, 1914–1915.* London: Spellmount, 2006.

Das, Santanu (ed.). *Race, Empire and First World War Writing.* New York: Cambridge University Press, 2011.

———. *1914–1918: Indian Troops in Europe.* Ahmedabad: Mapin, 2015.

Deshpande, Anirudh. 'Sailors and the Crowd: Popular Protest in Karachi, 1946'. *Indian Economic and Social History Review* vol. 26, no. 1 (1989): 1–28.

———. 'Hopes and Disillusionment: Recruitment, Demobilisation and the Emergence of Discontent in the Indian Armed Forces after the Second World War'. *Indian Economic and Social History Review* vol. 33, no. 2 (1996): 175–207.

———. *British Military Policy in India, 1900–1945: Colonial Constraints and Declining Power.* New Delhi: Manohar, 2005.

Dewey, C.J. 'The Education of a Ruling Caste: The Indian Civil Service in the Era of Competitive Examination'. *The English Historical Review* vol. 88, no. 347 (1973): 262–85.

Doorn, Jacques van. *Armed Forces and Society.* The Hague, Paris: Mouton, 1968.

———. *The Soldier and Social Change.* London and BH, California: SAGE, 1975.

Dutta, Vipul. 'Educating Future Generals: An Indian Defence University and Educational Reform'. *Economic and Political Weekly* vol. 53, no. 32 (2018): 47–54.

———. 'The "Indian" Staff College: Politics and Practices of Military Institution-Building in Twentieth Century India'. *Journal of Strategic Studies* vol. 42, no. 5 (2019): 600–25. doi: https://doi.org/10.1080/01402390.2019.1570148.

Ganachari, Aravind. 'First World War: Purchasing Indian Loyalties: Imperial Policy of Recruitment and Rewards'. *Economic and Political Weekly* vol. 40, no. 8 (19–25 February 2005): 779–88.

Gaylor, John. *Sons of John Company: The Indian and Pakistan Armies, 1903–91.* Tunbridge Wells: Spellmount, 1992.

Gegner, Martin and Bart Ziino (eds). *The Heritage of War.* Key Issues in Cultural Heritage Series. Abingdon and New York: Routledge, 2012.

Gray, T.I.G., Brig. (ed.). *The Imperial Defence College and the Royal College of Defence Studies, 1927–1977.* London: HM Stationery Office, 1977.

Green, Nile. *Islam and the Army in Colonial India: Sepoy Religion in the Service of Empire.* New York: Cambridge University Press, 2009.

Gupta, Narayani. *Delhi between Two Empires, 1803–1931: Society, Government and Urban Growth.* Delhi: Oxford University Press, 1981.

Gupta, P.S. *Power, Politics and the People: Studies in British Imperialism and Indian Nationalism.* New Delhi: Permanent Black, 2001.

Gupta, P.S. and Anirudh Deshpande (eds). *The British Raj and Its Indian Armed Forces, 1857–1939.* New Delhi: Oxford University Press, 2002.

Gutteridge, W.F. *Military Institutions and Power in the New States.* Essex: Pall Mall, 1964.

Guyot-Rechard, Berenice. 'Reordering a Border Space: Relief, Rehabilitation, and Nation-Building in Northeastern India after the 1950 Assam Earthquake'. *Modern Asian Studies* vol. 49, no. 4 (2015): 931–62.

Habibullah, E., Maj. Gen., in collaboration with Col B.K. Narayan. *The Sinews of Indian Defence.* New Delhi: Lancers Publishers, 1981.

Harries-Jenkins, Gwyn and Jacques van Doorn (eds). *The Military and Problem of Legitimacy.* London and BH, California: SAGE Studies in International Sociology, 1976.

———. *The Military in British India: The Development of British Land Forces in South Asia, 1600–1947.* Manchester: Manchester University Press, 1995.

Heimsath, C.H. and S. Mansingh. *A Diplomatic History of Modern India.* Delhi: Allied Publishers, 1971.

Holmes, Richard. *Sahib: The British Soldier in India, 1750–1914.* London: Harper Collins, 2005.

Hughes, M. and William J. Philpott (eds). *Palgrave Advances in Modern Military History.* Basingstoke and New York: Palgrave Macmillan, 2006.

Jackson, Ashley. *Botswana 1939–1945: An African Country at War.* Oxford: Clarendon Press; Oxford University Press, 1999.

Janowitz, M. *The Military in the Political Development of New Nations.* Chicago and London: University of Chicago Press, 1964.

Jeffery, Keith. 'An English Barrack in the Oriental Seas? India in the Aftermath of the First World War'. *Modern Asian Studies* vol. 15, no. 3 (1981): 369–86.

Jeffreys, Alan and Patrick Rose (eds). *The Indian Army, 1939–47: Experience and Development.* Farnham, Surrey, and Burlington, VT: Ashgate, 2012.

Kamtekar, Indivar. 'A Different War Dance: State and Class in India, 1939–1945'. *Past and Present* vol. 176, no. 1 (2002): 187–221.

Kant, Vedica. *'If I Die Here, Who Will Remember Me?': India and the First World War*. New Delhi: Roli, 2014.

Karnad, Raghu. *Farthest Field: An Indian Story of the Second World War*. Delhi: 4th Estate/Harper Collins, 2015.

Karsten, Peter. 'The "New" American Military History: A Map of the Territory, Explored and Unexplored'. *American Quarterly* vol. 36, no. 3 (1984): 389–418.

Khalidi, Omar. 'Ethnic Group Recruitment in the Indian Army'. *Pacific Affairs* vol. 74, no. 4 (Winter 2001–2): 529–52.

Khan, Yasmin. *The Great Partition: The Making of India and Pakistan*. New Haven and London: Yale University Press, 2007.

———. 'The Ending of an Empire: From Imagined Communities to Nation States in India and Pakistan'. *The Round Table: The Commonwealth Journal of International Affairs* vol. 97, no. 398 (2008): 693–704.

———. 'Sex in an Imperial War Zone: Transnational Encounters in Second World War India'. *History Workshop Journal* vol. 73, no. 1 (2012): 240–58.

———. 'The Raj at War: A People's History of India's Second World War'. Talk at the Oxford University Department for Continuing Education, 28 September 2015 (published online). Available at https://www.youtube.com/watch?v=tPyAnqXrTAA; accessed on 20 August 2020.

———. *The Raj at War: A People's History of India's Second World War*. Gurgaon: Random House India, 2015.

Khilnani, Sunil. *The Idea of India*. New Delhi: Penguin, 2003.

Killingray, David. 'The Idea of a British Imperial African Army'. *The Journal of African History* vol. 20, no. 3 (1979): 421–36.

Killingray, David and David Omissi (eds). *Guardians of Empire: The Armed Forces of the Colonial Powers c. 1700–1964*. Manchester and New York: Manchester University Press, 1999.

Killingray, David and R. Rathbone (eds). *Africa and the Second World War*. Basingstoke: Macmillan, 1986.

Killingray, David. *Fighting for Britain: African Soldiers in the Second World War*. London: James Currey, 2010.

Kitchen, J.E., A. Miller, and L. Rowe (eds). *Other Combatants, Other Fronts: Competing Histories of the First World War*. Newcastle upon Tyne: Cambridge Scholars Publishing, 2011.

Kudaisya, Gyanesh. '"In Aid of Civil Power": The Colonial Army in Northern India, c.1919–42'. *The Journal of Imperial and Commonwealth History* vol. 32, no. 1 (2004): 41–68.

Kundu, Apurba. *Militarism in India: The Army and Civil Society in Consensus.* London and New York: Tauris Academic Studies, 1998.

Lal, Kishori. *The National Defence Academy.* Pune: Parashuram Process Publishers, 1999.

Liebau, H., K. Bromber, K. Lange, D. Hamzah, and R. Ahuja (eds). *The World in the World Wars.* Leiden and Boston: Brill, 2010.

Longer, V. *Red Coats to Olive Green: A History of the Indian Army, 1600–1974.* New Delhi: Allied Publishers, 1974.

Luckham, Robin. 'Officers and Gentlemen of the Nigerian Army'. *Transition* no. 39 (October 1971): 38–55.

————. *The Nigerian Military: A Sociological Analysis of Authority and Revolt, 1960–67.* Cambridge: Cambridge University Press, 1971.

Marston, Daniel. *Phoenix from the Ashes: The Indian Army in the Burma Campaign.* Westport, CT: Praeger, 2003.

————. *The Indian Army and the End of the Raj.* Cambridge: Cambridge University Press, 2014.

Marston, Daniel and Chander Sundaram (eds). *A Military History of India and South Asia.* Westport: Praeger Security International, 2007.

Mason, Phillip. *A Matter of Honour: An Account of the Indian Army, Its Officers and Men.* London: Jonathan Cape, 1974.

Mazower, Mark. 'Violence and the State in the Twentieth Century'. *American Historical Review* vol. 107, no. 4 (2002): 1158–78.

Mazumder, Rajit. *The Indian Army and the Making of the Punjab.* Ranikhet, Bangalore: Permanent Black, 2003.

Mehrotra, S.R. *India and the Commonwealth: 1885–1929.* London: George Allen and Unwin, 1965.

Menon, V.P. *The Story of the Integration of the Indian States.* Calcutta: Orient Longmans, 1956.

Metcalf, Thomas R. *Ideologies of the Raj.* In *The New Cambridge History of India,* Volume 3, Part 4. Cambridge: Cambridge University Press, 1994.

Modak, G.V., Capt. *Indian Defence Problem.* Poona: Capt. G.V. Modak, 1933.

Moreman, Timothy. *The Army in India and the Development of Frontier Warfare: 1849–1947.* London: Macmillan, 1998.

Moreman, Timothy. *The Jungle, the Japanese and the British Commonwealth Armies at War, 1941–1945: Fighting Methods, Doctrine and Training for Jungle Warfare.* London: Frank Cass, 2005.

Morton-Jack, George. *The Indian Army on the Western Front: India's Expeditionary Force to France and Belgium in the First World War.* Cambridge: Cambridge University Press, 2014.

Murphy, Andrew R. (ed.). *The Blackwell Companion to Religion and Violence.* Oxford: Wiley-Blackwell, 2011.

Nawaz, Shuja. *Crossed Swords: Pakistan, Its Army, and the Wars Within.* Oxford: Oxford University Press, 2008.

Omissi, David. *The Sepoy and the Raj: The Indian Army, 1860–1940.* Basingstoke: Macmillan, 1994.

———. (ed.). *Indian Voices of the Great War: Soldiers' Letters, 1914–18.* Basingstoke: Macmillan, 1999.

Parker, Geoffrey. *The Military Revolution: Military Innovation and the Rise of the West, 1500–1800.* Cambridge: Cambridge University Press, 1988.

Perlmutter, A. *The Military and Politics in Modern Times: On Professionals, Praetorians, and Revolutionary Soldiers.* New Haven and London: Yale University Press, 1977.

Prakash, Arun. *The Young Warriors: A History of the Rashtriya Indian Military College, Dehra Dun.* Dehradun: RIMC, 2004.

Praval, K.C. *Indian Army after Independence.* New Delhi: Lancer International, 1987.

Raghavan, Pallavi. 'The Making of the India–Pakistan Dynamic: Nehru, Liaquat, and the No War Pact Correspondence of 1950'. *Modern Asian Studies* vol. 50, no. 5 (2006): 1645–78. doi:10.1017/S0026749X15000554.

Raghavan, Srinath. 'Protecting the Raj: The Army in India and Internal Security, c. 1919–39'. *Small Wars & Insurgencies* vol. 16, no. 3 (2005): 253–79.

———. *War and Peace in Modern India.* Delhi: Palgrave Macmillan, 2010.

———. *India's War: The Making of Modern South Asia, 1939–1945.* Delhi: Allen Lane, 2016.

Raina, T. (ed.). *National Defence Academy: Three Decades of Development, 1949–1978,* Memorial Volume. Pune: The Commandant, NDA, 1978.

———. *Cradle for Leadership: The National Defence Academy, 1949–1996.* New Delhi: Oxford University Press, 1997.

Rajan, M.S. *India and the Commonwealth: Some Studies.* Delhi: Konark, 1990.

Ramusack, Barbara N. *The Indian Princes and Their States.* Cambridge and New York: Cambridge University Press, 2004

Robb, Peter (ed.). *The Concept of Race in South Asia.* New Delhi: Oxford University Press, 1995.

Rose, Sonya O. *Which People's War?: National Identity and Citizenship in Wartime Britain 1939–1945.* Oxford and New York: Oxford University Press, 2003.

Rosen, Stephen P. *Societies and Military Power: India and Its Armies.* Delhi: Oxford University Press, 1996.

Roy, Franziska, Heike Liebau, and Ravi Ahuja (eds). *'When the War Began We Heard of Several Kings': South Asian Prisoners in World War I Germany.* New Delhi: Social Science Press, 2011.

Roy, Kaushik (ed.). *War and Society in Colonial India.* Delhi: Oxford University Press, 2006.

————. *Brown Warriors of the Raj: Recruitment and the Mechanics of Command in the Sepoy Army, 1859–1913.* Delhi: Manohar, 2008.

————. 'Military Loyalty in the Colonial Context: A Case Study of the Indian Army during World War II'. *Journal of Military History* vol. 73, no. 2 (2009): 497–529.

————. 'Discipline and Morale of the African, British and Indian Army Units in Burma and India during World War II: July 1943 to August 1945'. *Modern Asian Studies* vol. 44, no. 6 (2010): 1255–82.

————. 'From Defeat to Victory: Logistics of the Campaign in Mesopotamia, 1914–18'. *First World War Studies* vol. 1 (2010): 35–55.

————. *The Armed Forces of Independent India: 1947–2006.* Delhi: Manohar, 2010.

————. (ed.). *The Indian Army in the Two World Wars.* Leiden: Brill, 2012.

————. 'Race and Recruitment in the Indian Army: 1880–1918'. *Modern Asian Studies* vol. 47, no. 4 (2013): 1310–47.

————. *Sepoys against the Rising Sun: The Indian Army in the Far East and South-East Asia, 1941–45.* Leiden: Brill, 2016.

Sarkar, Sumit. *Modern India: 1885–1947.* New Delhi: Macmillan, 1983.

Saxena, K.M.L. *The Military System of India 1850–1900.* New Delhi: Sterling Publishers, 1974.

Saxena, S.N., Lt Col. *Role of Indian Army in the First World War.* Delhi: Bhavna, 1987.

Seal, Anil. *The Emergence of Indian Nationalism: Competition and Collaboration in the Later Nineteenth Century.* Cambridge: Cambridge University Press, 1968.

Sharma, Gautam. *Indian Army through the Ages.* Bombay: Allied Publishers, 1966.

Sherman, T.C. 'The Integration of the Princely State of Hyderabad and the Making of the Postcolonial State in India, 1948–1956'. *Indian Economic and Social History Review* vol. 44, no. 4 (2007): 489–516.

————. 'Migration, Citizenship and Belonging in Hyderabad (Deccan), 1948–1956'. *Modern Asian Studies* vol. 45, no. 1 (2011): 81–107.

Singh, Gajendra. *The Testimonies of Indian Soldiers and the Two World Wars: Between Self and Sepoy.* London and New York: Bloomsbury Academic, 2014.

Singh, I.A. 'Keeping India in the Commonwealth: British Political and Military Aims, 1947–49'. *Journal of Contemporary History* vol 20, no. 3 (1985): 469–81.

Singha, Radhika. 'The Great War and a "Proper" Passport for the Colony: Border-Crossing in British India, c.1882–1922'. *Indian Economic and Social History Review* vol. 50, no. 3 (2013): 289–315.

Sinha, B.P.N. and Sunil Chandra. *Valour and Wisdom: Genesis and Growth of the Indian Military Academy.* New Delhi: Oxford and IBH Publishing, 1992.

Sinha, Mrinalini. 'Britishness, Clubbability, and the Colonial Public Sphere: The Genealogy of an Imperial Institution in Colonial India'. *Journal of British Studies* vol. 40, no. 4 (2001): 498–521.

Stanley, Peter. *Die in Battle, Do Not Despair: The Indians on Gallipoli, 1915.* Solihull (UK): Helion, 2015.

Strachan, Hew. *History of the Cambridge University Officer Training Corps.* Tunbridge Wells: Midas Books, 1976.

——. *Financing the First World War.* Oxford and New York: Oxford University Press, 2004.

Sundaram, Chandar S. 'A Grudging Concession: the Origins of the Indianisation of the Indian Army's Officer Corps, 1817–1917'. Unpublished PhD Thesis. Montreal: McGill University, 1996.

——. '"Treated with Scant Attention": The Imperial Cadet Corps, Indian Nobles, and Anglo-Indian Policy, 1897–1917'. *The Journal of Military History* vol. 77, no. 1 (2013): 41–70.

——. *The Garrison State: The Military, Government and Society in Colonial Punjab, 1849–1947.* New Delhi: SAGE, 2005.

Tan Tai Yong and Gyanesh Kudaisya. *The Aftermath of Partition in South Asia.* London: Routledge, 2001.

——. (eds). *Partition and Post-colonial South Asia: A Reader*, 3 Vols. Oxon and New York: Routledge, 2008.

Tilly, Charles (ed.). *The Formation of National States in Western Europe.* Princeton, London: Princeton University Press, 1975.

Tooze, Adam and Michael Geyer (eds). *The Cambridge History of the Second World War, Volume 3.* Cambridge: Cambridge University Press, 2015.

Wald, Erica. 'Health, Discipline and Appropriate Behaviour: The Body of the Soldier and Space of the Cantonment'. *Modern Asian Studies* vol. 46, no. 4 (2012): 815–56.

——. *Vice in the Barracks: Medicine, the Military and the Making of Colonial India, 1780–1868.* London and New York: Palgrave Macmillan, 2014.

Wickremesekera, Channa. *'Best Black Troops in the World': British Perceptions and the Making of the Sepoy, 1746–1805.* Delhi: Manohar, 2002.

Wilkinson, Steven. *Army and Nation: The Military and Indian Democracy since Independence.* Cambridge, MA, and London: Harvard University Press, 2015.

Wilkinson, Steven and Saumitra Jha. 'Does Combat Experience Foster Organizational Skill? Evidence from Ethnic Cleansing during the Partition of South Asia'. *American Political Science Review* vol. 106, no. 4 (2012): 883–907.

FURTHER READING

Bond, Brian. *The Victorian Army and the Staff College, 1854–1914.* London: Eyre Methuen, 1972.

Hamid, Shahid, Maj. Gen. *Disastrous Twilight: A Personal Record of the Partition of India.* Barnsley, UK: Leo Cooper, 1986.

Heathcote, T.A. *The Indian Army*. London: David and Charles, 1974.

Jackson, Ashley. *The British Empire and The Second World War*. London and New York: Hambledon Continuum, 2006.

Kolff, D.H.A. *Naukar, Rajput and Sepoy: The Ethnohistory of the Military Labour Market in Hindustan, 1450–1850*. Cambridge: Cambridge University Press, 1990.

Menon, V.P. *The Transfer of Power in India*. Orient Longman, Calcutta: Orient Longmans, 1957.

Palsokar, R.D., Col. *Defence Services Staff College 1947–1987*. New Delhi: DSSC, 1987.

Partin, John W. (ed.). *A Brief History of Fort Leavenworth, 1827–1983*. Kansas: Combat Studies Institute, 1983.

Peers, Douglas M. *Between Mars and Mammon: Colonial Armies and the Garrison State in India, 1819–1835*. New York: Tauris Academic Press, 1995.

Roy, Kaushik. *From Hydaspes to Kargil: A History of Warfare in India from 326 BC to AD 1999*. Delhi: Manohar, 2004.

———. *The Army in British India: From Colonial Warfare to Total War, 1857–1947*. London, New York: Bloomsbury Academic, 2013.

Singh, Jagjit, Maj. Gen. *While Memory Is Fresh*. New Delhi: Lancer Publishers, 2006.

Smyth, John. *Before the Dawn: A Story of Two Historic Retreats*. London: Cassell, 1957.

Strachan, Hew. *The Politics of the British Army*. Oxford: Clarendon Press, 1997.

Tan Tai Yong. 'Maintaining the Military Districts: Civil–Military Integration and District Soldiers' Boards in the Punjab, 1919–1939'. *Modern Asian Studies* vol. 28, no. 4 (October 1994): 833–74.

Tuker, Sir Francis, Lt Gen. *While Memory Serves*. London: Cassell, 1950.

Warner, Philip. *Auchinleck, the Lonely Soldier*. London: Buchan and Enright, 1981.

Index

About the Author

Vipul Dutta is assistant professor of history at the Department of Humanities and Social Sciences, Indian Institute of Technology Guwahati, Assam, India. He has a PhD from King's College London, UK, and combines research and teaching interests in South Asian diplomatic, military, and economic history of the twentieth century.